Business Knowledge for IT in Insurance

A complete handbook for IT Professionals

Essvale Corporation Limited
The Forward Thinking Company

bizle
PROFESSIONAL SERIES

Essvale Corporation Limited
63 Apollo Building
1 Newton Place
London E14 3TS
www.essvale.com

This is the first edition of this publication.

A CIP record for this book is available from the British Library

ISBN (10-digit) 0955412439
ISBN (13-digit) 9780955412431

Cover design by Essvale Design Team
Printed by Lightning Source Ltd, Milton Keynes

Preface

Ever since the advent of the credit crunch, the world of finance has been given a wake-up call, but among the financial sectors that have been hit by the credit crisis, the insurance industry appears to be one of the more resilient ones.

To gain an understanding of the factors that help insurance companies thrive in the wake of the financial turmoil, it would be prudent to provide a background to insurance that allows us to draw this conclusion.

Insurance firms are foremost holders of financial assets. If there are fluctuations in the value of these assets, the balance sheets of insurers as well as the value of their shareholders' equity can be impacted. A major concern, however, is an excessive drop in the value of these assets, which could also affect the capability of insurance firms to meet claims in the future. That said, insurers have been less exposed, in the wake of the credit crisis, to toxic sub-prime assets and have not suffered the liquidity problems that banks have. Furthermore, the distinctive cash-flow nature of the insurance industry is expected to be an advantage in cash-hungry times.

This distinctive cash flow can be explained as follows.

Insurance firms receive cash premiums, which are invested, followed by the cash payment of claims. This is contrary to the situation faced by other businesses in the sense that before the receipt of cash flows from the end customer, up-front short- and long-term capital investments must be made. There is also the likelihood that customers will be more reluctant to withdraw money impulsively from insurers than from banks because of both their longer-term expectations and the significant tax and redemption penalties.

From the above, it can be seen that the insurance industry could be a stable industry for an IT professional to specialise in as it is one of the industries that can survive sharp economic downturns and the seemingly unending boom-and-bust cycles witnessed in recent years in the global financial services industry.

Acknowledgements

Essvale Corporation Limited would like to thank all authors and publishers of all materials used in compiling this publication. Also thanks to all the respondents to the research carried out to justify writing this publication.

We would like to acknowledge Vince Smith and Lucy Chapman of IBM, Nick Garner of FIS Software, Peter Hughes and Isobel McCalman of Standard and Poor's, Magda Ponce De LeonLijs of Swiss Reinsurance.

Our thanks also go to Pat Winfield of Bookworm Editorial Services, Barney Lodge of Lodge Consulting, the helpful staff of City Business Library and Idea Store Canary Wharf, the editors and support staff at Nielsen Book Data, Lucy Sharp of Lightning Source, Trey Smith of Ingram Digital ,Graham Morris and Vic Daniels of Hereisthecity.com, the staff of Amazon and other bookstores worldwide .Thanks for supporting Bizle Professional Series thus far.

Contents

Introduction

There are predictions that in the near future the insurance industry will be dampened by concerns over the future of stock market performance, as well as insurers' weakened balance sheets. In addition, the global insurance industry will witness a spate of mergers and acquisitions as a consequence of falling demand from retail customers.

The way the insurance industry is regulated is also predicted to change as regulators make fresh assessments of the risk management capabilities of local and international insurers and their ability to meet the rising capital infusion requirements of insurance operations.

While this may appear not to bode well for insurance professionals, IT professionals with business knowledge of the insurance industry can benefit from the integration of systems that usually occur when companies merge or when a company acquires another company. An increase in the regulations will also provide insurance companies with the impetus to execute IT projects that will ensure compliance. This could lead to a demand for the services of IT professionals with the right business skills who can deliver these projects according to the demands of the resulting regulatory initiatives.

IT professionals who are seeking to exploit the current and future opportunities in the insurance industry will find the content of this book very useful.

The first chapter provides an overview of insurance – the various definitions and the history, as well as a discussion of the global market for insurance products, while Chapter 2 discusses the various types of insurance products. Chapter 3 provides an overview of reinsurance – the different providers, the purchasers and the nature of reinsurance contracts.

Chapters 4 and 5 discuss the business environment in the insurance industry, and the recent trends in the insurance industry, respectively.

Chapter 6 is about some of the business processes, including underwriting and claims administration, in the insurance industry, while Chapter 7 discusses risk management in both insurance and reinsurance.

Common systems used in the insurance industry are discussed in Chapter 8. The discussion includes the history of the IT function in insurance and the use of legacy systems in the industry.

Chapter 9 contains information about some of the IT projects that can be executed in the insurance industry. In Chapter 10, the methodologies, skills and tools used in IT in insurance are discussed.

A list of common terminology used in the insurance industry is presented in Chapter 11. In chapter 12, the final chapter, the future of IT and business in insurance is discussed.

It is advisable to read this book in conjunction with Business Knowledge for IT in Investment Banking and Business Knowledge for IT in Investment Management in order to gain a better understanding of discussions on financial assets that insurance companies invest in and the section on insurance securitisation.

Overview of Insurance

1

This chapter introduces the concept of insurance and includes the history of insurance and an overview of the global insurance market.

Introduction

Insurance and risk management make up an immense global industry. From an economics standpoint, insurance is a form of risk management tool primarily used to hedge against the risk of a contingent loss. It is designed to protect the financial security of an individual, company or other entity in the case of unexpected loss. Some forms of insurance, such as car insurance, are required by law while others are optional.

The following describes how insurance typically works. A business that provides insurance (referred to as the 'insurer') agrees to take on the risk on behalf of the business or individual concerned (referred to as the 'insured'). Following that, it provides the insured with an insurance contract, sometimes referred to as a 'policy'. Stated in this contract is an agreement by the insurer to the risks it will insure against and how much it will pay out should the risk happen so that the insured is put back into the same position as if the risk had not occurred. The policy may also contain a list of things that are not insured against, known in the industry as 'exclusions'. An example of an exclusion is if someone insures their car against theft and the car gets stolen; the insurance may include an exclusion if the insured, due to negligence, left the keys in the car, thereby increasing the possibility of the car being stolen. In return, the insurer receives a fee from the insured, and this is referred to as the insurance 'premium'.

The insurer will gather premiums on a number of policies and pool these funds together, which it then invests to make the fund grow. The insurer pays out to any insured person in the event of a claim on a policy from the pool of funds. This raises the question: how do insurance companies make profits? The insurance business model is based on the hope that total premiums received in a year and the gains from investment of the funds will exceed the total claims paid out.

From a contract law perspective, insurance can be viewed as a risk transfer arrangement. It can also be considered a risk financing arrangement, given that the insured can use the promise from the insurer as contingent capital that can be depended upon for future use, subject to terms and conditions stipulated in the contract. The insured might experience lower cash flow volatility if a risk transfer/financing arrangement is in place.

The essence of the contract of insurance is mutuality. The major operations of an insurance company include underwriting – the determination of which risks the insurer can take on – and rate making, the decisions regarding necessary prices for such risks. It is the underwriter's responsibility to guard against adverse selection, in which there is excessive coverage of high-risk candidates in proportion to the coverage of low-risk candidates. So as to prevent adverse selection, the underwriter must take into account physical, psychological and moral hazards in relation to applicants. Physical hazards include those dangers which surround the individual or property, and put the well-being of the insured at risk. The amount of the premium is determined on the basis of calculations made by actuaries.[1] Insurance companies generally invest premium payments in a vast array of revenue-generating projects and in so doing have become key suppliers of capital.

Definition of Insurance

The following are definitions of insurance.

Insurance is a contract (policy) in which an individual or entity receives financial protection, or reimbursement, against losses from an insurance company, which pools clients' risks to make payments more affordable, in exchange for a premium. (The Free Dictionary)

Insurance is a protection against possible hazard that can be bought against an event which may or may not happen, such as a burglary, an illness, loss of property or a legal liability.

Insurance is a guard against property loss or damage that involves making payments in the form of premiums to an insurance company, which pays an agreed-upon sum to the insured in the event of loss.

Insurance, sometimes referred to as assurance, is a device for indemnifying or guaranteeing an individual against loss.

Insurance from an individual perspective is an economic device whereby the individual substitutes a small certain cost (the premium) for a large uncertain financial loss (the contingency insured against) which would exist if it were not for the insurance.

Definition of Indemnity

Indemnity is a word that is closely associated with insurance and is commonly used in the wording of insurance policies. The following are some definitions of indemnity.

Indemnity is a contractual agreement made between different parties to compensate for any damages or losses. (Investopedia)

An indemnity is a sum paid by a party to another party by way of compensation for a particular loss suffered by that party.

Indemnity is the legal philosophy upon which the concept of most insurance policies is based. In a strict sense, indemnity is protection from loss and damage claims filed by another person.

1 An actuary is a person who computes premium rates, dividends, risks, etc., according to probabilities based on statistical records.

Different Variations of Premiums

A standard definition of an insurance premium is the amount paid by one party (in most cases, the insured) as a consideration for insurance provided by another party (the insurer). However, while this is a practical and legal definition, it is worthwhile to define premiums from a more technical standpoint:

- **Written premium** – This is the premium registered on the books of an insurer or a reinsurer[2] at the time a policy is issued and paid for.
- **Direct premium** – This is an insurer's premium income calculated before reflecting reinsurance assumed (sold) or ceded (purchased).
- **Net premium** – This is used to denote the difference between premiums received for direct business and reinsurance sold, and premiums paid for reinsurance purchased.

History of Insurance[3]

The origins of insurance can be traced to ancient Babylonia whereby a practice was in place that encouraged traders to take on the risks of the caravan trade through loans that were repaid (with interest) only after the safe arrival of the goods. There was a similar practice in place among the Phoenicians and the Greeks for seaborne trading activities. A form of life insurance was also practised by the Romans through burial clubs that provided funeral expenses for members and later payments to the survivors.

As towns and trade grew in Europe, the medieval guilds felt the need to protect their members from loss by fire and shipwreck, to ransom them from captivity by pirates, and to provide decent burial and support in sickness and poverty.

By the middle of the 14th century, marine insurance was practically universal among the maritime nations of Europe, given the evidence of the earliest known insurance contract (Genoa, 1347). In 17th-century London, the merchants, ship owners, and underwriters convened to transact business in Lloyd's Coffee House. However, by the end of the 18th century, Lloyd's had evolved into one of the first modern insurance firms. Other notable milestones include the construction of the first mortality table, based on the statistical laws of mortality and compound interest. The table, which was corrected in 1756 by Joseph Dodson, allowed for scaling of the premium rate to age; previously the rate had been the same for all ages.

2 This is a company that sells a form of insurance that insurance companies buy for their own protection.

3 This section is an extract from The Columbia Encyclopedia, Sixth Edition, Copyright 2008, Columbia University Press.

Development of insurance gathered pace with the expansion of British commerce in the 17th and 18th centuries. Before the formation of corporations devoted exclusively to the business of writing insurance, the policies were signed by a number of individuals, each of whom wrote their name and the amount of risk they were assuming underneath the insurance proposal. This is what gave rise to the term 'underwriter'.

The first stock companies to be involved in insurance were chartered in England in 1720, and in 1735, the first insurance company in the American colonies was incorporated at Charleston, S.C. Fire insurance corporations were formed in New York City in 1787 and in Philadelphia in 1794. In 1759, The Presbyterian Synod of Philadelphia sponsored the first life insurance corporation in America for the benefit of Presbyterian ministers and their dependants. After 1840, with the decline of religious prejudice against the practice, life insurance entered a boom period. In the 1830s, the practice of classifying risks had begun.

Events such as the New York fire of 1835 created an awareness of the need to have adequate reserves to cater for unexpectedly large losses. The state of Massachusetts pioneered the legal requirement for maintaining such reserves. The great Chicago fire in 1871 highlighted the costly nature of fires in structurally dense modern cities.

Reinsurance, meanwhile, was devised to meet such situations and is now widespread in other lines of insurance. The Workmen's Compensation Act of 1897 in Britain decreed that employers should insure their employees against industrial accidents. Public liability insurance, promoted by legislation, emerged in the 1880s and attained major importance with the advent of the automobile.

In the 19th century, many friendly or benefit societies were created to provide insurance for the life and health of their members, and many fraternal orders were founded to offer low-cost, members-only insurance. Fraternal orders[4] continue to offer insurance coverage, as do most labour organisations. Many employers fund group insurance policies for their workers; such policies usually include life insurance, sickness and accident benefits and old-age pensions, and the employees generally put in a certain percentage of the premium.

Since the late 19th century there has been a growing inclination for the state to enter the field of insurance, especially with regard to protecting workers against sickness and disability, either temporary or permanent, destitute old age, and unemployment. The US government has also tested out a range of crop insurances, a milestone in this field being the Federal Crop Insurance Act of 1938. In World War II, the government provided life insurance for members of the armed forces and ever since has provided other forms of insurance such as pensions for veterans and government employees.

4 Fraternal orders were associations based on the Masonic model of social brotherhood that, on a practical level, sought to insure the well-being of their brothers via organised systems of mutual aid.

After 1944, the US Congress, under the interstate commerce clause of the US Constitution, became responsible for the supervision and regulation of insurance companies, a role that was previously the sole responsibility of the states. Until the 1950s, there was a restriction on the type of insurance offered by insurance companies to just one type. However, legislation was then passed to permit fire and casualty companies to underwrite several classes of insurance. Many companies have since grown, many mergers have taken place, and multiple-line companies are now dominant in the field.

Insurance Classifications

In the insurance industry, there are a number of ways in which insurance is classified. However, we have decided on the following classes.

Social versus Private Insurance

Social insurance is typically provided by governments as opposed to private organisations. In a number of countries around the world there are comprehensive social security systems in place that offer benefits including disability, unemployment, health and retirement benefits to eligible citizens.

Social insurance is typically provided by governments and take-up is compulsory, with financing being reliant upon government-mandated premiums, i.e. taxes. In addition, there is provision for well-defined risks such as unemployment and retirement through income security and there is no requirement for an economic needs test. Furthermore, social equality is stressed and this differentiates it from private insurance that places emphasis on actuarial equity[5] on an individual basis.

Private insurance is provided by insurance companies that operate in the private sector. The purchase is in some cases compulsory, for example in the case of car insurance, and in other cases optional. The insured's expected losses are reflected in the premiums paid.

Life versus Non-life

The insurance business has historically been divided into life insurance and non-life insurance.

Life insurance or life assurance is a contract between the policy owner and the insurer, where the insurer agrees to pay a sum of money upon the occurrence of the insured individual's or individuals':

5 This is the calculation of an insurance premium on the basis of factors such as the applicant's age, sex, health record, family history and type of insurance plan applied for.

- Death covered by life assurance;
- Incapacity covered by disability insurance;
- Injury or the contracting of a disease covered by health insurance;
- Living a certain period covered by endowments, pensions and annuities.

Non-life or general assurance is mainly concerned with protecting the policy-holder from loss or damage caused by specific risks such as:

- Property – Risks that can be incurred as a result of damage to homes, automobiles, business, or aircraft;
- Liability – Risks incurred as a result of negligent operation of an automobile, product defects and professional negligence that involve payments to third parties.

Personal versus Commercial

Insurance can also be categorised according to the target group of entities that purchase insurance, i.e. individuals and commercial entities. The class of insurance designed for individuals is known as personal insurance while that designed for organisations is known as commercial insurance. Examples of personal insurance include home and contents insurance designed for homeowners, motor insurance designed for family automobiles, and life and health insurance designed for individuals. Professional liability insurance is an example of commercial insurance.

Direct Insurance versus Reinsurance

Direct insurance is the type of insurance sold to the general public and the insurance companies that sell this type of insurance are known as direct insurers or primary insurers and the associated premiums are referred to as direct premiums.

Reinsurance is the type of insurance that insurance firms purchase for the purpose of hedging their own portfolio of risks. This is discussed in more detail in Chapter 3.

Table 1.1 shows the selected compulsory insurance laws in some countries around the world.

The Global Insurance Market

The global insurance market is enormous and the constituent markets vary in size and nature. The size of a country's insurance market is proportional to the size of its economy. At the time of writing, there was limited data on the state of the global insurance market as the effects of the credit crisis witnessed

Table 1.1 Compulsory Insurance Laws

	Automobile Third Party	Workers' Compensation	Others (Selected)
Belgium	√		Liability arising from fire and explosion in public buildings
Canada	√	√	
China	√		Nuclear liability
France	√	√	Risk relating to construction, other people's welfare and use of aircrafts Major risk relating to the nuclear industry and oil transport Professional indemnity risk
Germany	√	√	Oil pollution from ships
India	√	√	Professional indemnity by insurance brokers
Japan	Bodily injury only		Liability for nuclear risk Liability for maritime oil pollution
Korea	√		Fire Insurance Atomic energy risk
Malaysia	√	√	Professional indemnity by insurance brokers
Saudi Arabia	√		Health Insurance for expatriates
South Africa	√	√	Third party for commercial flight operators
United Kingdom	√	Employer's liability	Third party (selected) Professional Indemnity (selected)
United States	√	√	Aviation liability

Source: Lloyd's of London (2006) – Country Guide

across the world from 2007 are unknown. However, the following is a brief rundown of events during the credit crisis that could impact on insurers.[6]

The credit crisis began with the sub-prime mortgage meltdown in mid-2007 and has precipitated a broader economic crisis in the United States and around the world that has challenged every industry in ways that were not anticipated a year before that –insurers included. The insurance industry's financial performance in 2008 has been severely impacted by the bloodshed on Wall Street. Nevertheless, insurance is perceived as the most resilient of the financial services sectors.

6 The information in this section is drawn from 2008 – First Half Results by Dr. Robert P. Hartwig, CPCU President Insurance Information Institute.

The scope of destruction arising from the US's credit crisis is both terrifying and overwhelming. In the midst of the carnage are all five of the US's investment banks – all highly leveraged institutions that made too many bad bets in risky sub-prime mortgages and related securities. Lehman Brothers, despite having had a knack for surviving countless crises in its 158-year history, filed for bankruptcy on 15 September 2008, while in March 2008, Bear Stearns had to be rescued by the US Federal Reserve, which took $29 billion in risky debt off its books and this led to a takeover by Wall Street rival JPMorgan Chase. On the same day another major investment bank, Merrill Lynch, having witnessed the plight of Lehman's bankruptcy, offered itself to Bank of America for about $50 billion, which was half of its value in 2007. Given the turmoil in the stock market, and with the decline in the value of financial stocks, the two remaining investment banks, Morgan Stanley and Goldman Sachs, knowing that the investment banking operating model had been severely damaged by the collapse of the credit markets, had to recourse to petitioning the Federal Reserve to allow them to convert to bank holding companies, which in effect signalled the demise of the once-revered Wall Street model that had been supreme since 1929, the year of the Great Depression.

There was even more to come. Also in 2008, some of the largest bank failures in US history occurred. On 26 September, Washington Mutual declared bankruptcy and given its asset size ($307 billion), it was by far the country's largest. Prior to that, on 12 July, the US government seized IndyMac Bank, with $32 billion in assets, ranking the collapse as the third largest (now the fourth) of all time. Another major event was on 29 September when Wachovia (the sixth largest US bank by assets) was purchased by Citigroup with the assistance of FDIC in a bid to prevent the bank from also declaring bankruptcy.

Fannie Mae and Freddie Mac, the nation's largest mortgage lenders, were seized by federal regulators on 7 September 2008. Between these two institutions they owned or guaranteed $5.4 trillion in mortgages – about half of the US total.

Governments around the world also had to react to contain the financial pollution through timely injection of liquidity. Notable in this respect was the unprecedented measure taken on 29 September by the governments of Belgium, the Netherlands and Luxembourg to nationalise Fortis, a bank and insurance conglomerate that is one of Europe's largest financial institutions, with an injection of 11.2 billion euro ($16.4 billion). Fortis' problems arose from its exposure to certain structured credit assets and a loss of confidence among investors.

One of the most dramatic events in the financial crisis as of the time of writing, and most definitely the event that would have had the utmost impact on the insurance industry on a global scale, was the near bankruptcy of American International Group (AIG). AIG suffered a severe liquidity crisis at the holding company level (not in its insurance subsidiaries) and would have been bankrupt were it not for the intervention of the Federal Reserve, which provided an $85 billion loan to allow it time to sell off certain assets in an orderly manner.

How did AIG find itself in this situation? The root of AIG's problems was traced to a non-insurance financial products subsidiary based in London, UK. According to the statements made by the company and state regulators, its 71 US-domiciled insurance subsidiaries were continually solvent and held capital that met or exceeded requirements in every jurisdiction in which they operated.

Industry experts opine that the property/casualty insurance industry has fared relatively well since the beginning of the global credit crisis in mid-2007. They assert that investment portfolios are generally conservatively managed. Despite the spotlight on AIG and its near bankruptcy, insurance regulators in most countries and the USA maintained that the insurance subsidiaries they supervised were solvent and that the problems were limited to non-insurance operations.

It could be argued that insurance companies, due to their superior risk management model, have avoided most of the problems of the investment banks and many other financial institutions. Insurers have been more adept at ascertaining and underwriting risks. Many banks 'threw caution to the wind' and authorised mortgage brokers to flog loans to people with increasingly poor credit characteristics. Given that these mortgages could effectively be pooled and sold as mortgage-backed securities, originators of mortgages had no stake in the long-term performance of the loan. This division of underwriting and risk is in sharp contrast to insurers' approach to underwriting and risk management. Insurer control over underwriting authority is much tighter. While insurers typically spread risk through the use of reinsurance, they always retain some share of the losses.

In addition, insurers are much less dependent on borrowed money than are banks and investment banks. Most of the major investment banks in the United States, for instance, were reported to have borrowed 25 to 30 dollars for every dollar they held in capital. These high levels of leverage are rare in the insurance landscape.

Nevertheless, it is worthwhile providing data on the global insurance market prior to this period for illustration purposes.

According to International Financial Services London (IFSL) November 2007 Research, global insurance premiums grew by 8.0% in 2006 (or 5% in real terms) to reach $3.7 trillion (see Table 1.2) due to improved profitability and a benign economic environment characterised by solid economic growth, moderate inflation and strong equity markets. There was an improvement in the profitability in both life and non-life insurance in 2006 compared to the previous year. Life insurance premiums also experienced growth of 10.2% in 2006 as demand for annuity and pension products was on the increase. Non-life insurance premiums grew by 5.0% as a result of a growth in premium rates. From 1996 to 2006, global insurance premiums rose by more than half as annual growth fluctuated between 2% and 11%.

The research also shows that advanced economies account for the bulk of global insurance. Europe was shown to be the most important region with premium income of $1,485 billion (see Figure 1.1), followed by North

Table 1.2 Largest Insurance Markets

		1996 Premium income $bn	% share	2006 Premium income $bn	% share
1	US	653	31	1,170	31
2	Japan	520	25	460	12
3	UK	137	7	418	11
4	France	137	7	251	7
5	Germany	152	7	205	6
6	Italy	44	2	139	4
7	Canada	63	3	101	3
8	South Korea	36	2	88	2
9	Netherlands	62	3	71	2
10	Spain	30	1	66	2
11	PR China	36	2	63	2
12	Australia	33	2	53	1
13	Taiwan	16	1	52	1
14	Switzerland	7	0	47	1
15	Belgium	7	0	43	1
	Other	173	8	496	13
	World	2,106	100	3,723	100

Source: Swiss Re

America ($1,258bn) and Asia ($801bn). It can be seen in Table 1.2 that the top four countries accounted for nearly two-thirds of premiums in 2006. The USA and Japan alone accounted for 43% of world insurance, much higher than their 7% share of the global population. Despite generating only around 10% of premiums, emerging markets accounted for over 85% of the world's population.

The UK insurance market was the largest in Europe and, after the USA and Japan, the third largest in the world in 2006. Between 1996 and 2006, the USA maintained its 31% share of the global market, Japan's share fell from 25% to 12%, while the UK increased its share from 7% to 11%. The UK's life market premiums were almost twice those of any other European country. The UK is also the second largest European non-life insurer, after Germany.

There are a number of factors that can determine the premium levels in a country. Fast-growing countries such as India and China are perceived as having great potential due to their size. However, stifled demand in these countries has been attributed to low average income. In many emerging markets, there appears to be inadequate awareness of the economic importance

Figure 1.1 Global Volumes by Region

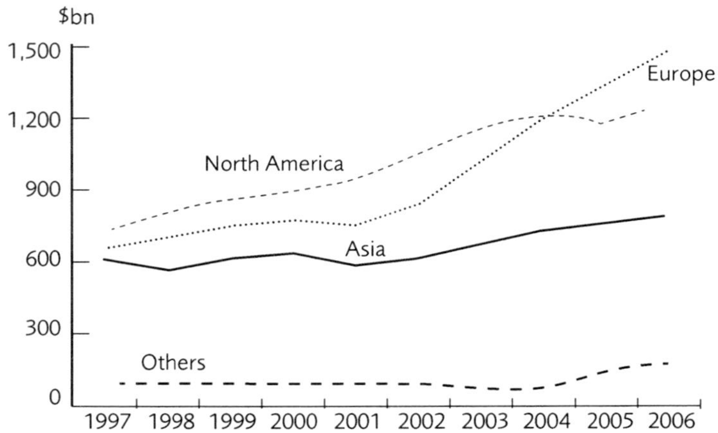

Source: Swiss Re

of insurance by both individuals and businesses. Another major factor is the degree of the state's involvement in insurance provision.

Insurance business is becoming more international in its organisation and operation in a similar way to other financial services. This has been possible because of the reduction of barriers to international trade and advancements in information technology, and also changes in both the demand and the supply sides of the industry. Overall, insurance is less liberalised internationally than banking and is particularly predisposed to new regulatory obstacles. However, there are changes afoot that could result in the removal of many of the types of barrier that are currently in existence.

Analysis of a Pre-eminent Global Insurance Centre – United Kingdom

The justification for selecting the United Kingdom is London's (the capital city) place at the top of the league table of financial centres according to the Global Financial Centres Index (GFCI). Table 1.3 shows the top GFCI centres as of September 2008.

It shows that London is in the top spot with 791 points out of a possible 1000. The ranking is included in the GFCI reports that have been published every six months since their inception in March 2007.

Table 1.3 Top GFCI centres 2008

Financial Centre	GFCI 4 Rank	Change in Rank Since GFCI 3	GFCI 4 Rating	Change in Rating Since GFCI 3
London	►1	0	791	▼– 4
New York	►2	0	774	▼–12
Singapore	▲3	1	701	▲26
Hong Kong	▼4	–1	700	▼5
Zurich	►5	0	676	▲11
Geneva	▲6	1	645	▲5
Tokyo	▲7	2	642	▲14
Chicago	►8	0	641	▲4
Frankfurt	▼9	–3	636	▼–6
Sydney	►10	0	630	▲9

Source: City A.M.

The following is a snapshot of the UK Insurance Market in 2006:[7]

- The UK insurance industry was the largest in Europe and at the time the second largest in the world, accounting for 11% of total worldwide premium income.
- It controlled 15% of investment in the London stock market in 2006. This compares to 13% held by company pension funds, 3% by banks, 2% by unit trusts and 10% by other financial institutions.
- It was a major contributor to the UK's tax take. In the 2006/07 tax year, the industry contributed £9.7 billion in taxes,[8] of which £2.9 billion was Corporation Tax and £2.3 billion was Insurance Premium Tax.
- It was a major exporter. One fifth of its net premium income came from overseas business. Premium income from overseas was £48 billion, of which long-term business accounted for £34 billion and general business £14 billion.

In 2007, the UK insurance industry paid out:

- £211 million per day in pension and life insurance benefits. This included:
  - £193 million to pensioners and long-term savers;
  - £18 million in death and disability benefits.

- £59 million per day in general insurance claims. This included:
  - £17.1 million in private motor car claims (more than one in six private car drivers make a claim each year);

7 Source: Association of British Insurers, 'UK Insurance – Key Facts', September 2008.
8 2007 Total Tax Contribution Survey conducted by PwC for the ABI.

- £12.4 million to householders for property damage or the loss of possessions;
- £5.9 million to businesses for property damage;
- £6.2 million in liability claims, such as for accidents at work, professional liability, and injuries to the public on commercial premises.

There are different types of insurance available to consumers in the UK. Figure 1.2 shows, for 2005/06, the percentage of households with different types of insurance products, and the average annual expenditure on insurance products by those households.[9]

Figure 1.2 UK Households buying products and the price they pay each year[a]

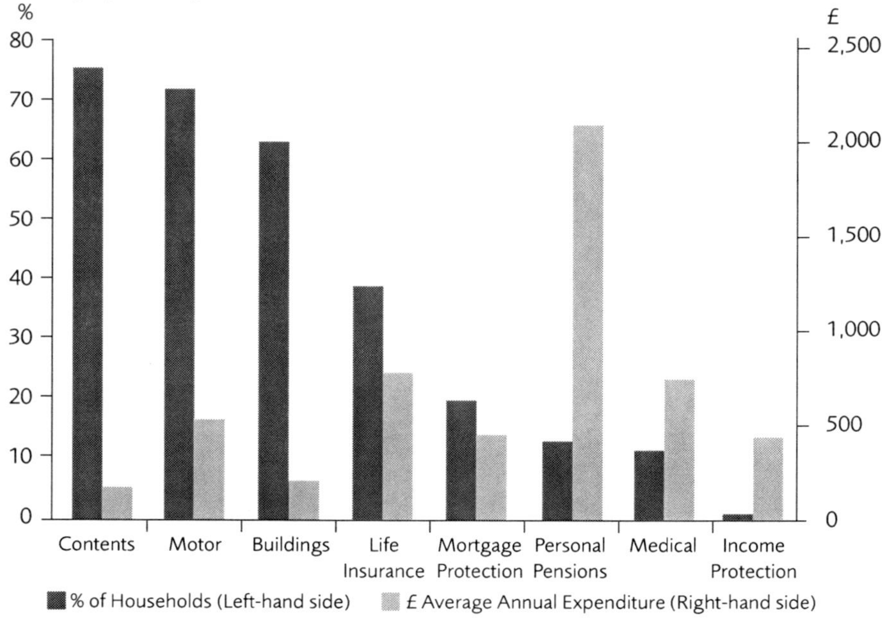

[a] This does not include insurance provided by employers (e.g. medical cover). Insurance products are discussed further in Chapter 2.

9 Source: National Statistics© Crown Copyright 2006. The Expenditure and Food Survey is Crown Copyright. Figures relate to 2005/2006, the latest available.

The World's Largest Insurance Companies

In this section, details of the world largest life insurance companies, property/casualty and insurance brokers by their 2006 revenue will be given.

Life Insurance Companies

The largest life insurance company in the world in terms of revenue in 2006 was ING group with revenues of $158.3 billion. This was followed by French insurer AXA with revenues of $139.7 billion.

Figure 1.3 shows the top ten largest life insurance companies in the world, their countries of origin and the revenues they generated in 2006 in descending order.

Figure 1.3 Largest Life Insurance Companies

2006		Country	Revenues $bn
1	ING Group	Netherlands	158.3
2	AXA	France	139.7
3	Assicurazioni Generali	Italy	101.8
4	Aviva	UK	83.5
5	Prudential	UK	66.1
6	Nippon Life Insurance	Japan	56.6
7	CNP Assurances	France	55.6
8	MetLife	US	53.3
9	Aegon	Netherlands	45.9
10	Dai-ichi Mutual Life Insurance	Japan	40.1

Source: Fortune, Insurance Information Institute

Property/Casualty Insurance Companies

The largest property/casualty insurance company in the world in terms of revenue in 2006 was Allianz with revenues of $125.4 billion. This was followed by American Insurance Group (AIG) with revenues of $113.2 billion.

Figure 1.4 shows the top ten largest property/casualty insurance companies in the world, their countries of origin and the revenues they generated in 2006 in descending order.

Insurance Brokers

Insurance brokers are firms that source (broke) contracts of insurance on behalf of their customers. A few large insurance brokers emerged in the early

Figure 1.4 Largest Property/Casualty Insurance Companies

2006		Country	Revenues $bn
1	Allianz	Germany	125.4
2	American International Group	US	113.2
3	Berkshire Hathaway	US	98.5
4	Zurich Financial Services	Switzerland	65.0
5	State Farm Insurance Cos.	US	60.5
6	Munich Re Group	Germany	58.2
7	Millea Holdings	Japan	36.1
8	Allstate	US	35.8
9	Swiss Reinsurance	Switzerland	32.1
10	Hartford Financial Services	US	26.5

Source: Fortune, Insurance Information Institute

and mid 1990s as a result of a great number of mergers and acquisitions. Notable among these large brokers are Marsh and Aon and they acquired significant business around the world.

In 2006, US companies dominated the rankings with seven out of the top ten companies. Marsh, with brokerage revenue of $10,000 million, and Aon, with $6,522 million, were by far the largest and they generated revenue of over 66% of the top ten brokers.

Figure 1.5 shows the top ten largest insurance brokers in the world, their countries of origin and the revenues they generated in 2006 in descending order.

Figure 1.5 Largest Insurance Brokers

2006	Country	Brokerage revenues ($m)
Marsh & McLennan Cos. Inc.	US	10,000
Aon Corp.	US	6,522
Willis Group Holdings Ltd.	UK	2,194
Arthur J. Gallagher & Co.	US	1,351
Wells Fargo Insurance Serv. Inc.	US	959
Brown & Brown Inc.	US	882
Jardine Lloyd Thompson Group plc	UK	776
BB&T Insurance Services Inc.	US	757
Hilb Rogal & Hobbs Co.	US	682
Lockton Cos. L.L.C.	US	658

Source: Business Insurance

2

Types of Insurance Products

The different types of products offered by insurance companies are discussed in this chapter.

Introduction

The sale of insurance products generates revenue for firms that sell these products to both individuals and businesses. Insurance products vary from country to country depending on the local demand. In this chapter the various types of insurance products will be categorised broadly as life – mortality based and morbidity based – and non-life – property, liability and package.

Selling insurance products to customers can allow companies that are not traditional insurance companies to complement their existing products and services, and generate extra revenue. Under this rationale, travel operators, for example, sell travel insurance. Others may want to offer various insurance products to their employees as part of their benefits packages.

As seen in Chapter 1, insurance companies sell policies (insurance contracts) for which the payments are reliant on the occurrence of an event.

Insurers use demographic factors to segment their target markets and market segmentation is one of the ways by which they choose their desired distribution channels. Market segmentation and distribution channels will also be discussed in this chapter.

Life Insurance

Life insurers generally sell insurance to cover death, survival to a certain age, incapacity and injury or disease. Typical life insurance policies can be categorised on the basis of mortality and morbidity. Thus, the first two classifications that demand life insurance are mortality based while the last two are morbidity based. These classifications are, however, not always consistent internationally. While in some countries such as the USA, Canada and a number of countries in Asia both mortality- and morbidity-based insurance are included in life insurance that is sold to individuals or organisations, in others morbidity-based insurance usually falls within the realms of non-life insurance. In this chapter, the former convention will be adopted.

Mortality-based Insurance Policies

Mortality-based insurance policies can be classified in two ways:

1. Policies where the policyholder's beneficiaries receive a benefit if he or she dies during the policy term, commonly referred to as life insurance policies or life assurance policies. The latter term is universally used in the UK and other Commonwealth countries.
2. Policies that pay a benefit should the policyholder (insured) survive for a fixed time or to a certain age are commonly called annuities (or pensions) or endowments. Given that endowments normally pay a death benefit, they are commonly considered as life insurance policies. In the related discussions in the rest of this chapter, this tradition will be adhered to.

It is worthwhile to note the potentially confusing aspect of this terminology as life insurance includes not just life insurance policies but also annuities and endowments, as well as the morbidity-based policies (see next section). Likewise, life insurance firms are insurers that may engage in writing any mortality- or morbidity-based policy.

Life insurance policies

Upon the death of the insured, a stated amount of money known as the face amount or sum assured is paid by the life insurance policy as a death benefit. The parties involved in a life insurance policy are as follows:

- **The insured** – This is the individual whose death results in the payment of the face amount.
- **The applicant** – This is the individual that applies for the policy.
- **The policyholder** – This is the person that the insurer deals with and who is capable of exercising all policy rights.
- **The beneficiary** – This is the person nominated by the applicant as the recipient of the face amount in the event of the death of the insured.

Insurance companies make the decision on issuing or declining the insurance policy requested on the basis of the applications they receive and, on occasion, on the basis of the outcome of laboratory tests, physical examination and sundry information. Contained in these applications are questions designed to determine the insurability of the applicant. Apart from establishing the proposed insured's health status, the underwriter also wants to ascertain that the amount of insurance applied for is reasonably related to the economic loss that the beneficiary would suffer on the insured's death.

In the modern day insurance industry, there are thousands of different life policies. Experts generally acknowledge that all life insurance policies are one of two generic types – term life insurance and cash-value life insurance.

Term life insurance

Term life insurance or term assurance is life insurance which provides coverage during the policy term, typically a specified number of years, such as 10 or 20 years, or to a specified age, such as 65. After that period, the insured can either drop the policy or pay annually increasing premiums to continue the coverage. If the insured dies during the term, the death benefit will be paid to the beneficiary. In the event that the insured survives until the end of the set term, the policy expires, i.e. it terminates without any payment. Figure 2.1 illustrates a term-to-age-65 policy. Under this £200,000 term life policy, the insurer typically pays the sum of £200,000 to the beneficiary only if the insured dies before the age of 65. No amount of money is paid if the insured happens to survive the policy term.

Figure 2.1 Diagrammatic Illustration of Term-to-Age 65 Life Insurance Policy

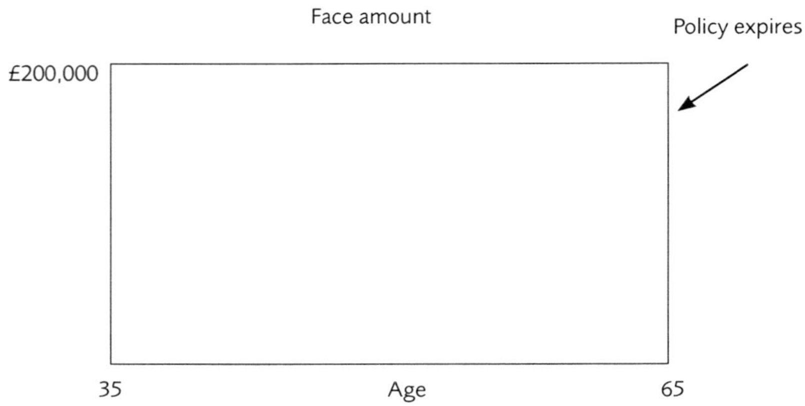

Cash-value life insurance policies

A cash-value life insurance policy pays a benefit on the death of the insured and also provides a savings element,[10] the cash value, where benefits are payable before death. In today's insurance marketplace, there are a large number of variations of cash-value policies as a result of insurers' desire to achieve product differentiation with a view to gaining market power. Industry experts point out that the terminology used for cash-value insurance policies is not standardised, but acknowledge that almost every cash-value policy that is sold is categorised broadly into one of three types, regardless of whether or not the insurer labels the policy as such. Universal life insurance, endowment insurance and whole life insurance are the three categories in question.

Virtually all cash-value life insurance policies are structured in much the same way. They are essentially a combination of yearly renewable term (YRT) insurance and a savings account designed in such a way that these combinations are always accurately equal to the policy face amount. Therefore, in the case of policies that have level face amounts, the amount of term insurance bought each year changes by exactly the same amount but in the opposite direction as the cash value changes. The difference between the insurance policy's face amount (death benefit) and its cash-value amount is referred to as the net amount at risk (NAR). Figure 2.2 is an illustration of a cash-value policy whose cash value increases each year and thus whose NAR decreases each year.

Universal life insurance

Universal life (UL) policies are contracts designed in such a way that the premiums payable by the insured are flexible and the death benefit payable

10 This saving element is akin to accumulated funds that are available to the policy owner in the same way as a savings account with a bank.

Figure 2.2 A Graphic Illustrating a Whole Life Insurance Policy

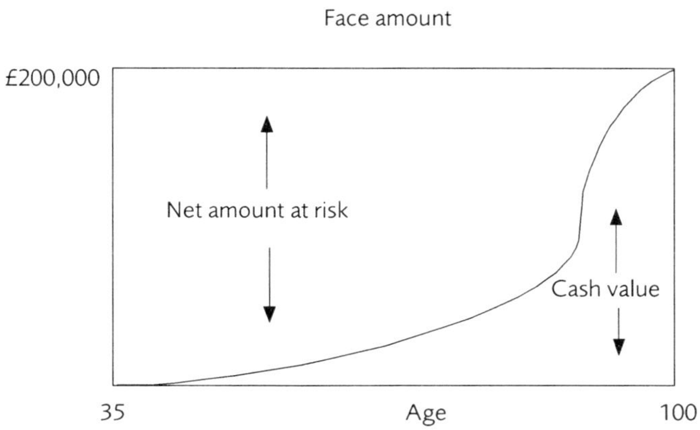

by the insurer is adjustable. The cash values and durations of these types of policies are dependent on the premiums paid into them. In order to get the policy started, and after the decision on the policy face amount, the applicant pays a premium of at least a certain amount. Subsequently, the policy owner is at liberty to pay as little or as much money into the policy as they wish. The magnitude of the savings is dependent on the amount that is paid into the policy.

There are three types of UL policies:

- **Single Premium** – The policy is paid for by a single, substantial initial payment. The policy is valid so long as the costs of insurance (COI) charges have not depleted the account.
- **Fixed Premium** – The policy is paid for by periodic premium payments. In general, these payments will be for a shorter period of time than the policy is in force; for example, payments may be made for 10 years, with the intention that thereafter the policy is paid-up. If the experience of the plan is not as good as predicted, the account value at the end of the premium period may not be adequate to continue the policy as originally written. In this case, the policyholder may have the choice to either:
  1. Leave the policy alone and allow it to potentially expire early (if COI charges deplete the account);
  2. Make additional or higher premium payments to keep the death benefit level;
  3. Lower the death benefit.
- **Flexible Premium** – This policy allows the policyholder to determine the amount they wish to pay on every occasion that the premium is due. Additionally, a flexible premium UL offers two different death benefit options:
  1. A level face amount (often called Option A), whereby the NAR varies inversely with the cash value;

2. A level amount at risk (often called Option B). This is also referred to as an increasing death benefit. Under this option pattern, the face value varies directly with the cash value.

Policyholders frequently purchase a flexible premium UL with a large initial deposit, thereafter making payments irregularly.

Whole life insurance policies

Whole life insurance is a policy that will pay out on death at any time of the person whose life is assured (insured), so long as the whole life insurance policy is still valid.

Unlike universal life policies, premiums for whole life insurance policies have the following characteristics:

- They are directly related to the amount of insurance that is bought.
- They must be paid when due otherwise the policy will terminate.
- Calculation of these premiums is done in such a way that the policy will be valid for the entire lifetime.

The main difference between whole life insurance and term insurance is that payment of the benefit will be inevitable (hence the difference between 'assurance' and 'insurance'). With term insurance, premiums only go towards a mortality element, as it will only pay out if the policyholder dies within the term. With whole of life, the premiums go partly towards a mortality element and partly towards a savings element, which builds up an investment fund in order to pay the benefit on death. Whole of life policies tend to be more expensive than term policies as a result of this.

The following are the main types of traditional whole life policies:

- **Non-participating whole life insurance** – This type of life policy has a level premium and face amount during the policyholder's entire life. The advantages of such a policy are its fixed costs and relatively low out-of-pocket premium payments. Since the policy is non-participating, it does not pay the policyholder any dividends.
- **Participating whole life insurance** – A participating whole life policy pays dividends. The dividends represent the favourable experience of the company and result from excess investment earnings, favourable mortality and expense savings. Dividends can be paid in cash, used to reduce premium payments, left to accumulate at a specified rate of interest or used to purchase paid-up additional insurance which will increase the policyholder's face amount of coverage. Dividends are not guaranteed to be paid to the policyholder.

Within the two broad categories of traditional non-participating whole life insurance and participating whole life insurance, there are various whole life policies such as level premium whole life insurance, limited payment whole life insurance, single premium whole life insurance and indeterminate premium whole life insurance. These types of policies are described below:

- **Level premium whole life insurance** – With this type of whole life insurance the premium payments are level and are required to be paid as long as the insured is living. In the early years, the premium is more than enough to pay the current cost of insurance protection. The excess, including interest earnings, makes up the deficiency of premiums in later years when the annual premium is not sufficient to pay the annual cost of insurance. These extra premiums are held and invested by the insurer, creating the 'cash value' of the policy.
- **Limited payment whole life insurance** – This allows the policyholder to pay a limited number of premium payments for a limited time and gives the policyholder lifetime protection. Given that the premiums are paid over a shorter span of time, the premium payments will be higher than under the ordinary whole life plan. Limited payment plans can provide for the payment of premiums for a set number of years, e.g. ten-payment or twenty-payment whole life insurance. Limited payment plans can also be based on age, e.g. whole life paid up at age 65 or at age 85.
- **Single premium whole life insurance** – This type of policy is a limited payment whole life insurance plan with one relatively large premium payment due at issue. The policy is fully paid up and no further premiums are required. Due to the single premium payment, the policy will have an instant cash value and loan value that could be considerable, depending on the amount of the single premium payment. Since a substantial single premium payment could be involved, this type of plan may be viewed more as an investment-oriented type of whole life insurance product.
- **Indeterminate premium whole life insurance** – An indeterminate premium whole life policy is akin to an ordinary whole life plan of insurance except that it provides for adjustable premiums. The insurer will charge a 'current' premium based on its current estimate of investment earnings, mortality and expense costs. If these estimates change in later years, the insurer will adjust the premium accordingly but never above the maximum guaranteed premium stated in the policy.

There is another type of whole life insurance policy – **unit-linked whole of life** – whereby the assets backing the policyholder's cash values are lodged in accounts that are separate from the insurer's general investments. With this type of policy, the 'mix' between life cover and investment is decided at the outset. Each monthly premium is used to buy units in a selected fund at an offer price.

Then every month the insurer calculates the cost of the life assurance for the next month only and deducts this charge by 'cancelling' just enough of the policyholder's accumulated units to pay for the cover.

In this way, the policy grows in value as the number of units held in the policy accumulates and (hopefully) the value of each unit also increases. The investment growth will depend on fund performance, how much is being deducted to pay for the life cover, and any other optional benefits selected (e.g. critical illness cover). Initial charges are made to recoup the set-up cost of this type of policy. This is done either by a low allocation to investment units or by creating special initial units.

The premium is usually reviewed on the 10th anniversary and may need to increase at that point (or the sum assured to reduce) depending on the level of unit growth.

Endowment insurance

This is a type of life insurance contract designed to pay a lump sum after a specified term (on its 'maturity') or on earlier death. With endowment insurance, the insured is given assurances, which are mutually exclusive, of payment of the face amount if the insured dies during the policy period or lives to the end of the period. The former is identical to that given under a term policy while the latter encompasses the concept of pure endowment. Pure endowment gives the assurance of payment of face value only if the insured survives to the end of the stated endowment period, with nothing paid if the insured dies during the endowment period. Few, if any, of these policies are sold as a separate policy; instead they are often entrenched within policies that offer other benefits.

Typical maturities of endowment insurance are 10, 15 or 20 years up to a certain age limit.

Annuities

An annuity is a contract between the insured and an insurer, under which the insured makes a lump-sum payment or series of payments. In return, the insurer agrees to make periodic payments to the insured, beginning immediately or at some future date.

The relationship between life insurance and an annuity is that while life insurance has the main task of the creation of a fund, an annuity's task is to systematically liquidate a fund and serves the purpose of protecting against the possibility of the insured outliving their income (the direct opposite of life insurance).

The following are some important terms that relate to annuities:

- **Annuitant** – This is the beneficiary of an annuity. He or she can be the contract holder or someone else to whom the title is designated. Proceeds of the contract are given to the beneficiary upon the annuitant's death in order to protect the beneficiary from a loss of income.
- **Pure life annuity** – This is an annuity contract under which annuity payments stop when the annuitant dies. Also known as a straight-life annuity.
- **Whole life annuity** – This pays over the life of an individual from a certain date, regardless of how long that may be.

- **Annuity certain** – This type of annuity pays a specific amount on a monthly basis for a set amount of time and is unrelated to whether the annuitant is alive.
- **Temporary life annuity** – This is an annuity that makes regular payments to a person (the annuitant) for a specified number of years.

There are generally two types of annuities – fixed and variable.

With a fixed annuity, the insured can expect a guaranteed rate of return for a specified time. With variable annuities, where the underlying investments are in stocks and bonds, the insured has the potential for a greater return on their investment, coupled with higher risk.

Annuities may also be classified by the payout options, either deferred or immediate. When an insured purchases an annuity, they will need to decide how they want the proceeds paid to them. An immediate annuity will begin payments to the insured immediately. With a deferred annuity, the insured will receive payments at a later date.

Fixed annuities

Fixed annuities earn a guaranteed rate of interest for a specific time period, such as one, three or five years. Once the guarantee period is over, a new interest rate is set for the next period. The guaranteed interest rate of a fixed annuity is based on the claims-paying ability and financial health of the insurer that issues the annuity.

Variable annuities

Variable annuities normally offer a range of funding options from which the insured may choose. These funding options may include portfolios comprising stocks, bonds and money-market instruments. The account value of variable annuities can go up or down based on market fluctuations. The insured's contributions and earnings are not guaranteed but instead depend on the performance of the underlying investment options. If the funding options the insured chooses for his or her annuity perform well, they may exceed the inflation rate or fixed annuity returns. If they don't perform well, the insured may lose not only any earnings he or she has made, but even some of the contributions.

Some variable annuities offer, in addition to a range of funding options, a fixed account option that guarantees both principal and interest, much like a fixed annuity. A fixed account option can give the insured the security of allocating some of their premium payments more conservatively while still taking advantage of market potential. Again, the guaranteed rate is based on the claims-paying ability of the issuer.

Variable annuities also allow the insured to transfer money from one funding option to another without triggering a taxable event. In other words, if the insured transfers money to a different funding option within their variable annuity, they will not have to pay income taxes on any earnings they have accumulated at the time of transfer. Income tax-free transfer means they can reallocate money to suit changing investment goals (e.g. due to life events) without worrying about income tax burdens.[11]

Types of annuity contract

Annuities fall into one of two general categories, based on when the annuity's payments are scheduled to begin. These categories are **immediate** and **deferred** annuities.

A contract is designated as an immediate annuity if income payments to the annuitant are scheduled to begin one payout interval (for instance, one month or one year) after the purchase date of the annuity. The contract is called a deferred annuity if income payments are to begin at some further point in the future – perhaps as much as several years from the date of purchase.

As for immediate annuities, there is some confusion surrounding this name. It should be noted that although the contract is called an immediate annuity, payments don't begin on the very next day after the contract is purchased. Rather, payments begin after one full payment period has elapsed following the date of purchase. For instance, if the contract calls for monthly instalments, payments will begin one month after the date of purchase. If the contract specifies that annual payments will be made, the annuitant will receive the first payment one year after the purchase date of the annuity.

That said, the following are some of the more common types of annuity contract:

- **Flexible-premium deferred annuity**[12] – FPDA is a contract under which the premium payment frequency (monthly, quarterly, semi-annually, yearly) may vary and the amount of each premium payment (usually subject to a minimum value) may vary. This contract pays a monthly (or quarterly, semi-annual, or annual) income benefit for the life of a person (the annuitant), for the lives of two or more persons, or for a specified period of time. These income payments are scheduled to begin at a specified later date. The annuitant can never outlive the income from the annuity. While the basic purpose of life insurance is to provide an income for a beneficiary at the death of the insured, the annuity is intended to provide an income for life for the annuitant.
- **Single-premium deferred annuity**[13] – is a tax-deferred investment whereby an investor makes a lump-sum payment to an insurance company and the lump sum is invested in either a fixed-return instrument like a certificate of deposit (CD) or a variable-return portfolio that can be switched among stocks, bonds, and money-market accounts.
- **Single-premium immediate annuity**[14] – SPIAs are designed for

11 MetLife (2007), 'Annuities – Answering Your Questions about Annuities', Life Advice Booklet.
12 Descriptions of this type of annuity may vary from market to market.
13 Ibid.
14 Ibid.

people who need a guaranteed income on a regular basis. Under the SPIA, payments are made to the annuitant immediately after the insurer has received a single premium payment.

Morbidity-based Insurance Policies

There are essentially three major types of economic loss relating to health risk that individuals typically face and they are:

1. Medical expenses that they incur if they happen to become sick or injured;
2. Expenses incurred for the provision of long-term care (LTC) in the event of mental or physical illness, old age frailty or injury that may hamper their ability to engage in daily activities;
3. Incapacity or poor health that can be devastating to the extent that employment may be prevented and the implication would likely be a reduction, or in some cases elimination, of income.

The types of morbidity-based insurance policies – health insurance, LTC insurance and disability income insurance policies – described below are usually designed to respectively cover each of the three loss exposures.

Health insurance policies

Health insurance protects the insured and their dependants against any financial constraints arising on account of a medical emergency. Government programmes and employers are usually the financiers of healthcare expenses. In some cases these expenses are financed from personal financial resources. While most health insurance cover is employer based, individuals without access to employer-sponsored insurance may obtain health insurance on their own, usually through the individual health insurance market, although in some instances health insurance may be available to individuals through professional associations or similar arrangements.

Commercial health insurers (sometimes called indemnity insurers), generally organised as stock companies (owned by stockholders) or as mutual insurance companies (owned by their policyholders), write some form of health insurance in many countries.

For health coverage arrangements to perform well, the risk pooling should result in expected costs for the pool that are reasonably predictable for the insurer and relatively stable over time (e.g. the average level of health risk in the pool should not vary dramatically from time to time, although costs will rise with overall changes in price and utilisation).

To accomplish this, health coverage providers endeavour to maintain risk pools of people whose health, on average, is the same as that of the general population. In other words, health coverage providers take steps to avoid attracting a disproportionate share of people in poor health into their risk pools, which is often referred to as adverse selection.

Health coverage providers use underwriting to maintain a predictable and stable level of risk within their risk pools and to set terms of coverage for people of different risks within a risk pool. Underwriting is the process of determining whether or not to accept an applicant for coverage and determining what the terms of coverage will be, including the premium.

A primary underwriting decision is whether or not the health coverage provider will accept an applicant for coverage. Health coverage providers typically underwrite each person seeking to purchase coverage in the individual insurance market (where people buy insurance on their own), reviewing the person's health status and claims history.

Insurers offer, amongst others, health insurance policies, hospital-medical and major medical insurance policies, and also special individual policies. These special policies include: supplemental health insurance, hospital confinement indemnity, and specified disease policies:

- Supplemental health insurance is a type of insurance policy designed to cover the gaps that regular health insurance may have due to deductibles and co-payments. Supplemental health insurance covers additional expenses that primary insurance doesn't cover, such as lost income and living expenses.
- Hospital confinement indemnity is a policy that pays a fixed sum for each day the insured is confined to the hospital, usually regardless of other health insurance coverage.
- A specified disease policy, sometimes called a 'dread disease policy', is individual coverage that pays benefits only when the insured person is diagnosed with the specific illness or condition named in the policy. In general, policy provisions are very specific and may limit benefit payments to narrowly defined conditions. For instance, a policy might only provide coverage if an insured person is admitted to hospital for a condition.

  Specified disease policies are not an alternative to comprehensive health coverage, such as a major medical policy that provides benefits in the event of a variety of illnesses or injuries. Rather, the main purpose of specified disease insurance is to provide supplemental coverage on top of an existing health policy. For this reason, specified disease coverage is often sold as a special amendment to an existing insurance plan, rather than as a stand-alone policy and is limited in scope.

Long-term care insurance policies

The second type of health risk that individuals are faced with is as a result of the possibility of their being incapable of caring for themselves; usually associated with old age.

Long-term care refers to the many services beyond medical care and nursing care used by people who have disabilities or chronic (long-lasting) illnesses. Long-term care insurance helps individuals pay for these services, which can be very expensive. A policy also ensures that these individuals can make their own choices about what long-term care services they receive and where they receive them.

Long-term care insurance normally covers the cost of:

- Help in their homes with daily activities like bathing, dressing, eating and cleaning;
- Community programmes, such as adult day care;
- Assisted living services that are provided in a special residential setting other than their own home; these services may include meals, health monitoring, and help with daily activities;
- Visiting nurses;
- Care in a nursing home.

Those that seek insurance under individually issued policies typically choose from a wide range of options, including the length of the benefit period, which may range from one to five years to a lifetime.

Disability insurance policies

Individual disability insurance is an insurance product designed to replace gross income on a tax-free basis should a sickness or illness prevent a person from earning an income in their occupation.

Types of disability insurance include:

- **National social insurance programmes** – In most developed countries, the government is responsible for providing the single most important form of disability insurance for all of its citizens. Typical examples are part of the UK's National Insurance and the US's Social Security (SS) schemes – specifically, several parts of SS including Social Security Disability Insurance (SSDI) and Supplemental Security Income (SSI). These programmes provide a floor beneath all the other separate forms of disability insurance available in the various societies around the world. Said in another way, they are the 'safety net' that catches everyone who is either (a) otherwise uninsured or (b) otherwise underinsured. In this capacity, they are very large, very important programmes, with a large number of beneficiaries. Experts assert that the general theory of the benefit formula is that the benefit is not large but is enough to prevent abject poverty.
- **Employer-supplied disability insurance** – The second most important form of disability insurance is that provided by employers to cover their employees, which is obvious given that one of the top causes of becoming disabled is sustaining injury on the job. There are several subtypes that may or may not be separate parts of the benefits package: workers' compensation and more general (but very basic) disability insurance policies.
- **Individual disability insurance policies** – There are instances when employers do not provide benefits and employees desire disability cover-

age and so have to purchase their own policies on the open market. There are variations in the premiums and available benefits for individual coverage between different companies, for individuals in different occupations, and by country.

Self-employed individuals also buy their disability insurance policies on the market as they have to make these provisions since they do not have employers to take care of this for them.

Non-life Insurance

Non-life insurance (or general insurance as it is known in some markets) is generally associated with the more descriptive terms property and liability (P&L) insurance and property and casualty (P&C) insurance.

Non-life insurance can be broadly categorised into property insurance and liability insurance. We will take into account two other categories for classifying insurance, personal insurance and commercial insurance, to be used in conjunction with the latter categories for the relevant discussions in this section.

A classification is offered by OECD (see Figure 2.3) that accentuates the various forms of non-life insurance.

Property Insurance Policies

Property insurance offers protection against most risks to property, such as fire, theft and some weather damage. This includes specialised forms of insurance such as fire insurance, flood insurance, earthquake insurance, home insurance or boiler insurance. Property insurance is carried out in two principal ways – open perils and named perils. Open perils provides cover for all the causes of loss not specifically excluded in the policy. Common exclusions on open peril policies include damage that occurs as a result of earthquakes, floods, nuclear incidents, acts of terrorism and war. In order for insurance to be provided for named perils there is usually a requirement for the actual cause of loss to be listed in the policy. Common named perils include such damage-causing events as fire, lightning, explosion and theft.

Types of policies

Property insurance policies are offered by insurers for coverage of a business's building and its contents – money and securities, accounts-receivable records, inventory, furniture, machinery, supplies and even intangible assets such as trademarks – in the event of damage, theft or loss. Property insurance is issued for both commercial and personal purposes.

Some insurance companies offer property insurance by named peril, such

Figure 2.3 OECD Classifications of Non-life Insurance

Category	Product Type
Motor Vehicle	▪ *Land Vehicles* (other than railway rolling stock) covering all damage to or loss of: land motor vehicles or land vehicles other than motor vehicles ▪ *Motor Vehicle* Liability covering all liability arising out of the use of motor vehicles operating on land (including carrier's liability)
Marine, Aviation and Transportation (MAT)	▪ *Railway Rolling Stock and Other Transport* covering all damage to or loss of railway rolling stock ▪ *Aircraft* covering all damage to or loss of aircraft ▪ *Ships* (sea, lake, and river and canal vessels) covering all damage to or loss of: river and canal vessels, lake vessels, and sea vessels ▪ *Aircraft Liability* covering all liability arising out of the use of aircraft (including carrier's liability) ▪ *Liability for Ships* (sea, lake, and river and canal vessels) covering all liability arising out of ships, vessels, or boats on the sea, lakes, rivers, or canals (including carrier's liability)
Freight	▪ *Goods in Transit* (including merchandise, baggage and all other goods) covering all damage to or loss of goods in transit or baggage, irrespective of the form of transport
Fire and Other Property Damage	▪ *Fire and Natural Forces* covering all damage or loss of property due to fire, explosion, storm, natural forces other than storm, nuclear energy or land subsidence (excluded is property included in land vehicle, railway rolling stock and other transport, aircraft, ships and goods in transit) ▪ *Other Damage to Property* covering all damage or loss of property (other than property included in land vehicle, railway rolling stock and other transport, aircraft, ships and goods in transit) due to hail or frost, and any event such as theft, other than those mentioned under fire and natural forces
Pecuniary Loss	▪ *Credit* covering insolvency (general), export credit, instalment credit, mortgages and agricultural credit ▪ *Surety* ▪ *Miscellaneous Financial Loss* covering employment risk, insufficiency of income (general), bad weather, loss of benefits, continuing general expenses, unforeseen trading expenses, indirect trading losses other than those mentioned above, other financial loss (non-trading), and other forms of financial loss
General Liability	▪ *General Liability* covering all liability other than those forms mentioned under motor vehicle liability, aircraft liability and liability for ships
Accident and Sickness	▪ *Accident* (including industrial injury and occupational diseases) covering: fixed pecuniary benefits, benefits in the nature of indemnity or injury to passengers
Other Non-life Insurance	▪ *Legal Expenses* covering legal expenses and costs of litigation ▪ *Assistance* ▪ *Miscellaneous*
Treaty Reinsurance	▪ *Treaty Reinsurance*

Source: OECD (2003).

as fire and theft, while others offer policies that cover multiple perils. Some policies offer coverage for only direct destruction and damage to property. Others offer coverage for both direct and indirect losses.

- **Fire insurance policies** – These types of insurance policy are named-perils contracts that provide comprehensive cover against fire, lightning and smoke damage to the insured's property and contents. Insurance companies sell fire insurance policies for residential and commercial purposes and offer coverage for both movable and immovable property. The exact features and cost of cover will vary on the level of cover that the insured takes out, as well as on a possible assessment of the property and the degree of fire risk.
- **Commercial property insurance policies** – These types of policy are for those that intend to insure their businesses against both direct and indirect property losses. In most cases, insurers target them at large businesses. They typically take a different approach to small and medium-sized enterprises as they tend to provide a package policy that covers both liability and property risks. The most common types of business property, both movable and immovable, are covered by this type of insurance policy and they include buildings, fixtures, inventory, computers and so on.
- **Consequential loss insurance** – Consequential losses are secondary losses suffered as a consequence of an original loss. For example, if a fire destroys a shopping mall (the original loss), a business may suffer loss of profit through inability to trade for an extended period. Consequential loss insurance, as the name implies, is used to indemnify the insured for specific indirect losses that the insured can incur as result of the loss of or damage to the covered property directly from an insured peril.
- **Industrial all-risk insurance policies** – These are all-risk contracts that provide wide protection by providing coverage for a variety of high-value movable and immovable properties. Large industrial and commercial enterprises are the types of companies that use this type of insurance cover. Settlement of losses is carried out on a replacement cost basis[15] apart from inventory, which may be settled on a market-value basis.
- **Contractors' all-risk (CAR) insurance policies** (also called **builders' all-risk policies**) – These insure against physical loss or damage to works, plant, equipment and materials during the course of construction. They are sometimes called **course of construction** policies.

  The major characteristic that differentiates this type of insurance policy from other types of insurance is that CAR insurance is not limited by reference to specified perils – in other words, everything is covered unless it is excluded (expressly or by implication). CAR insurance is usually combined with liability insurance.

15 On this basis, the policyholder suffers no reduction in loss recovery due to depreciation of owned property from its original value.

- **Fidelity/crime insurance policies** – These are named-peril contracts designed to protect organisations from loss of money, securities or inventory resulting from crime. Common fidelity/crime insurance claims allege employee dishonesty, embezzlement, forgery, robbery, safe burglary, computer fraud, wire transfer fraud, counterfeiting, and other criminal acts. These schemes involve every possible angle, taking advantage of any potential weakness in a company's financial controls. From fictitious employees, dummy accounts payable and non-existent suppliers to outright theft of money, securities and property.
- **Motor vehicle insurance** – The policy for this type of insurance is a contract by which the insurer assumes the risk of any loss the owner or operator of a car – individual and business – may incur through damage to property or persons as the result of an accident. There are many particular forms of motor vehicle insurance, varying in the sort of risk that they cover and also in the legal principles underlying them.
- **Marine insurance** – This type of insurance covers the loss or damage of ships, cargo, terminals, and any transport or property by which cargo is transferred, acquired or held between the point of origin and final destination. The policy provides both hull insurance and cargo insurance (described below). Hull insurance covers the vessel or hull, the cargo, the freight revenue to be received by the ship owner, and legal liability for negligence of the shipper or the carrier.
- **Aircraft hull insurance** – This type of coverage is on an all-risk basis, regardless of where the aeroplane is – on the ground or in the air – and is also known as **hull aircraft insurance**. Exclusions, although none are standard, include illegal use of an aircraft; using an aircraft for purposes other than that described in the policy; wear and tear; piloting of the aircraft by someone not named in the policy; operating an aircraft outside stipulated geographical boundaries; and damage or destruction of an aircraft resulting from war, riots and strikes. The hull value may include instruments, radios, autopilots, wings, engines, and other equipment attached to or carried on the plane, as described in the policy.
- **Cargo insurance** – This type of insurance, also called **marine cargo insurance**, covers physical damage to or loss of goods whilst in transit by land, sea and air. The insurance is taken out by either the exporter or the importer, depending on the shipping terms, from the departure point to the final destination.

Liability Insurance Policies

In many countries around the world, liability insurance is a compulsory form of insurance for those at risk of being sued by third parties for negligence or other tortuous actions. The most usual classes of mandatory policy provide coverage for the drivers of vehicles, those who provide professional services to the public, those who manufacture products that may be capable of causing harm, constructors and those who employ staff. The rationale behind such laws is that the classes of insured are intentionally engaging in activities that put others at risk of injury or loss. Public policy therefore requires that such individuals should carry insurance so that, should their activities happen to cause loss or damage to another, money will be available to pay compensation. Additionally, there are a further range of perils that people insure against and, as a consequence, the number and range of liability policies have increased in line with the increase in the contingency fee litigation offered by lawyers (sometimes on a class action basis).

The following are some of the more popular liability policies:

- **General (public) liability insurance policy** – This type of insurance is absolutely essential to every business owner. Public liability insurance offers all-risk protection for any business where the general public frequent from legal and medical costs that arise from an incident on its property, even if the insured is not to blame.
- **Professional liability insurance policy** – This is an insurance policy that offers protection for an individual or company in the event a client alleges they have suffered a financial loss as a result of an error or an omission committed by the individual or company in the delivery of professional services. It is also known as error and omissions (E&O) insurance. Professional liability coverage is separate from a general liability (GL) policy, which would cover you mainly for bodily injury or property damage liability. These policies are popular with healthcare professionals, directors and officers, engineers and other professionals who seek cover for liability resulting from their professional negligence.
- **Product liability insurance policy** – In product liability insurance terms, a product is any physical item that is sold or given away. Product liability is the area of law in which manufacturers, distributors, suppliers, retailers, and others who make products available to the public are held responsible for the injuries those products cause.
- **Automobile (motor) liability insurance policy** – This type of insurance policy is compulsory in most countries for automobile owners and users and provides cover for the insured's legal liability to a third party for bodily injury or property damage as a result of negligent operation of an automobile.
- **Workers' (workmen's) compensation policy** – This is a type of legally required insurance provided by employers to all employees for work-related illnesses and injuries, and even death.

Package Insurance Policies

These are essentially several basic property and/or liability policies combined to create a single policy. A typical example, the Home-owner's Insurance Policy, is made up of such basic coverages as Broad Form Personal Theft Insurance, Comprehensive Personal Liability and Fire Insurance–Standard Fire Policy. Other examples of commercial multi-peril insurance and business-owners' insurance are:

- **Commercial multi-peril insurance** – This is a policy that includes several different coverage forms for both the property and general liability loss exposures of large businesses.
- **Business-owners' insurance policies (BOPs)** – These are insurance packages that provide both direct and indirect property and liability coverage for owners of businesses. These packaged policies are commonly purchased by most small and medium-sized companies. They include property protection for an office building and its contents as well as other people's property brought into the office building and indemnity for the insured for consequential expenses that arise from a direct property loss, and agree to pay any judgments against the insured as a result of business-related tortuous actions. Depending on the markets for which they are targeted, insurers offer these policies on a named-peril and all-risks basis.

Market Segmentation

Behavioural profiling is an effective method used by insurers to segment their customers in most mature insurance markets. One interesting method of segmentation that uses behavioural profiling is contained in the World Insurance Report 2008 by Capgemini and EFMA. The report segments the market for insurance products into Traditionalists, Opportunists, Indifferent and Average users. The segmentation is a reflection of important customer perceptions and attitudes toward insurance, its value and potential, as well as actual buying patterns according to the report.

Figure 2.4 shows a brief description of the characteristics of these market segments.

Figure 2.4 Descriptions of the Characteristics of Identified Market Segments

Indifferent	Traditionalists
Have a tendency toward minimal coverage and their income may be insufficient to build a comprehensive insurance portfolio, especially on life products. Are unconvinced, at best, about the value of insurance, and have a tendency to view insurance as no more than an enforced requirement. Are generally unconcerned to search for the best products, or carry out their own research. Are mainly too indifferent to be volatile.	Usually more mature in age, from middle-to-higher income brackets, and are more likely to be multi-equipped (i.e. they have several types of policy). Take a classic view of insurance as a means of guaranteeing against risk (in particular property and family), but are aware of the financial potential of insurance, given that they have savings. Like to be reassured when purchasing (e.g. by advice and/or brand). Are characteristically loyal and rarely self-motivated to switch insurers.
Opportunists	**Average**
Are characteristically middle class, and hold an above-average number of policies. Perceive insurance from a classic viewpoint of a means of guaranteeing against risk. Continually search the market for more suitable products. Are pragmatic and technical in their approach to buying, and therefore pay special attention to price and/or product specifics. Aim to obtain independent data and research, and frequently use the Internet to gather basic knowledge before developing their own opinions on insurance. Are a potentially volatile group, ready to switch insurers if the transition is straightforward, and admit that they would defect after a bad claims experience.	Could be described as pedestrian, in that they take a classic view of insurance as a way of risk-protection, and are inclined to be averagely equipped with coverage (i.e. they have about the average number of policies in a given country). Most countries display a block of Average users, except for the USA and the UK.

Source: Adapted from descriptions in the World Insurance Report 2008 by Capgemini and EFMA

Distribution Channels

Historically, most insurance companies used a simple distribution model whereby they had one distribution network, which was classically generalist, or possibly multi-specialist, and the agent (whether the distribution was intermediated or not) was the single point of contact for all customer requirements.

In recent times, there have been many different types of distributors competing for customers, and each is seeking to differentiate itself with a view to gaining a competitive edge. As a consequence, distribution networks are inclined to remain generalist to the extent that a wide net can be cast for customers and specialist to the extent that they can adequately serve specific product segments.

This contradiction in terms has challenged insurers as they attempt to identify the optimal distribution strategy and at the same time manage and plan multiple distribution networks to approach customers effectively and increase wallet share.

An analysis carried out by Capgemini, also contained in the 2008 World Report, using data on customer demographics, usage and attitudes, reveals many important differences in network profiles as well as the strengths and weaknesses of different networks (see Figure 2.5). This shows the profile and demographics of the customers that make use of these channels. Also shown are characteristics of each distribution network (channel), the product specialty, and the strengths and weaknesses of each network.

It is worth noting that distribution channels have, in recent times, become more specialised. The level of specialisation is illustrated in Figure 2.6, also extracted from the 2008 World Insurance Report. Notably, the usage of each type of distribution network and the perception by customers is demonstrated by the dispersion on this matrix. Each usage has a specialty in terms of the products sold, the manner in which products are sold, their appeal to customers, and the type of customers served. The matrix exhibits the distribution networks' high level of specialisation in recent times, or at least, the perception of customers about their degree of specialisation. This would suggest that insurers in mature countries haven't had the need to deviate from their conventional (traditional) models. Each distribution channel provides for a specific need of a specific segment of the population.

Figure 2.5 Distribution Networks in Mature Markets: Profile and Attributes

	Customer demographics	Customer Profile	Network Characteristics	Product Speciality (by premium)	Network Strengths/Weaknesses
Tied agents	Older customers (11% more of 41-to-55-year-olds 10% more of 71+ year-olds	Customers slightly more equipped Fewer users of multiple distributors	Customers are likely to switch after a poor claims experience More customers who perceive insurance as a means to improve finance	58% Non-Life	**Strengths** Professional advice especially in Non-Life (+11%) **Weaknesses** Ease of purchase especially in Non-Life (−12%)
Multi-tied agents/Brokers/ IFAs	More high-income customers (+18%)	Customers much more equipped (higher number of policies owned)	More customers who perceive insurance as a means to protect against financial loss	53% Life	**Strengths** Professional advice (+27% in Non-Life and +20% in Life) **Weaknesses** Brand/Trust (−14% in Non-Life and −12% in Life)
Direct writing companies	Older customers (20% more of the 56-to-70-year-olds, 32% more of 71-year-olds Fewer high-income customers (−22%)	Customers slightly less equipped, but with a higher concentration of policies with a smaller number of distributors	Longer contract longevity (+29%)	61% Non-Life	**Strengths** Brands/Trusts (+10% in Non-Life and +11% in Life **Weaknesses** Professional advice (−10% in Non-Life and −11% in Life)
Banks	More middle-aged customers (14% more of 26-to-40-year-olds)	Customers more equipped More users of multiple distributors	Shorter contract longevity (−30%) Customers more likely to switch after a poor claims experience	68% Life	**Strengths** Professional advice (+14% in Non-Life and +6% in Life) Product, especially in Non-Life (+8%) **Weaknesses** After-sales service (−19% in Non-Life adnd −27% in Life)

Mobile sales forces	More low-income customers (+11%)	Customers with average equipment but a higher concentration of policies with a smaller number of distributors	Much longer contract longevity (+31%) Customers less likely to switch after a poor claims experience More customers who perceive insurance as a means to protect family and improve finance	65% Non-Life	**Strengths** After-sales service (+40% in Non-Life and +48% in Life) Professional advice especially in Non-Life (+37%) Fees/returns (only in Life) **Weaknesses** Ease of purchase (−20% in Non-Life and −18% in Life) Product (−27% in Non-Life and −23% in Life) Price only in Non-Life (−13%)
Internet	Younger customers (65% more of 18-to-25-year-olds) More high-income customers (+41%)	Customers with much lower equipment On average, customers tend to use slightly more distributors	Shorter contract longevity (−60%) More customers who perceive insurance as a means to protect against financial loss	80% Non-Life	**Strengths** Ease of purchase (+51% in Non-Life and −32% in Life) Price Product but to a lower extent **Weaknesses** Professional advice (−49% in Non-Life and −25% in Life) Brand/Trust, especially in Non-Life
Telephone sales (not phone communications e.g. by agent)	More of both younger and older customers (25% more of the 18-to-25-year-olds. 43% more of 71+ year-olds) More low-income customers (+24%)	Higher number of distributors used	Shorter contract longevity (−14%)	81% Non-Life	**Strengths** Ease of purchase (+22% in Non-Life and +20% in Life) **Weaknesses** Professional advice (−27% in Non-Life and −10% in Life)
Alternative networks	More of both younger and older customers (21% more of the 18-to-25-year-olds. 15% more of 71+ year-olds) More high-income customers (+11%)	Higher number of distributors used		51% Non-Life	**Strengths** Ease of purchase (+13% in Non-Life and +24% in Life) **Weaknesses** Professional advice (−25% in Non-Life and −22% in Life)

Source: Capgemini analysis, 2007.

Note: This is a comparison among distribution networks. Value differences (+/– %) for each network are relative to the mean of all distribution networks. Product speciality percentages are the network's concentration of life or non-life premiums, on aggregate across mature markets.

Figure 2.6 Distribution Networks in Mature Markets: Mapping of Product Speciality vs Strength of Professional Advice (%)

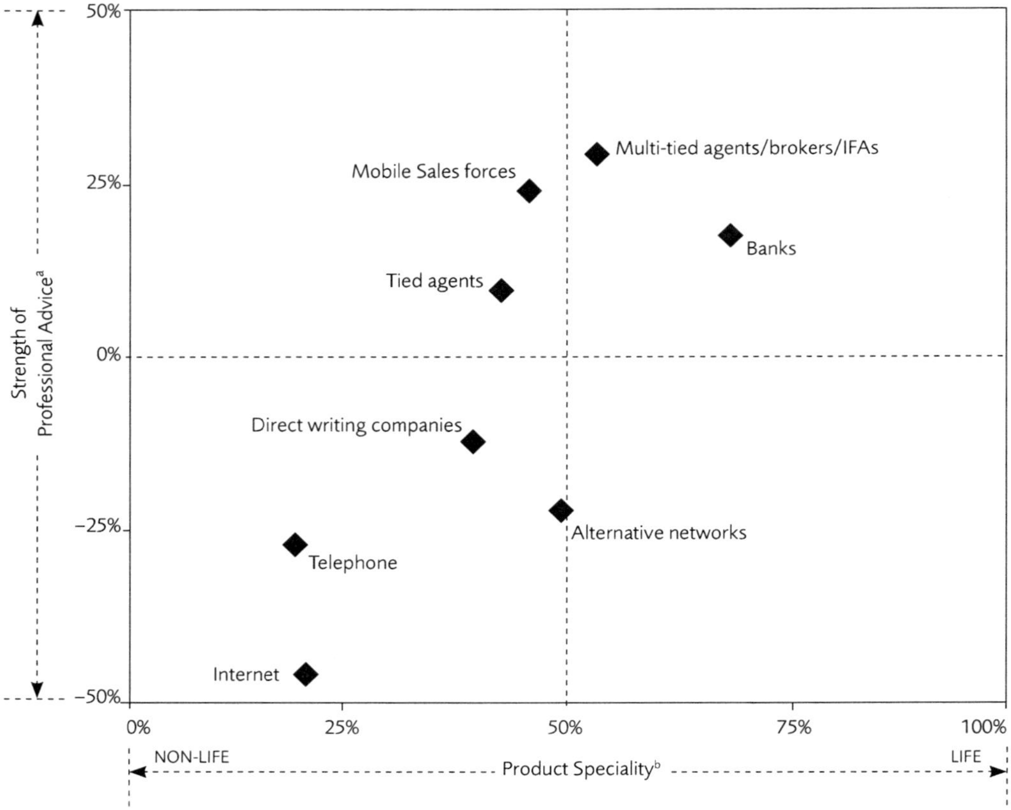

[a] Professional advice is the rating that customers gave to professional advice as a purchase influencer in a given distribution network. The percentage is derived by calculating the deviation of one distributor to the mean of all the distributors.

[b] Product speciality is expressed as the share of total premiums generated by life policies.

Source: Capgemini analysis, 2007

Overview of Reinsurance

3

This chapter provides an overview of reinsurance including the function of reinsurance and the forms of reinsurance.

Introduction

When observing the risks that insurers take on, it is to be expected that they themselves might be in need of insurance. When insurers insure a risk again, it is called reinsurance. Hence reinsurance can be described as insurance for insurers and is one of the major risk and capital management tools accessible to primary insurance companies.

Reinsurance can be described as an extension of the concept of insurance, in that it passes on part of the risk for which the original insurer is liable. Reinsurance contracts are somewhat more specialised than insurance contracts but for the most part they work in exactly the same way; the difference being that the 'insured' is another insurer, known as the 'reinsured'.

Reinsurance entails financing by the insurer of a portion of a risk, a policy or portfolio of risks by taking out a contract with another insurance company, the reinsurance company, which is also referred to as the assuming company. In this case the insurer is referred to as the cedant or the ceding company. The amount of risk transferred is referred to as the cession and that not reinsured and retained by the cedant is referred to as the retention.

A contract of reinsurance is between the insurer and reinsurer only and legally there is no direct link between the original insured and any reinsurer. The original insurer is still the one who must pay any claim from the insured – the insurer must then make its own separate claim against the reinsurer.

There are two fundamental types of reinsurance companies: direct writers, which have their own employed account executives who generate business, and broker companies with expert knowledge of the market, which get business through reinsurance intermediaries. However, some direct writers get a fraction of their business through brokers, and similarly, some brokers in reinsurance receive some business directly from the insuring company.

Brokers vs Direct Writers

From a ceding company's standpoint, both the broker market and the direct market have advantages as well as disadvantages. A ceding company's choice of one market over the other will be influenced by its view of such advantages and disadvantages in relation to the reinsurance coverage being placed. For example, broker coverages usually involve a number of participating reinsurers that have been assembled by a broker, each assuming a specified portion of the risk being reinsured. A ceding company may find it easier to arrange such coverage in a difficult underwriting environment where risk capacity is constrained and reinsurers are seeking to limit their risk exposure. In contrast, direct coverage is usually structured by ceding companies directly with one or a limited number of reinsurers.

Definition of Reinsurance

Reinsurance is the practice undertaken by insurers to transfer portions of risk portfolios to other parties by a form of agreement with a view to lessening the likelihood of having to pay a large obligation as a result of an insurance claim. Insurance companies use reinsurance to reduce the risks associated with underwritten policies by spreading risks across alternative institutions.

A reinsurance contract is an insurance contract between one insurer or pure reinsurer (the reinsurer) and another insurer or pure insurer (the cedant) to indemnify against losses on one or more contracts issued by the cedant in exchange for a consideration (the premium). (IAIS Standard on reinsurance cover of primary insurers, January 2002)

A reinsurer is an insurer that offers protection through the sale of a reinsurance contract to a risk-transferring policyholder who is an insurer. If the risk-transferring policyholder is a (re)insurer itself, the risk-assuming insurer is called the reinsurer, and the risk transfer is known as retrocession. (IAIS Guidance paper on risk transfer, disclosure and analysis of finite reinsurance, October 2005)

Functions of Reinsurance

Reinsurance provides three essential functions:

1. It helps to stabilise direct insurers' earnings when unusual and major events occur, by assuming the high layers of these risks or relieving them of accumulated individual exposures.
2. It allows insurers to increase the maximum amount they can insure for a given loss or category of losses by facilitating the underwriting of a greater number of risks, or larger risks, without burdening them with the need to cover their solvency margin, and hence their capital base.
3. It makes substantial quantities of liquidity available to insurers in the event of major loss.

Providers of Reinsurance

Ever since reinsurance emerged in the 19th century out of the need on the part of the primary insurers to insure themselves against payment difficulties by means of a broad international distribution of their obligations, there has been a proliferation of reinsurance providers.

Types of Reinsurance Companies

Reinsurance providers can be classed as:

- **Professional reinsurers** – This type of provider's business is confined solely to reinsurance and the peripheral services offered by a reinsurer to its customers as opposed to primary insurers who exchange reinsurance or operate reinsurance departments as an addition to their central business of primary insurance. The majority of professional reinsurers provide complete reinsurance and services from one source directly to the ceding company.
- **Reinsurance departments of primary insurers** – Primary insurers are also permitted by insurance law to sell reinsurance and they use this to diversify their risk and also increase their product offering.
- **Pools** – Sometimes known as associations, these are organisations of insurers or reinsurers through which particular types of risk are underwritten, with the premiums, losses and expenses shared in agreed ratios. Pools provide a way of writing larger limits of insurance than a single reinsurer may be willing to assume. Examples are the Turkish Reinsurance Pool and States of the Gulf Aviation Pool.
- **Lloyd's associations** – Syndicates of Lloyd's of London, an insurance market providing specialist insurance services to businesses, accept reinsurance and a considerable inter-syndicate reinsurance business also exists at Lloyd's.

Table 3.1 Global Reinsurance Companies

Ranking	Company	Country	Net Reinsurance Premiums Written (Mil. $)	
			2007	2006
1	Munich Reinsurance Co.	Germany	30,292.9	27,425.2
2	Swiss Reinsurance Co.	Switzerland	27,706.6	23,841.1
3	Berkshire Hathaway Re	US	17,398.0	11,576.0
4	Hannover Rueckversicherung AG	Germany	10,630.0	9,353.5
5	Lloyd's	UK	8,362.9	8,445.3
6	SCOR SE	France	7,871.7	4,885.2
7	Reinsurance Group of America, Inc.	US	4,906.5	4,343.0
8	Transatlantic Holdings Inc.	US	3,952.9	3,633.4
9	Everest Reinsurance Co.	Bermuda	3,919.4	3,875.7
10	PartnerRe Ltd	Bermuda	3,757.1	3,689.5

Source: Standard and Poor's Global Reinsurance Highlights, 2008

Purchasers of Reinsurance

Reinsurers' professional corporate counterparties, i.e. firms that purchase reinsurance, include primary insurers, reinsurance intermediaries, multinational companies and their captive insurers or banks. Primary insurers from all classes form the majority of reinsurance clients.

Factors that determine the volume of business that an insurer will reinsure include the business model it adopts, its risk appetite and capital strength as well as the prevailing market conditions.

The following are categories of insurers that typically purchase reinsurance:

- Insurers with portfolios that are heavily exposed to catastrophic events such as windstorms, earthquakes or floods and have a strong need for reinsurance cover;
- Relatively small local players that require more insurance coverage than large international insurers, given their inability to diversify their insurance risks over a larger client base;
- Life insurers with a greater fraction of contracts containing a mortality or disability risk element;
- Insurers that are writing many lines of business and have a relatively better balanced portfolio than specialised insurers that have focused customer groups or few business lines;
- Insurers, particularly life insurers, that are pursuing an expansion strategy involving development of new products or entry into new geographical regions;
- Insurers that are exiting markets or lines of business.[16]

Nature of Reinsurance Contracts

In the reinsurance industry, contracts are not standardised. The terms and conditions attached to an individual contract differ from market to market as well as from product line to product line. Nevertheless, the classifications below – treaty and facultative – can be used to categorise contracts.

Treaty Reinsurance

In treaty reinsurance, the ceding company is contractually bound to cede (buy) and the reinsurer is bound to assume a specified portion of a type or

16 These types of insurer use run-off reinsurance, i.e. the management of liabilities and exposures when an insurance company stops underwriting a business, to transfer to reinsurers the closed books of business where liabilities continue to exist under the contracts.

category of risks insured by the ceding company. For instance, they may be in agreement to share risks proportionally up to, say, $2 million written by the insurer for commercial property risks situated in Mexico, Brazil and Venezuela for a period of 12 months subject to renewal.

A treaty automatically relates to the whole portfolio of risks it covers unless there are specific exclusions. Included in a treaty are the maximum size of risk, the reinsurance limit and the business territories to which it is applicable. Reinsurance treaties are written on a term or continuous basis. A term agreement has a built-in expiration date when the contract ceases, while a continuous contract does not have an expiration date but continues indefinitely. In general, there is a notice period attached to a continuous contract that allows either party to inform the other of its aim to cancel or amend the treaty.

Treaty reinsurers typically do not separately appraise each of the individual risks assumed under their treaties and as a result, after a review of the ceding company's underwriting practices, are dependent on the original risk-underwriting decisions made by the ceding primary policy writers.

Given this dependence, reinsurers are subject to the likelihood that the ceding companies have not sufficiently weighed up the risks to be reinsured and, thus, that the premiums ceded in connection to the treaty may not adequately compensate the reinsurer for the risk assumed.

Pricing of the treaty is therefore impacted by the reinsurer's evaluation of the ceding company's risk management and underwriting practices as well as claims settlement practices and procedures.

Facultative Reinsurance

Facultative reinsurance allows insurers to purchase protection on a single policy, so they can manage peak limits or different exposures within their overall portfolios. For instance, FacInsure, a fictional insurer, may be considering a large risk (policy) for which it does not have sufficient capacity to underwrite. The solution will be to approach a reinsurer or a group of reinsurers that is ready to take on a portion of the risk. The issuer carries out this process again for another risk. This method allows the insurer to place risk or policies on an individual basis. The word facultative thus connotes that both FacInsure and the reinsurer have the faculty or option of accepting or rejecting the individual submission (approach).

Ceding companies typically purchase facultative reinsurance for individual risks not covered by their reinsurance treaties, for amounts in excess of the monetary limits of their reinsurance treaties and for unusual risks. Since each risk is individually underwritten and administered, underwriting expenses and, in particular, personnel costs, are higher in relation to premiums written on facultative business. The probability that the underwriter can price the contract to more accurately reflect the risks involved is increased by their ability to separately evaluate each risk reinsured.

The classifications of reinsurance contracts are shown in Figure 3.1.

Figure 3.1 Classifications of Reinsurance Contracts[17]

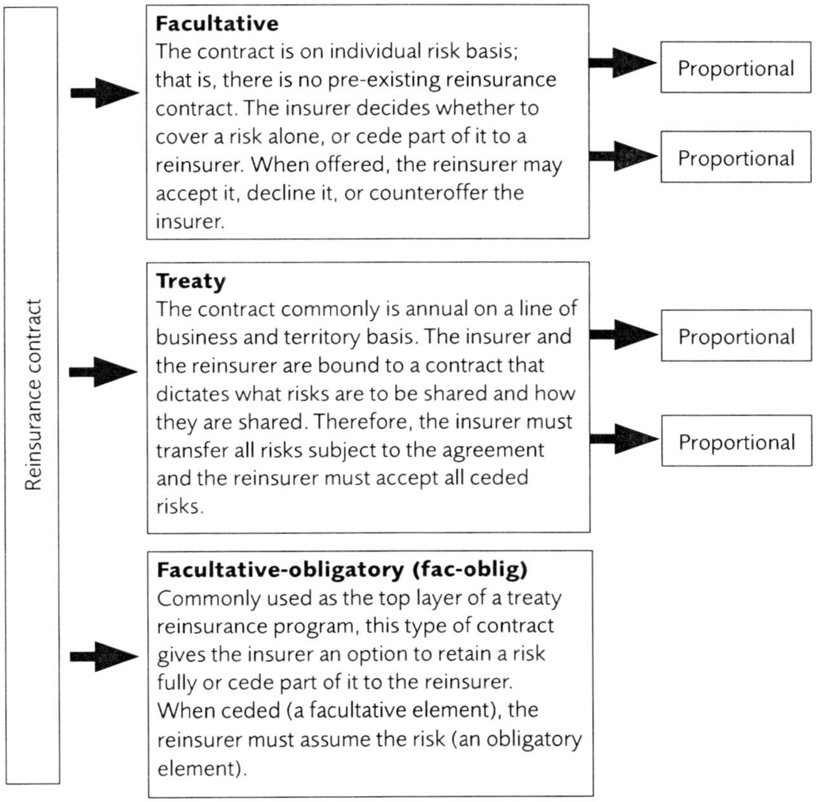

Types/Forms of Reinsurance

Reinsurance may assume the form of proportional and non-proportional. In either case, the contract can be drafted on a facultative or treaty basis. There are differences in the manner in which the insurer and the reinsurer share the premiums and losses as well as the amount of insurance.

Proportional Reinsurance

Proportional reinsurance involves one or more reinsurers taking a stated fraction of each risk that an insurer produces (writes) and receiving shares in the premium and losses in the same proportion.

17 Kwon, W. J. (1999), *Risk Management and Insurance in Singapore*, Singapore College of Insurance.

There are two types of proportional insurance: quota share and surplus share.

Figure 3.2 Forms of Reinsurance[18]

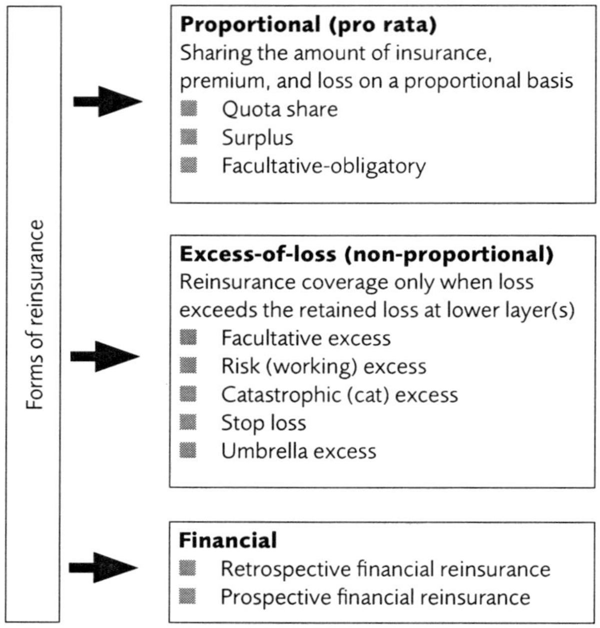

Quota Share Reinsurance

Quota share (QS) reinsurance is a form of reinsurance that stipulates that premiums and losses are to be shared proportionately between the ceding company and the reinsurer. Under quota share, the same percentage applies to all reinsured policies in a given class of business. The contract specifies a maximum amount above which the reinsurer is not ready to commit on any one risk. For example, in the case of a 20% quota share, the insurer transfers 20% of its liability and premiums on every risk to the reinsurer, who must pay 20% of any loss sustained, whether total or partial. The percentage is constant throughout and applies to both premiums and losses.

The ceding company may seek such coverage for several reasons. First, it may not have adequate capital to practically retain all of the business that it is capable of producing. For example, it may only be able to offer $2 million in coverage, but by buying proportional reinsurance it might double or triple that limit. Premiums and losses are then shared on a pro rata basis. For

18 Ibid.

example, an insurance company might buy a 50% quota share treaty; in this case they would share half of all premiums and losses with the reinsurer. In a 75% quota share, they would be responsible for three quarters of all premiums and losses. The reinsurance company usually pays a commission on the premiums back to the insurer in order to compensate them for costs incurred in sourcing and administering (e.g. retail brokerage, taxes, fees, home office expenses) the business. This is known as the ceding commission.

An illustration follows.

A direct insurer, Q-Insure, writes the following contacts

Policy	Sum Insured ($)	Premium (100%)
1	20,000	200
2	50,000	300
3	80,000	500

Under a 30% quota share reinsurance contract, the following sums would be reinsured on each contract:

Policy	Sum Insured ($)	Premium (100%)	Sum reinsured ($)	Premium to Quota Share*
1	20,000	200	7,500	75
2	50,000	300	15,000	90
3	80,000	500	30,000	187.5

*Sum Reinsured x Premium/ Sum Insured

If a claim on policy 1 is $15,000 is paid then the reinsurer will pay $4,500 (30% of $15,000).

A claim of $36,000 on policy 2 would result in the reinsurer paying $10,800 (30% of $36,000).

The reinsurer will pay out $24,000 on a claim of $80,000 on policy 3 (30% of $80,000).

An insurer uses quota share reinsurance for a number of reasons including:

- To increase its competence in writing policies with higher limits;
- To take advantage of the reinsurer's expertise;
- To support a new line of business for which it lacks sufficient experience.

Surplus Reinsurance

Surplus reinsurance entails an insurer determining the amount it can retain per risk for every risk in a portfolio (e.g. commercial property risks in Mexico City, Mexico) and approaching one or more reinsurers ready to provide additional capacity. The cedant's retention in this case is referred to as a 'line'. The risks falling within this line are the sole responsibility of the direct insurer. In the industry, the reinsurance coverage on any ceded risk is conveyed as a multiple of lines. Therefore, a three-line surplus treaty implies that the maximum reinsurance on any risk is triple the amount of the insurer's retention. All premiums and losses that exceed the insurer's retention, up to the reinsurance limit, are pro rated. In essence, the higher the retention, the greater the share of risk retained and the lower the insurance premium.

In the case of a line defined as a certain policy limit of $100,000 and a 9-line surplus share treaty, the reinsurer could then accept up to $900,000 (9 lines). So if the insurance company issues a policy for $100,000, they would keep all of the premiums and losses from that policy. If they issue a $200,000 policy, they would give (cede) half of the premiums and losses to the reinsurer (1 line each). If they issue a $500,000 policy, they would cede 80% of the premiums and losses on that policy to the reinsurer (1 line to the company, 4 lines to the reinsurer, 4/5 = 80%). If they issue the maximum policy limit of $1,000,000 then the reinsurer would then get 90% of all of the premiums and losses from that policy.

The following is another illustration.

SpInsure, a direct insurer, writes the following contract.

Policy	Sum Insured $	Premium (100%)
A	20,000	200
B	45,000	300
C	100,000	500

Suppose a 5-line surplus reinsurance is entered into with a retention of $15,000. The limit is therefore calculated as 5 x $15,000 which equals $75,000. Reinsurance payments are calculated using the following formula.

(Limit of reinsurer's liability – Retention)/Sum Insured x Claim

If a claim on policy A of $10,000 is paid, then SpInsure will pay out $2,500.

[(20,000 – 15,000)/20,000 x $10,000]

A claim of $30,000 on policy B would result in SpInsure paying $20,000.

[(45,000 – 15,000)/45,000 x $30,000]

SpInsure will pay out $30,000 on a claim of $50,000 on policy C.

[(75,000 – 15,000)/100,000 x $50,000]

Premiums (gross of reinsurance commission) are allocated on a similar basis:

- Policy A (20,000 – 15,000)/20,000 x $200 = $50
- Policy B (45,000 – 15,000)/45,000 x $300 = $200
- Policy C (75,000 – 15,000)/100,000 x $500 = $250

A surplus treaty offers the insurer considerable automatic reinsurance capacity. With this type of reinsurance, the insurer is able to fully retain small risks, which enables it to stabilise its risk and loss portfolios.

In addition, the insurer is able to build surplus, thus extending its capacity to write larger lines and at the same time minimise its exposure to large losses and catastrophic events.

Non-proportional Reinsurance

Non-proportional reinsurance, also known as excess of loss reinsurance or XL insurance, provides for a reinsurer making payments to an insurer (cedant) whose losses exceed a predetermined retention level. An example of this form of reinsurance is where the insurer is prepared to accept a loss of $2 million for any loss which may occur and purchases a layer of reinsurance of $5 million in excess of $2 million – if a loss of $4 million occurs, the insurer pays the $4 million to the insured(s) and then recovers $3 million from their reinsurer(s). In this case, the insurer will therefore retain any loss exceeding $7 million unless they have purchased a further excess layer (second layer) of, say, $12 million in excess of $5 million.

Excess of loss reinsurance can be bought to provide indemnification for a variety of circumstances. Two of the most common are as follows:

- **Facultative or per risk (sometimes referred to as XL) reinsurance** is designed to provide coverage for losses of an individual risk or policy that exceed the cedant's reinsurance retention. For example, an insurance company might insure commercial property risks with policy limits up to $10 million and then buy per risk reinsurance of $5 million in excess of $5 million. In this case a loss of $7 million on that policy will result in the recovery of $2 million from the reinsurer. The larger the risk that can pose considerable loss exposure to insurers, the higher the facultative XL reinsurance.
- **Catastrophe excess of loss (sometimes referred to as per occurrence XL) reinsurance** protects the insurance company against an accumulation of losses due to single events such as major natural or human-made disasters. The reinsurance will pay out to the insurer only when there are two or more losses per event and when the accumulation of losses paid by the cedant exceeds the per occurrence reinsurance retention. A typical example would be if an insurance company issues homeowner's policy limits of up to $500,000 and then purchases catastrophe reinsurance of $22,000,000 in excess of $3,000,000. In that case, the insurance company would only recover from reinsurers in the event of multiple losses in one event (i.e. hurricane, earthquake, etc.).

Figure 3.3 Reinsurance Premium Assumed by Class of Business and Class across the Globe in 2006

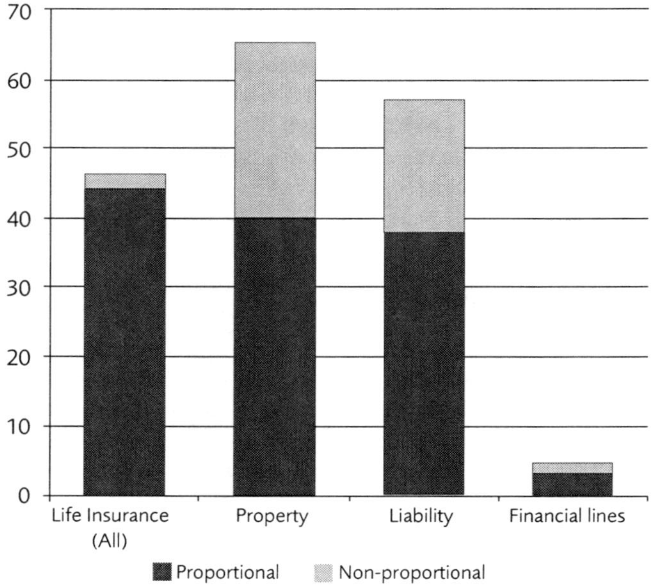

Source: IAIS, Data displayed in US$ millions

Benefits of Reinsurance

- **To guard against large claims** – For instance, if an earthquake hits a large city or a hurricane sweeps across a province, insurers will need to spread the risk by reinsuring a portion of what they have agreed to insure with other reinsurers in order to reduce the severity of the loss for any one insurer.
- **To avert unnecessary fluctuations in underwriting results** – Insurers want a model situation whereby a balanced set of results, without 'peaks and troughs', can be guaranteed each year. To this end, they get reinsurance which will cover them against any unusually large losses. This keeps a cap on the claims the insurer itself is exposed to having to pay.
- **To achieve an international spread of risk** – This is essential in situations where a country is susceptible to natural disasters and an insurer is heavily committed in that country. Insurance may require reinsurance in order to spread the risk outside the country.
- **To boost the capacity of the direct insurer** – Occasionally insurers intend to insure a risk but are incapable of doing so on their own. This problem can be solved by using reinsurance and in doing so the insurer

can accept the risk by insuring the whole risk and then reinsuring the part it cannot keep for itself to other reinsurers.

- **Facilitation of growth and social welfare** – Given that reinsurance allows insurers to take advantage of economies of scale, insurers can use their capital more efficiently, allowing them to offer their policyholders the same level of security at a better price. Additionally, many large and complex risks would not be insurable without reinsurance.
- **Allows for efficient risk and capital management** – Ultimately, reinsurance allows primary insurers to efficiently manage their risks and capital so as to make insurance more secure and less costly (see Figure 3.4). In addition, it extends the range of products and coverage that primary insurers can provide.

Figure 3.4 Micro and macro dimension of reinsurance

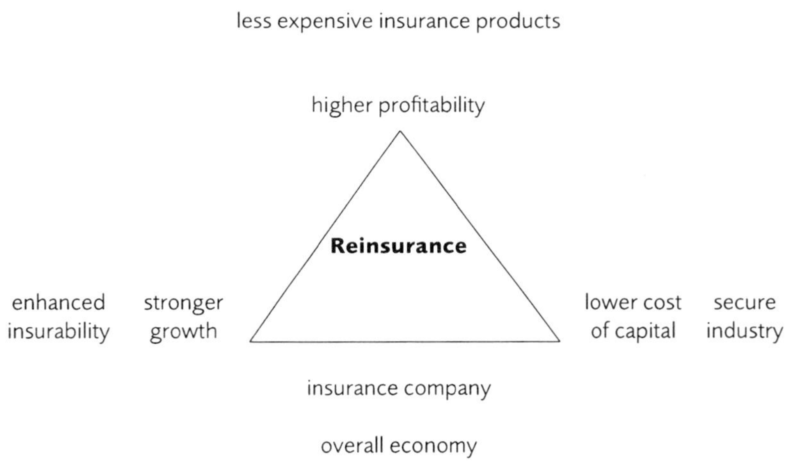

Source: Understanding Re Insurance, Swiss Re

The Business Environment

4

This chapter describes the business environment in which insurance companies operate.

Introduction

The insurance industry plays a major role in the transfer of risk and the provision of risk management services within an economic system. There are two measures that are used customarily to demonstrate the relative significance of insurance within national economies. One measure is referred to as **insurance density**, which indicates the average annual per capita premium within a given country. This is used as an indicator for the state of development of a country's insurance sector.

Figure 4.1 Ten Countries with Highest Insurance Density (2005)

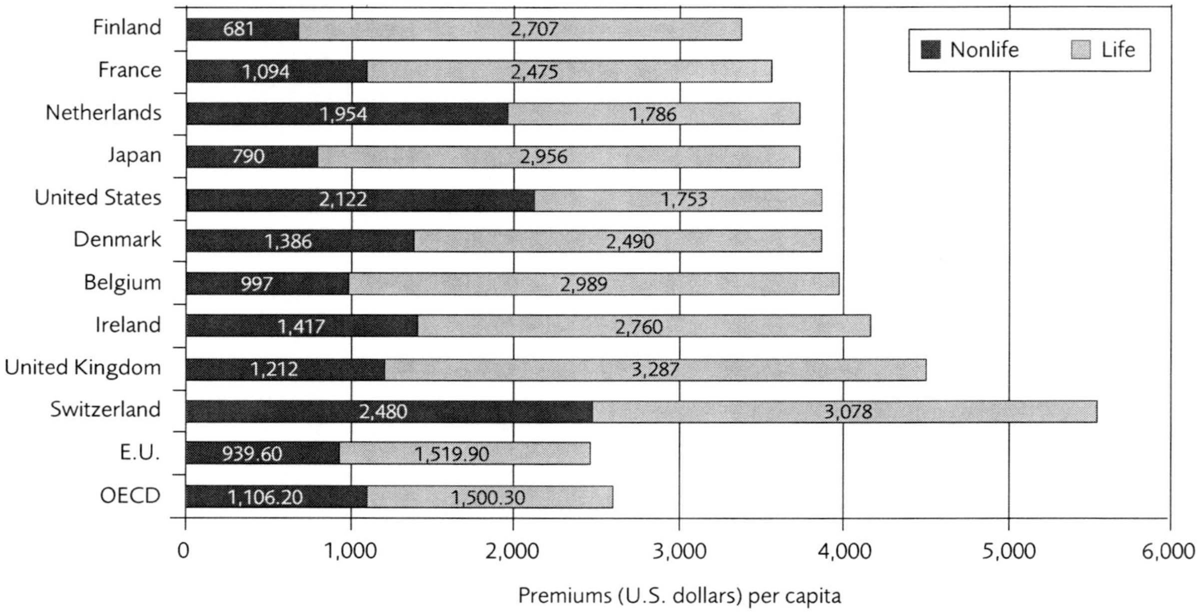

Source: Swiss Re (2006)

The other is **insurance penetration**, which measures insurance premiums as a percentage of the gross domestic product (GDP). It is used as an indicator for the state of development of a country's insurance sector.

Figure 4.2 Ten Countries with Highest Insurance Penetration (2005)

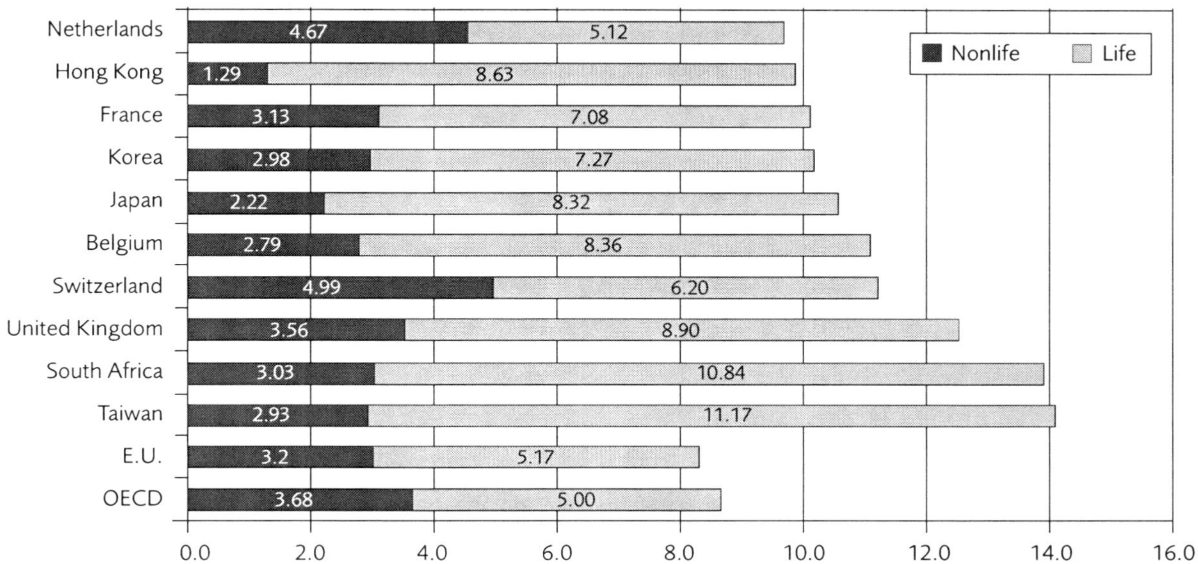

Source: Swiss Re (2006)

Some of the benefits of insurance for the economic growth of countries are listed below:

- Promotion of financial stability;
- Facilitation of trade and commerce;
- Promotion of a more efficient capital allocation;
- Fostering of more efficient risk management;
- Encouragement of loss mitigation;
- Facilitation of the mobilisation of savings.

Environmental Factors Affecting the Insurance Industry

Political and Legal

Environmental factors categorised as political and legal also incorporate regulatory factors. Industry experts assert that research findings substantiate the relationship between a country's political environment and demand for insurance products. These findings have revealed that insurance demand is proportional to improvements in a country's political climate and that the converse holds true, i.e. an unstable political climate depresses demand for insurance.

Government policies can also be a determinant of which insurance products are compulsory and the ones that are optional or discretional. They can also determine the tax concessions that could be afforded to the purchase of certain types of insurance products.

Impact: Insurance companies take regulatory factors into account when creating and marketing insurance products to their target market segments. They also cater for the effects of political instability in each jurisdiction in which they have a presence as this may impact on their expansion plans. Regulations such as Solvency II, which require capital adequacy on the part of insurance companies, could trigger mergers and acquisitions as firms seek to be compliant.

Economic

- **GDP** – The demand for insurance products is also proportional to income at both the macroeconomic and microeconomic levels. The higher an economy's income, the higher the level of insurance consumption. Similarly, the higher the income of households in a given economy, the higher the level of insurance consumption.
- **Inflation** – Another important economic factor that affects insurance consumption is inflation. Inflation rates are known to typically influence insurance consumption, and life insurance supply and demand are usually subject to the detrimental effects of inflation.

Impact: Insurance companies' profitability will be impacted by variation in these economic factors. Those companies operating in emerging markets, where the GDP has been on the rise in recent times, can not only increase output, but also charge more for insurance services on the back of the resulting increase in demand for insurance products.

Socio-cultural

Socio-cultural factors shape perceptions of the role of insurance products from country to country. In a number of countries, particularly in Asia, life insurance products are purchased largely as savings instruments and this aligns with their cultural tendency to save. In other countries, especially those with a sizeable Muslim population, Islamic scholars consider the classic risk transfer model through insurance to be improper for use in Islamic communities. This religious doctrine, often compounded by cultural issues, contributes to the relatively poor demand for insurance in Islamic regions.

Demographic factors are also included in this category. Research shows that changes in demographic factors affect the demand for insurance products. For instance, according to research findings, both men and women delay marriage longer than ever before nowadays. This practice is especially prevalent in Western countries. At the same time, the years of higher education have also lengthened.

Other notable demographic changes that affect insurance demand include:

- Married couples bearing fewer children, and in some cases choosing not to have any children at all;
- An increase in the number of dual-income families and also single-parent families;
- Changing attitudes towards fitness and adopting a healthier lifestyle;
- People living longer, resulting in a higher ageing population;
- Changes in household structures that have resulted in the decline of the nuclear family structure;
- Increased industrialisation, and hence urbanisation, which results in a new social order that emphasises the need for greater financial self-reliance as opposed to dependence on family and friends for both economic and social security.

Impact: Insurance companies are designing culture-specific products such as those for the Muslim community. They are rapidly expanding the Islamic insurance (Takaful) business model to bring insurance to Islamic adherents across the world.

In addition, insurers have to design new products, especially life-insurance products, to cater for the aforementioned demographic changes.

Technological

Since the early 2000s, there has been an increase in the number of catastrophe events, both natural and human-made, an increased number of people in the Western world entering retirement and an increase in people's lifespan as a result of better healthcare and lifestyles. Within this context of risk and opportunity, the most momentous development in the realms of technology that is applicable to business is the Internet, which is now a major commercial channel. More so in recent years with the increasing maturity of Web 2.0, which is now the infrastructure for social computing and is set to include innovations such as the Semantic Web.[19]

The role of technology (IT) in insurance is increasingly business-process driven and on-demand. The introduction of innovations such as service-oriented architecture (SOA) means that business processes can be stream-

19 Wikipedia describes Semantic Web as '*an evolving extension of the World Wide Web in which the semantics of information and services on the web is defined, making it possible for the web to understand and satisfy the requests of people and machines to use the web content*'.

lined over time and these processes can be assigned ownership within an insurance company.

Impact: Insurers are increasingly leveraging the Internet's ubiquity and ease of use to help them reduce expenses, do away with paperwork, and boost the speed with which they do business. These benefits, in turn, are drivers for agent loyalty, helping customers find loyal insurance agents, and in turn become drivers for steadily increasing sales and retention of business.

SOA is being increasingly adopted by insurers to align IT to the business and decompose the business processes to increase their efficiency.

Competitive Landscape

The insurance industry is typically regarded as being very mature, and has rich customer information, established distribution channels, favourable product positioning, and years of sound business practices and solid investment reputation. These fundamentals have been the critical success factors for insurers.

In recent times, insurance companies have been facing stiff competition in the global financial services marketplace. It has become increasingly necessary for them to evaluate the customary product-centric business model of the insurance industry and evaluate opportunities to increase their customer focus.

In the current business environment, a number of agile financial services players are making inroads by developing customer-centric models and advice-driven approaches not bound by insurance tradition. The balance of power has been shifted to the customers, who now have new choices, and in response, insurers are taking steps to update the traditional business model, which is encumbered with legacy systems, and position their firms against the future.

Additionally, insurance companies around the world have for some time been witnessing the changing external competitive landscape in the financial services industry and are continuing to manage the competing realities of the insurance business.

They are increasingly under pressure from customers, regulators and the marketplace in general. A combination of these elements influences business strategies and technology decisions that have a direct impact on the business, the customer and the bottom line. Insurers now find that managing these competing realities and leveraging technology strategically can be appropriately challenging.

Insurers that are seeking to expand their customer base have become customer-focused with an emphasis on customer needs, demands and changing demographics.

Technology is also becoming the cornerstone for understanding and managing customer relationships and customer data, and is increasingly vital for growing market share and increasing share of wallet as well as achieving client satisfaction.

Marketplace Convergence

An interesting recent development has been the blurring of lines between financial services institutions as companies seek to provide a wide range of products and services. Products are now less of a differentiator, and insurers have found themselves having to increase their range of service options with competitive pricing.

In most jurisdictions, such as the USA, the continuation of financial services' convergence, consolidation and demutualisation have all contributed toward a changing competitive landscape. This is evidenced on the home web page of any of the top financial service players – they all support banking, insurance, and retirement planning centres. Without looking at the names of the companies, a customer is unable to tell if they are a bank or an insurance company.

Insurance companies are not only competing against other insurers, they are competing against the financial services industry. A recent development has been the offering of insurance products by firms that are not traditional financial services firms. For example, in the UK, big supermarket chains such as Tesco, Asda and Sainsbury's, and also Virgin, are selling insurance products.

Profile of Major Insurers around the World

Life Insurance Companies

ING Group[20]

ING is a global financial services company headquartered in the Netherlands that provides life insurance services amongst other services. It serves more than 85 million customers in Europe, the United States, Canada, Latin America, Asia and Australia.

ING was established in 1991 as the result of a merger between Nationale-Nederlanden and NMB Postbank Group. Over the last decade, ING has become a multinational with very varied international activities.

The company's history shows that its roots can be traced to the insurers De Nationale Levensverzekering Bank and De Nederlanden van 1845 and to the public bank services such as De Rijkspostspaarbank and De Postcheque- and

20 Source: www.ing.com/group/showdoc.jsp?docid=092825_EN&menopt=abolfct #P7_1253.

Girodienst, as well as to the Nederlandsche Middenstands Bank. These are the legal predecessors of the 'founding fathers' of ING; Nationale-Nederlanden and NMB Postbank Group.

The insurance elements of its six clear business lines include Insurance Europe, Insurance Americas and Insurance Asia/Pacific.

Key figures for insurance operations for year end 2007 are:

- Income: €62,208 million;
- Profit before tax: €6,533 million;
- Profit by insurance business line (% based on full year 2007):
  - Insurance Europe (19%); Insurance Americas (22%); Insurance Asia/Pacific (6%).

AXA[21]

With group headquarters located in Paris, France, AXA is a French global insurance company. It was founded in 1985 by Claude Bébéar. Its organisational structure is such that AXA is not the name of a single company but a group of companies, independently organised and operated according to the regulations of many different countries.

The AXA insurance business lines include life, health and other forms of insurance. The AXA group has its operations located primarily in Western Europe, North America, the Asia Pacific region and the Middle East.

Major events in the history of AXA are the 2008 acquisition of Oyak's 50% stake in AXA Oyak, second largest Turkish insurer, for 525 million dollars, and penetration of high potential-growth markets, with the acquisition, also in 2008, of 100% of the 3rd largest Mexican insurer, ING Seguros (for an amount of 1.5 billion dollars).

Key figures for year end 2007 are:

- Revenue: €93.63 billion;
- Operating income: €7.695 billion;
- Net income: €5.666 billion.

Assicurazioni Generali[22]

Assicurazioni Generali, a major player in the global insurance marketplace, was founded in 1831 in Trieste, Italy. It is considered to be the industry market leader in Italy and as of October 2008 was operating in 40 countries. The Generali Group, and its consolidated partnerships with major international reinsurers, operates in all classes of insurance.

One of the major milestones in the company's history was in 1918 when it

21 Source: www.axa.co.uk/aboutus/global/index.html.

22 Source: www.generali.com/Generali_Group/About_us/sezionePSV/1098/index.html?idLanguage=EN.

obtained full Italian nationality status; the share capital was converted into lira. As of 31 December 2007, it operated through 331 consolidated subsidiaries of which 148 were insurance companies.

Key figures for year end 2007 are:

- Net profits: €1,401 million;
- Premiums: €66,218 (of which life was €45,373 and non-life €20,845).

Aviva[23]

Aviva, the world's fifth-largest insurance group on the basis of gross world-wide premiums for the year ended 31 December 2007, became the new name for the former CGNU in July 2002. CGNU was created by a merger of Norwich Union and CGU plc in 2000.[24] The Aviva brand brought together more than 40 different trading names around the world. As of 2007, it was considered to be the largest insurance services provider in the UK and one of the leading providers of life insurance products in Europe.

As of 30 June 2007, Aviva had a staff strength of 59,000.

Key figures for year 2007 are:

- Revenue: £40,645 million;
- Operating income: £2,228 million;
- Net income: £1,505 million.

Property/Casualty

Allianz[25]

Allianz Group is a global services provider in insurance, amongst other financial services, that is headquartered in Munich, Germany. Allianz is considered to be the market leader in the German insurance market and also has a strong international presence.

Allianz's roots can be traced to the summer of 1889 when the director of Münchener Rückversicherungs-Gesellschaft (Munich Re), Carl Thieme and Munich banker Wilhelm Finck decided on the creation of a primary insurance company, which they named Allianz. According to the history of Allianz on the corporate website (www.allianz.com), the founders of the company at the time recognised an increase in risk in the industrial age and had prescience of the opportunities of a service market that was undergoing rapid growth. The company's intention of becoming an international company was initially realised with the opening of a branch office in London in the late 19th century.

23 Source: www.aviva.com/index.asp?pageid=2.
24 BBC Business News, (21 February 2000), 'CGU and Norwich Union Merge', available from http://news.bbc.co.uk/1/hi/business/649600.stm.
25 Source: www.allianz.co.uk/aboutus/.

After World War II, global business activities began again in a gradual manner. Allianz opened an office in Paris in the late 1950s and a management office for Italy in the 1960s.

As of 30 June 2008, Allianz Group employed 181,124 people around the world and served more than 80 million customers in about 70 countries.

Key figures for year 2007 are:

- Revenue: €102.6 billion;
- Operating income: €10.91 billion;
- Profit: €7.966 billion.

American International Group (AIG)[26]

American International Group, Inc. (AIG) is a leading insurer headquartered in New York City, USA, with operations in more than 130 countries and jurisdictions. AIG companies serve commercial, institutional and individual customers through a worldwide property–casualty and life insurance network. There are listings of AIG's common stock on the New York Stock Exchange, as well as the stock exchanges in Ireland and Tokyo.

AIG's roots can be traced back to 1919 when Cornelius Vander Starr founded an insurance agency in Shanghai, China. Starr is regarded as the first Westerner in Shanghai to sell insurance to the Chinese.

A major milestone in the company's history was its near bankruptcy in September 2008. According to industry reports, its small London unit AIG Financial Products' involvement in complex credit derivatives transactions was responsible for the near collapse of the company.

These credit derivatives, mostly credit default swaps (CDSs) on collateralised debt obligations (CDOs), had been a major source for AIG as this small unit sold contracts that offered protection for clients from losses on debt. According to AIG company reports, AIG Financial Products insured $513 billion of debt against default using credit-default swaps, and $78 billion worth of insured debt was affected by the onset of the US sub-prime mortgage crisis.

However, as certain debts piled up, AIG was compelled to increase its own financial cushion and write down the value of some of the company's holdings.

At first, given its high credit rating, AIG did not require any collateral to sell the insurance. But the way the derivatives contracts were structured meant that AIG was compelled to increase the amount on hand as the value of the debt fell.

Credit rating agencies such as Standard and Poor's downgraded AIG's credit rating. By 15 September 2008, its credit rating was A- and the money

26 Source: AIG 2007 Annual Report and New York Times 'An Insurance Giant, Brought Down', available from www.nytimes.com/imagepages/2008/09/27/business/20080928_MELT_GRAPHIC.html.

it needed required more funds than it could borrow and so required the US Federal Reserve to bail it out.

Key financial figures for year 2007 are:

- Revenue: US$110.064 billion;
- Operating income: US$8.943 billion;
- Net income: US$6.20 billion.

Zurich Financial Services[27]

Headquartered in Zurich, Switzerland, Zurich Financial Services Group can be described as insurance-based financial services provider. The company currently has a global network of subsidiaries and offices in North America, Europe, Asia Pacific and Latin America amongst other markets.

Zurich was established in 1872 under the name Versicherung Verein/ Insurance Club as a subsidiary of the 'Schweiz' Marine Insurance Company. Its core business purpose was to write marine reinsurance from the parent company and to build up a marine book of its own.

Other notable milestones in the company's history include the establishment in 1885 of a branch office in Spain, which concluded the first wave of international expansion, the 1912 acquisition of the necessary licences to start business in the USA and the opening of a representative office in Beijing in 1993. In 2005, Zurich launched its global brand campaign, 'Because change happenz', which is regarded in the industry as a step towards building Zurich into a leading brand and ensuring sustainable growth.

Key financial figures for year 2007 are:

- Business operating profit: US$6.6 billion;
- General insurance business operating profit: US$4.02 billion;
- Net income: US$5.6 billion;
- Shareholders' equity: US$28.8 billion.

Reinsurers

Munich Reinsurance Co.[28]

Munich Re is a large reinsurance company with headquarters in Munich, Germany. It was founded in 1880 by one of the co-founders of Allianz, Carl Thieme. At the time, it was regarded as one of the first independent reinsurance companies, i.e. a reinsurer not run by a primary insurer.

One of the major milestones in the company's history was in the aftermath

27 Source: Zurich Financial Services, 'Global Factsheet' and 'Zurich at a Glance', May 2008, available from www.zurich.com/main/about/introduction.htm.

28 Source: Munich Re Company Profile and 2007 Annual Report available from www.munichre.com/en/corporate/default.aspx.

of the 9/11 terrorist attacks in the USA, when it was reported to have suffered the largest loss in its history as a result of its burden of the insurance on losses. Other notable events include its financial strain, estimated at US$1.6 billion, which resulted from events surrounding Hurricane Katrina in the USA in 2005.

As of 31 December 2007, Munich Re employed 38,634 people at more than 50 locations around the world.

Key financial figures for year 2007 are:

- Gross premiums written: €17,562 million;
- Profit/loss for the year: €1,443 million;
- Market capitalisation at 31 December: €28,966 million.

Swiss Reinsurance Co.[29]

Swiss Re is a diversified global reinsurer that was founded in Zurich, Switzerland, in 1863. Swiss Re was established by the Helvetia General Insurance Company (now using the trade name of Helvetia insurance) in St. Gallen, the Schweizerische Kreditanstalt (Credit Suisse) in Zurich and the Basler Handelsbank (predecessor of UBS AG) bank in Basel.

Swiss Re offers a wide variety of reinsurance products to manage risk and capital. In September 2006, it announced it would be offering reinsurance cover for private health insurance companies, starting in China and India.

Key financial figures for year 2007 are:

- Net income: CHF4.2 billion;
- Property and casualty insurance operating income: CHF5.9 billion;
- Life and health insurance operating income: CHF2.7 billion;
- Investment portfolio: CHF31.7 billion.

Hannover Rueckversicherung AG[30]

Hannover Rueckversicherung (Hannover Re) is a large reinsurance group with headquarters in Hannover, Germany. Established in 1966 under the name 'Aktiengesellschaft für Transport und Rückversicherung', its principal shareholder is HDI Haftpflichtverband der Deutschen Industrie V.a.G., which holds 50.2% of Hannover Re's shares via Talanx AG.

The company's business groups transact both life and health and non-life reinsurance. According to the Hannover Re Group's factsheet, its worldwide network consists of more than 100 subsidiaries, branches and representative offices in around 20 countries with total staff of around 1800.

29 Source: Swiss Re at a Glance, available from www.swissre.com/pws/about%20us/swiss%20re%20at%20a%20glance/swiss%20re%20at%20a%20glance.html.

30 Hannover Re Factsheet, available from www.hannover-re.com/about/index.html.

Key financial figures for year 2007 are:

- Net income: CHF4.2 billion;
- Property and casualty insurance operating income: CHF5.9 billion;
- Life and health insurance operating income: CHF2.7 billion;
- Investment portfolio: CHF31.7 billion.

Key milestones in the company's expansion in the international reinsurance markets are the establishment of catastrophe reinsurer Hannover Re (Bermuda) Ltd. in 2001, and the establishment of Hannover Rückversicherung AG, Bahrain Branch, for the underwriting of traditional reinsurance business in Arab countries in 2007.

Key financial figures for year 2007 (IFRS basis) are:

- Gross written premium: €8,259 million;
- Non-life reinsurance net income: €560 million;
- Life/health reinsurance net income: €189 million.

SCOR SE[31]

Scor Se, formerly known as Scor Regroupe, is a global reinsurance firm headquartered in Paris, France. The firm has more than 40,000 shareholders and 1,840 employees in 49 offices across 5 continents. Its reinsurance offerings cover both non-life and life and accident reinsurance.

SCOR was founded in 1970 and in 1988 acquired La Vittoria Riassicurazioni in Italy. In 2007 it acquired 98% of Converium to create a Top 5 global multi-line reinsurer.

Key financial figures for year 2007 (IFRS basis) are:

- Gross written premiums: €4,762 million;
- Operating income: €576 million;
- Net income: €407 million.

Insurance Brokers

Marsh & McLennan Companies Inc.

Marsh & McLennan Companies, Inc. (MMC) is a global insurance brokerage and professional services firm with headquarters in New York, USA.

Its subsidiary Marsh Inc., a risk and insurance brokerage, operates by collecting advisory fees from its clients – mainly large corporations but also small and mid-size businesses, municipal governments, school districts and some individuals – in exchange for locating property and casualty insurance coverage for them.

31 Source: 'SCOR in the World', available from www.scor.com/www/index.php?id=377&L=2.

Marsh & McLennan Companies' ancestor, Dan H. Bomar Company, was founded in 1871 in Chicago after the Great Chicago Fire. One of the co-founders of Marsh & McLennan, Henry Marsh, was, in 1897, credited with introducing the concept of a broker acting as a buyer of insurance representing the client, rather than as a seller of insurance. In 1906, Burrows, Marsh & McLennan was formed in Chicago, and was renamed Marsh & McLennan in 1906.

Key financial figures for year ending 31 December 2007 are:

- Total revenue: $11,350 million;
- Total risk and insurance services revenue: $5,565 million;
- Net income: $2,475 million.

Aon Corporation[32]

Aon (which means 'oneness' in Gaelic) is one of the world's leading insurance brokerages, as well as a top reinsurance broker. The company, headquartered in Chicago, United States, operates in the commercial brokerage segment. The company's Aon Risk Services brokerage unit offers retail property/casualty, liability, and other insurance products for groups and businesses. Aon Re Global handles reinsurance brokerage services for aviation, marine, energy, professional liability, and other niche and specialty business lines.

The roots of Aon can be traced back to the early 20th century, but its fast-paced growth commenced in 1982 when Ryan Insurance Group merged with Combined International Corporation, and by 1987 that company was renamed as Aon.

The firm grew both organically and through strategic acquisitions through the 1980s and 1990s. At the time of writing, Aon has 42,500 employees in 500 offices in more than 120 countries.

Key financial figures for year 2007 are:

- Revenue: $7,471 million;
- Operating income: $1,162 million;
- Net income: $864 million.

Arthur J. Gallagher & Co.[33]

Arthur J. Gallagher & Co. is a global insurance brokerage firm headquartered at the Gallagher Centre in Itasca, Illinois (a suburb of Chicago) in the USA. Founded in 1927 by Arthur Gallagher, the company began its international expansion with the formation of Gallagher, Hinton & Vereker, Ltd. in London

32 Source: 'About AON Corporation', www.aon.com/about-aon/company-overview.jsp.

33 Source: 'Corporate History', available from www.ajg.com/portal/server.pt?open=512&objID=359&&activetab=TabCTRL_DropDownTabsCompany1&mode=2&in_hi_userid=21938&cached=true.

in 1974. By 1982, the firm was ranked by Business Insurance magazine as the 10th-largest broker in the USA. The company acquired The Galtney Group, one of the 25 largest privately held brokers in the USA, in 2001.

Gallagher has operations in 14 countries and conducts business in more than 100 countries through a network of correspondent brokers and consultants.

Key financial figures for year 2007 are:

- Total revenue: $1,619 million;
- Total brokerage revenues: $1,114.2 million;
- Earnings from continuing operations after taxes: $112.3 million.

Rating Agencies

Standard & Poor's[34]

Standard & Poor's is a provider of financial market intelligence. Companies operating in the financial markets regard Standard & Poor's as a source of credit ratings, indices, investment research, risk evaluation and data.

Standard & Poor's roots can be traced to the publication, in 1860, of Henry Varnum Poor's *History of Railroads and Canals in the United States*, regarded in financial circles as a pioneer of modern stock reporting and analysis. Poor's Publishing and Standard Statistics merged in 1941 to create the Standard & Poor's Corporation. The McGraw-Hill Companies, Inc acquired the company in 1966.

At the time of writing, Standard & Poor's employs approximately 8,500 employees located in 23 countries and markets.

Standard & Poor's Insurer Financial Strength Ratings are discussed in detail in the latter part of this chapter.

Moody's[35]

Moody's Corporation is the holding company for Moody's Investors Service, which is famous for its financial research and analysis on commercial and government entities. The firm also performs ranking of the credit-worthiness of borrowers using a standardised ratings scale.

Historians credit John Moody, the founder of the company, as the creator of the credit-rating business. In 1900, the year in which the firm was established, John Moody & Company published *Moody's Manual of Industrial and Miscellaneous Securities*. Contained in this manual were information and statistics on stocks and bonds of financial institutions, government agencies, manufacturing, mining, utilities, and food companies.

34 Source: 'About S&P', available from /www2.standardandpoors.com.

35 Source: 'About Moody's'. available from www.moodys.com/moodys/cust/AboutMoodys/AboutMoodys.aspx?.

At the time of writing, Moody's offices are located in most of the world's major financial centres and employ approximately 3,000 people worldwide, including more than 1,000 analysts.

Moody's ratings determine the financial strength of providers. It is, like S&P's ratings, a measure of the capacity to meet policyholder obligations under a variety of economic and underwriting conditions.

The ratings are as follows:

Rating	Description	Notes
Aaa	Exceptional	Insurance companies rated Aaa offer exceptional financial security. While the financial strength of these companies is likely to change, such changes as can be visualised are most unlikely to impair their fundamentally strong position.
Aa	Excellent	Insurance companies rated Aa offer excellent financial security. Together with the Aaa group, they constitute what are generally known as high-grade companies and are rated lower than Aaa companies because long-term risks appear somewhat larger.
A	Good	Insurance companies rated A offer good financial security. However, elements may be present which suggest a susceptibility to impairment sometime in the future.
Baa	Adequate	Insurance companies rated Baa offer adequate financial security. However, certain protective elements may be lacking or may be characteristically unreliable over any length of time.
Ba	Questionable	Insurance companies rated Ba offer questionable financial security. Often the ability of these companies to meet policyholder obligations may be very moderate and thereby not well safeguarded in the future.
B	Poor	Insurance companies rated B offer poor financial security. Assistance of punctual payment of policyholder obligations may be very moderate and thereby not well safeguarded in the future.
Caa	Very poor	Insurance companies rated Caa offer very poor financial security. They may be in default on their policyholder obligations or there may be present elements of danger with respect to punctual payment of policyholder obligations and claims.
Ca	Extremely poor	Insurance companies rated Ca offer extremely poor financial security. Such companies are often in default on their policyholder obligations or have other marked shortcomings.
C	Lowest	Insurance companies rated C are the lowest-rated class of insurance company and are regarded as having extremely poor prospects of ever offering financial strength.

Source: www.sharingpensions.co.uk/financial_strength.htm

Moody's analytics contribute data modelling, among other capabilities, to develop solutions adapted to an individual insurance company's needs.

Fitch[36]

Fitch Ratings, dual-headquartered in New York and London, is a global rating agency that provides the world's credit markets with credit opinions. It operates offices and joint ventures in more than 49 locations and covers entities in more than 90 countries, including insurer financial strength ratings on over 2,000 insurance companies.

Fitch has a market presence in all insurance market sectors including life and non-life insurance. The group's analysts generate research on major issues affecting the insurance industry, such as finite risk reinsurance, insurance securitisation, natural catastrophes and enterprise risk management.

According to the Fitch Ratings Capabilities brochure, Fitch has two economic stochastic capital models, Prism and Matrix, suited to the insurance sector. Prism is a tool that was developed to measure ratings globally for both life and non-life insurers using a single platform. Similarly, Matrix is a model that enhances the firm's capabilities in evaluating financial guaranty insurers.

A.M. Best Company[37]

A.M. Best Company is a full-service credit rating organisation that services the insurance sector among other sectors. Best's ratings and analysis are used by policyholders as a means of assessing the financial strength and creditworthiness of risk-bearing entities and investment vehicles. The company was founded by Alfred M. Best in 1989.

A.M. Best issues reports and financial strength ratings about insurance organisations. Best's Insurance Reports, the firm's flagship publication and database, offers the largest coverage of insurers and reinsurers in the United States, Canada, the United Kingdom and worldwide.

Headquartered in Oldwick, New Jersey, in the USA, A.M. Best started its life, as Alfred M. Best Company, Inc., in an office in New York City. It began rating life insurance companies in 1928 and established Best's Insurance News Digest – Property/Casualty and Life/Health, now known as Best Week® – in 1953. In 1972, the Alfred M. Best Company became the A.M. Best Company.

A.M. Best's financial-strength ratings measure insurance companies' ability to pay claims. It also rates financial instruments issued by insurance companies, such as bonds, notes, and securitisation products.

The following list summarises A.M. Best's rating scale and associated descriptions.

36 Source: 'About Us', available from www.fitchratings.com/jsp/corporate/AboutFitch.faces?context=1&detail=1.
37 Source: 'About A.M. Best', available from www.ambest.com/about/.

Secure	**Vulnerable**	**Not Rated (NR)**
A++, A+ (Superior)	**B, B-** (Fair)	**NR-1:** Insufficient data
A, A- (Excellent)	**C++, C+** (Marginal)	**NR-2:** Insufficient size and/or operating experience
B++, B+ (Good)	**C, C-** (Weak)	**NR-3:** Rating procedure inapplicable
	D (Poor)	**NR-4:** Company request
	E (Under regulatory supervision)	**NR-5:** Not formally followed
	F (In liquidation)	
	S (Rating suspended)	

Source: A.M. Best

Sample Ratings

The following are sample ratings for a number of leading insurance companies using ING, AXA, Allianz, Zurich and Swiss Re as examples.[38]

Company	**S&P**	**Moody's**	**Fitch**	**A.M. Best**
ING	AA-	Aa2	AA-	NR-5
AXA	AA	Aa3	AA	N/A
Allianz	AA	Aa3	AA-	A+
Zurich	AA	A1	A+	A
Swiss Re	AA-	Aa2	withdrawn	A+

Insurer Financial Strength Ratings[39]

A Standard & Poor's Insurer Financial Strength Rating is a current opinion of the financial security characteristics of an insurance organisation with respect to its ability to pay under its insurance policies and contracts in accordance with their terms.

Insurer Financial Strength Ratings are also assigned to Health Maintenance Organisations (HMOs) and similar health plans with respect to their ability to pay under their policies and contracts in accordance with their terms. This opinion is not specific to any particular policy or contract, nor does it address the suitability of a particular policy or contract for a specific purpose or purchaser. Furthermore, the opinion does not take into account deductibles, surrender or cancellation penalties, timeliness of payment, or the likelihood

38 Please note that these are illustrative ratings for these companies recorded at different times and should not be used as definitive ratings for any particular date.

39 Source: Standard & Poor's, Global Reinsurance Highlights, 2008 Edition.

of the use of a defence such as fraud to deny claims. For organisations with cross-border or multinational operations, including those conducted by subsidiaries or branch offices, the ratings do not take into account the potential that may exist for foreign exchange restrictions to prevent financial obligations from being met.

Insurer Financial Strength Ratings are based on information furnished by rated organisations or obtained by Standard & Poor's from other sources it considers reliable. Standard & Poor's does not perform an audit in connection with any rating and may on occasion rely on unaudited financial information.

Ratings may be changed, suspended or withdrawn as a result of changes in or unavailability of such information, or based on other circumstances.

Insurer Financial Strength Ratings do not refer to an organisation's ability to meet non-policy (i.e. debt) obligations.

Assignment of ratings to debt issued by insurers or to debt issues that are fully or partially supported by insurance policies, contracts or guaranties is a separate process from the determination of Insurer Financial Strength Ratings, and follows procedures consistent with issued credit rating definitions and practices. Insurer Financial Strength Ratings are not a recommendation to purchase or discontinue any policy or contract issued by an insurer or to buy, hold or sell any security issued by an insurer. An Insurer Financial Strength Rating is not a guaranty of an insurer's financial strength or security.

'pi' ratings, denoted with a 'pi' subscript, are Insurer Financial Strength Ratings based on an analysis of an insurer's published financial information and additional information in the public domain. They do not reflect in-depth meetings with an insurer's management and are therefore based on less comprehensive information than ratings without a 'pi' subscript. 'pi' ratings are reviewed annually based on a new year's financial statements, but may be reviewed on an interim basis if a major event that may affect the insurer's financial security occurs. Ratings with a 'pi' subscript are not subject to potential CreditWatch listings.

Ratings with a 'pi' subscript generally are not modified with '+' or '–' designations. However, such designations may be assigned when the insurer's financial strength rating is constrained by sovereign risk or the credit quality of a parent company or affiliated group.

Insurer Financial Enhancement Ratings

A Standard & Poor's Insurer Financial Enhancement Rating is a current opinion of the creditworthiness of an insurer with respect to insurance policies or other financial obligations that are predominantly used as credit enhancement and/or financial guaranties in Standard & Poor's rated transactions. When assigning an Insurer Financial Enhancement Rating, Standard & Poor's analysis focuses on capital, liquidity and company commitment necessary to support a credit enhancement or financial guaranty business. The Insurer Financial Enhancement Rating is not a recommendation to purchase, sell or hold a financial obligation, inasmuch as it does not comment as to market price or suitability for a particular investor.

Insurer Financial Enhancement Ratings are based on information furnished by the insurers or obtained by Standard &Poor's from other sources it considers reliable. Standard & Poor's does not perform an audit in connection with any credit rating and may, on occasion, rely on unaudited financial information. Insurer Financial Enhancement Ratings may be changed, suspended, or withdrawn as a result of changes in, or unavailability of, such information or based on other circumstances. Insurer Financial Enhancement Ratings are based, in varying degrees, on all of the following considerations:

- Likelihood of payment capacity and willingness of the insurer to meet its financial commitment on an obligation in accordance with the terms of the obligation;
- Nature and provisions of the obligations; and
- Protection afforded by, and relative position of, the obligation in the event of bankruptcy, reorganisation or other arrangement under the laws of bankruptcy and other laws affecting creditors' rights.

Insurer Financial Strength Ratings

An insurer rated 'BBB' or higher is regarded as having financial security characteristics that outweigh any vulnerabilities, and is highly likely to have the ability to meet financial commitments.

AAA

An insurer rated 'AAA' has **extremely strong** financial security characteristics. 'AAA' is the highest Insurer Financial Strength Rating assigned by Standard & Poor's.

AA

An insurer rated 'AA' has **very strong** financial security characteristics, differing only slightly from those rated higher.

A

An insurer rated 'A' has **strong** financial security characteristics, but is somewhat more likely to be affected by adverse business conditions than are insurers with higher ratings.

BBB

An insurer rated 'BBB' has **good** financial security characteristics, but is more likely to be affected by adverse business conditions than are higher rated insurers.

An insurer rated 'BB' or lower is regarded as having vulnerable characteristics that may outweigh its strengths. 'BB' indicates the least degree of vulnerability within the range; 'CC' the highest.

BB

An insurer rated 'BB' has **marginal** financial security characteristics. Positive attributes exist, but adverse business conditions could lead to insufficient ability to meet financial commitments.

B

An insurer rated 'B' has **weak** financial security characteristics. Adverse business conditions will likely impair its ability to meet financial commitments.

CCC

An insurer rated 'CCC' has **very weak** financial security characteristics and is dependent on favourable business conditions to meet financial commitments.

CC

An insurer rated 'CC' has **extremely weak** financial security characteristics and is likely not to meet some of its financial commitments.

R

An insurer rated 'R' is under regulatory supervision owing to its financial condition. During the pendency of the regulatory supervision, the regulators may have the power to favour one class of obligations over others or pay some obligations and not others. The rating does not apply to insurers subject only to non-financial actions such as market conduct violations.

NR

An insurer designated 'NR' is **not rated**, which implies no opinion about the insurer's financial security.

Plus (+) or minus (–)

Ratings from 'AA' to 'CCC' may be modified by the addition of a plus or minus sign to show relative standing within the major rating categories.

CreditWatch highlights the potential direction of a rating, focusing on identifiable events and short-term trends that cause ratings to be placed under special surveillance by Standard & Poor's. The events may include mergers, recapitalisations, voter referenda, regulatory actions or anticipated operating developments. Ratings appear on CreditWatch when such an event or a deviation from an expected trend occurs and additional information is needed to evaluate the rating. A listing, however, does not mean a rating change is inevitable, and whenever possible, a range of alternative ratings will be shown. CreditWatch is not intended to include all ratings under review, and rating changes may occur without the ratings having first appeared on CreditWatch. The 'positive' designation means that a rating may be raised; 'negative' means that a rating may be lowered; 'developing' means that a rating may be raised, lowered, or affirmed.

National Scale Ratings, denoted with a prefix such as 'mx' (Mexico) or 'ra' (Argentina), assess an insurer's financial security relative to other insurers in its home market.

Trends in Insurance

5

This chapter discusses some of the recent trends in insurance including recent regulations.

Introduction

The insurance sector appears to be at saturation point in many Western European countries, and in North America. In these established markets, major insurance products have been available for quite some time, and the needs of the majority of customers have already been met. Thus, unlike other sectors of the financial services industry such as retail banking, investment banking and hedge funds, innovation in the industry is limited.

However, in recent times, with regulatory changes and the need to grow in mature markets, some trends have been observable in the industry that are shaping the interaction of insurance players with regulators, players in other sectors of financial services such as private bankers, hedge fund managers, investment bankers and players in other sectors such as attorneys.

In addition, the growing economies of the emerging markets with relatively young populations and expanding middle classes are driving sales across all products. Figure 5.1 shows the real premium growth in recent times in South and East Asia, which is indicative of the strong growth and potential future growth in these model emerging markets.

Figure 5.1 Premiums in 2007 in South and East Asia

	USD bn	World market share
Life	124	5.2%
Non-life	53	3.2%

Real premium growth

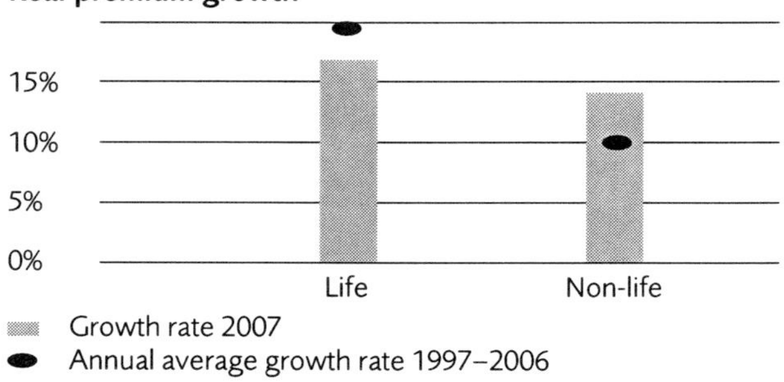

Source: Swiss Re, Sigma No 3/2008

Furthermore, industry reports show that governments in this region are breaking up monopolies and liberalising regulations, and the insurance industry is witnessing unprecedented growth driven by the recent economic boom and increasing presence of multinational insurance companies in the region. Deregulation in the sector has also created new opportunities in a region that is perceived as one of the most underserved in the world

A number of these observed trends are discussed in this chapter.

The Introduction of Solvency II

Solvency II is the project spearheaded by the European Commission with the aim of updating European insurance regulations. For the Commission, the objectives of the project include the following:

- Intensifying the integration of the European Union insurance market;
- Improving the protection of policyholders and beneficiaries;
- Making EU insurers more competitive in the international market;
- Improving regulation of the European Union insurance markets.

Often referred to as 'Basel for insurers', Solvency II is somewhat akin to the banking regulations of Basel II. For example, the proposed Solvency II framework has three main areas (pillars):

- **Pillar 1** consists of the quantitative requirements (for example, the amount of capital an insurer should hold).
- **Pillar 2** sets out requirements for the governance and risk management of insurers, as well as for the effective supervision of insurers.
- **Pillar 3** focuses on disclosure and transparency requirements.

Industry observers believe that the technical, organisational and strategic challenges of implementing Basel II and Solvency II are similar. Both frameworks attempt to align capital requirements with the risk profile of the business, with the assessment of risks and the associated capital charges placing huge demands on data collation, analytical systems and the people at the helm.

Many insurers recognise that learning the lessons of Basel II could help them to implement Solvency II more efficiently, while reaping the potential benefits more quickly and effectively. However, the financial services groups that combine banking and insurance, having gained valuable first-hand experience of what the data, people and organisational requirements of Basel II entail, would have an advantage when implementing this project.

Figure 5.2 shows an estimate of IT spending on Solvency II over the next decade.

Introduction of MiFID

MiFID (the Markets in Financial Instruments Directive) is considered one of the most wide-ranging and important pieces of financial services legislation introduced in Europe over recent years.

Figure 5.2 Estimated Solvency II Spending

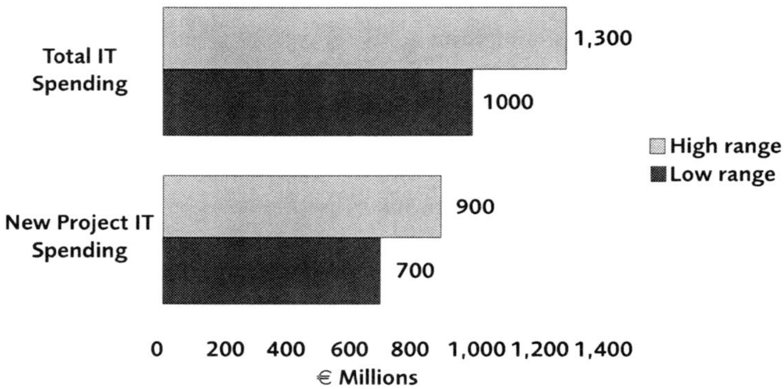

Source: Celent

What is MiFID?

MiFID (the Markets in Financial Instruments Directive) is a European Union directive intended to promote a single EU market for wholesale and retail transactions in financial instruments.

MiFID relates to 'investment firms', which are defined as '*any legal person whose regular occupation or business is the provision of one or more investment services to third parties and/or the performance of one or more investment activities on a professional basis*', i.e.:

- Investment banks;
- Portfolio managers;
- Stockbrokers and broker dealers;
- Corporate finance firms;
- Many futures and options firms; and
- Some commodities firms.

For some aspects, the position may not be clear-cut. For instance, retail banks and building societies will be subject to MiFID for some parts of their business (e.g., selling securities, or investment products which contain securities, to customers) but not others.

Impact on insurers: Although MiFID excludes insurance sales, industry watchers are of the opinion that national regulators may look to extend MiFID's impact to insurers. In the UK, for example, the FSA has stated their intention to consider extending some MiFID standards to non-MiFID firms and businesses (including the sales of certain insurance products).

Enforcement of AML/KYC in Insurance

The terrorist attack on 11 September 2001 in the USA has forced the issue of money laundering firmly into the spotlight in the insurance industry. Governments around the world have strengthened their resolve to block the access that money launderers – especially those that intend to move terrorist funds – have to the international financial system.

In recent times, regulators and law enforcement agencies have focused their attention on the banking system. However, in light of the increasing sophistication of criminals, the relative ease with which money can be transferred across the world and the need to be impartial to all sectors of the financial services industry, the regulators are increasingly focusing on other sectors, insurance included.

What is Money Laundering?

Money laundering is the process by which large amounts of illegally obtained money (from terrorist activity or other serious crimes) is given the appearance of having originated from a legitimate source.

There are three stages that constitute the money laundering process and these are shown in Figure 5.3.

The ability of criminals to convert illegitimate earnings to forms that permit the offender to freely spend and invest these earnings has continually been a source of concern for both criminals and governments around the world since at least the early days of the American Mafia. The infamous mobster, Meyer Lansky, was renowned for his proficiency at concealing the source of funds for his purchases of real estate and other legitimate commercial concerns. His aim was to avoid tax evasion charges that were responsible for the downfall of Al Capone by taking measures that could help cover the traces of the

Figure 5.3 Stages of Money Laundering

Placement	→	**Layering**	→	**Integration**
This is the stage where illegitimate funds (mostly cash) are placed in the financial system via payment into genuine accounts.		This is the stage where the audit trail is covered up between the funds and the original point of entry into the system by the use of several transactions, moving the funds around the world and through a range of financial products and institutions in an effort to conceal the origin.		At this stage the funds are reintroduced as legally acquired wealth that can be used to fund further activities or acquire more assets.

connections between his wealth and its criminal sources. During that period, laws that prohibited handling stolen property traditionally referred only to the physical property obtained in the course of the crime. Only in the last generation has the concealment of revenue obtained from crimes itself become a criminal activity, in a way created by a new set of laws and regulations aimed at money laundering.

The range of institutions that engage in anti-money laundering (AML) is extraordinary. The control regime in the USA, for instance, has extended beyond banks, the original focus, to a wide range of businesses such as real-estate developers, car dealers, casinos, businesses involved in money transmission, pawnbrokers and insurance companies. All these are now required to become actively involved in crime control through, inter alia, reporting on those customers whom they suspect of obtaining funds from crime or of using funds (whether from crime or legitimate sources) for terrorist activities. Figure 5.4 provides a more detailed illustration of the processes of money laundering and financing of terrorism.

Traditionally, there has been the notion that money launderers are least interested in the insurance industry for carrying out their nefarious activities. This has, however, not been the case in recent times. Insurance companies are now factoring anti-money laundering considerations into processes such as the issuance of policies, monitoring of policies, payment of claims and risk management. Before going into a discussion of how this is achieved, it would be prudent to provide a description of international standards and basic AML principles.

International standards

The crusade against money laundering across the world has been carried out primarily by the Financial Action Task Force (FATF). In response to growing concern over money laundering, the Financial Action Task Force on Money Laundering was set up by the G-7 Summit that was held in Paris in 1989. In recognition of the risk to the banking system and to financial institutions, the G-7 Heads of State or Government and the President of the European Commission assembled the Task Force from the G-7 member States, the European Commission and eight other countries.

It was tasked with the examination of money laundering methods and trends, reviewing the action which had already been taken at a national or international level, and outlining the measures that still needed to be taken to fight money laundering.

Additionally, in a bid to raise the standard of AML, the IAIS (International Association of Insurance Supervision) issued Guidance Notes for Insurance Supervisors and Entities so that they could be used in relation to AML.

Figure 5.4 The Process of Money Laundering and Financing of Terrorism[a]

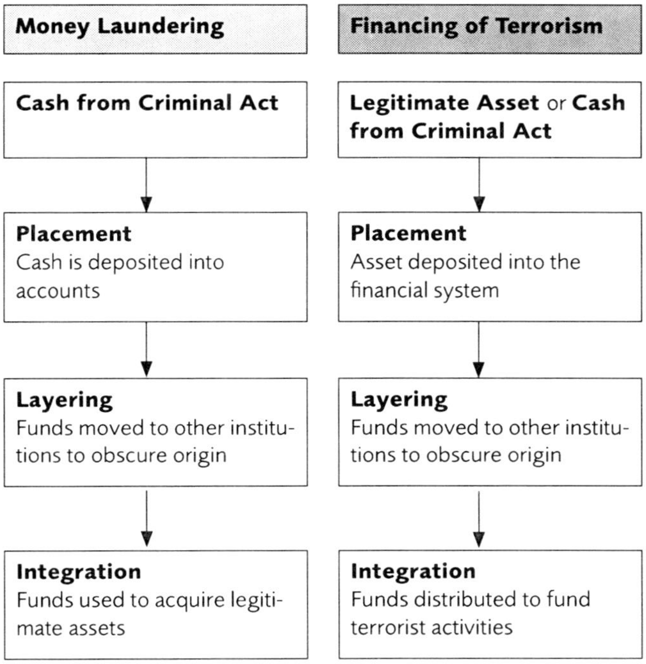

[a] Adapted from World Bank, 2003a, Reference Guide to Anti-Money Laundering and Combating the Financing of Terrorism, Washington DC, World Bank.

Source: Money Laundering, Michael Levi and Peter Reuter 2006

Basic AML principles

The following are some of the essential principles that are vital for any successful AML system:[40]

1. Conformity with the applicable AML laws of the appropriate jurisdiction;
2. Consideration of Know Your Customer (KYC) initiatives including due diligence in determining the source of wealth;
3. Co-operation with different law enforcement and supervisory bodies; and
4. Communication of the company's AML system through policies, procedures and staff training.

40 Drawn from Insurance Digest, May 2002, American Edition by Price Waterhouse Coopers.

Primary money laundering risks to insurance companies include:[41]

- Compliance or regulatory risk, or exposure for non-compliance with applicable existing AML rules and regulations;
- Reputational risk stemming from a money laundering 'accident' (inside or outside) and negative press coverage and associations;
- Operational risk, which will manifest itself throughout operations and transactions enterprise-wide; and
- Strategic risk, which can result from failure to consider ML vulnerability connected with mergers and acquisitions, planning and launching new products and services, entering new markets, and developing new technologies.

Suspicious activity monitoring and reporting

Some activities among insurance customers may indicate an element of money laundering. Some examples are:

- A customer that shows interest in a particular policy but does not appear to be concerned about the risks or costs associated with the policy or is having difficulty describing the nature of the business or source of funds;
- Payments made by a customer that are not proportional to the customer's stated occupation or income;
- Transactions where the business purpose is not defined;
- Customers assigning policies to third parties for cash;
- Customer paying premiums in cash, by an unrelated third party or using funds originating from abroad.

In response, insurance companies are increasingly putting systems in place that:

- Allow them to obtain sufficient knowledge about the reinsurers and agents with whom the firm does business;
- Allow them to identify customers with a history of policy terminations by monitoring early termination of policies;
- Allow the return of funds that have been held in suspense awaiting receipt of adequate KYC information;
- Allow refusal to accept business from customers, agents or reinsurers to protect them against the risks of money laundering.

They are implementing IT systems that are able to record and retrieve customer data as required by the new standards and expected by the current AML regime, and have the capability to monitor suspicious activity in an efficient and effective way.

41 Ibid.

AML/KYC programs at many insurance companies form the basis for executing a number of IT projects that ensure compliance with these initiatives.

Introduction of Islamic Insurance

The dictates of Islam provide that Muslims must find ways and means to avoid catastrophes and disasters wherever possible, and to minimise their family's losses should such events occur. One feasible solution is to purchase an insurance cover as in the conventional system.

Takaful, the Islamic insurance concept, is based on the social solidarity, cooperation and mutual indemnification of losses of members. The word 'takaful' is derived from an Arabic word which means joint guarantee. It is essentially a promise among a group of people who agree to jointly indemnify the loss or damage that may be inflicted upon any of them, out of the fund they donate to collectively. The core of a takaful system is 'tabarru', which means a donation, gift or contribution that makes the element of uncertainty allowable under a takaful contract.

The difference between traditional insurance and the takaful alternative is more evident with regard to investment of funds. While traditional insurance firms invest their funds in areas that generate interest and without any consideration for the concept of *Halal-o-Haram*,[42] takaful companies carry out only Shariah-compliant business and the profits are distributed in accordance with the pre-agreed ratios in the takaful agreement. Similarly, they receive a share in any surplus or loss[43] from the pool collectively. The takaful system has a built-in mechanism to counter any overpricing policies of the insurance companies because whatever the premium charged may be, the surplus would normally revert to the participants in proportion to their contributions.

There are three models and several variations on how takaful can be implemented. They are:

1. Mudharabah (profit-sharing model);
2. Wakalah model (agency model);
3. A combination of both.

The key features of both Mudharabah and Wakalah are shown in Figure 5.5.

The typical operational flow of short-term takaful products and that of long-term takaful products are shown in Figures 5.6 and 5.7 respectively.

In line with other types of Islamic finance products, the Islamic insurance

42 This concept is based on spiritual and moral factors involved in Islamic economics; while an activity may be economically sound, it may not be allowed in Islamic society if it is forbidden by the Shariah.

43 Muhammad Ayub (2003), 'An Introduction to Takaful – An Alternative to Insurance', available from www.islamic-world.net/economics/takaful_intro.htm.

Figure 5.5 Key Features of Mudharabah and Wakalah

Contract	Key features
Mudharabah (Profit-sharing model)	■ Participants are the capital provider to the Takaful fund; ■ Takaful operator is the manager of the fund; ■ Profits of the fund are shared between the participants and Takaful operator on a pre-agreed ratio (e.g. 50/50 for general Takaful or 70/30 for individual family Takaful etc.); ■ All acquisitions costs and management expenses incurred by the Takaful funds will be borne by the funds, before arriving at profits to be shared between participants and Takaful operators; ■ Losses of the Takaful funds are solely borne by the participants as capital providers (except in cases of negligence of the manager); and ■ Takaful operators will need to provide an interest-free loan ('Qardhul Hassan') to the Takaful funds in the event of deficiency.
Wakalah (Agency fee model)	■ Participants are the principals in the agency contract; ■ The work done by the agent (i.e. Takaful operator) will be remunerated with a fee; ■ Fees earned by the Takaful operator will be used to pay acquisition costs and management expenses of the Takaful funds; ■ Fees paid to the Takaful operator may include certain performance fees based on underwriting results and investment returns; ■ Losses of the Takaful funds are solely borne by the participants as capital providers (except in cases of negligence of the manager); and ■ Takaful operators will need to provide an interest-free loan ('Qardhul Hassan') to the Takaful funds in the event of deficiency.

Source: PricewaterhouseCoopers

market has experienced significant growth since the establishment of the first takaful operator in 1979.

Research has indicated that, as of March 2007, there were over 250 takaful companies in existence globally, and projections show that total takaful premiums are likely to reach over US$7 bn by 2015. A 2008 Ernst & Young report revealed that the Gulf Co-operative Countries (GCC) are at the heart of the worldwide takaful market. The report shows the takaful market is growing at an annual rate of 20% and it forecasts a worldwide takaful market worth $4.3 billion by 2010, and reaching $10–15 billion within the next decade.[44]

44 David Masters, 'Takaful Market Booming in GCC', *Insurance Daily*, 15 April 2008, available from www.insurancedaily.co.uk/2008/04/15/takaful-market-booming-in-gcc/.

Figure 5.6 Operational Flow of Short-term Takaful Products

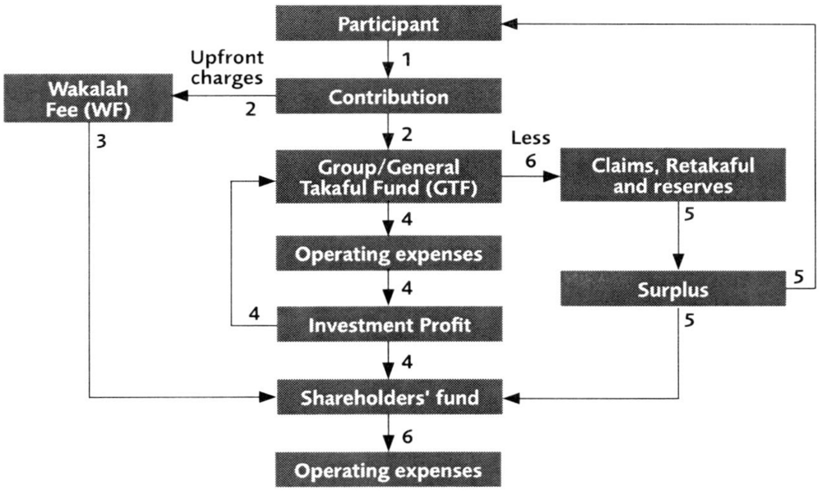

Description of operational flow:

1. Participant pays contribution under the scheme.
2. Contribution will be divided into:
   - Wakalah Fee ('WF') (applicable for Wakalah model); and
   - Group/General Takaful fund ('GTF').

   The allocation between WF and GTF is based on a pre-agreed ratio between the participant and takaful operator as specified in the contract and depending on the type of products.
3. WF that consists of commissions and management expenses will be paid to the shareholders' fund ('SHF' i.e. the takaful operator).
4. Excess in GTF [after deducting operating expenses (applicable for Mudharabah model)] will be invested in Shariah-compliant investments and investment income will be ploughed back to the fund. The takaful operator may receive an agreed portion of the investment income as a performance fee.
5. Surplus at the end of the year (after deducting claims, retakaful and reserves) will be distributed to the takaful operator and participants based on the pre-agreed ratio as stipulated in the contract (under the Mudharabah model).
6. Shareholders will use the WF and investment profit to pay for operating expenses of the SHF and takaful funds under the Wakalah model (only SHF's operating expenses under the Mudharabah model).

Source: Bank Negara Malaysia

Figure 5.7 Operational Flow of Long-term Takaful Products

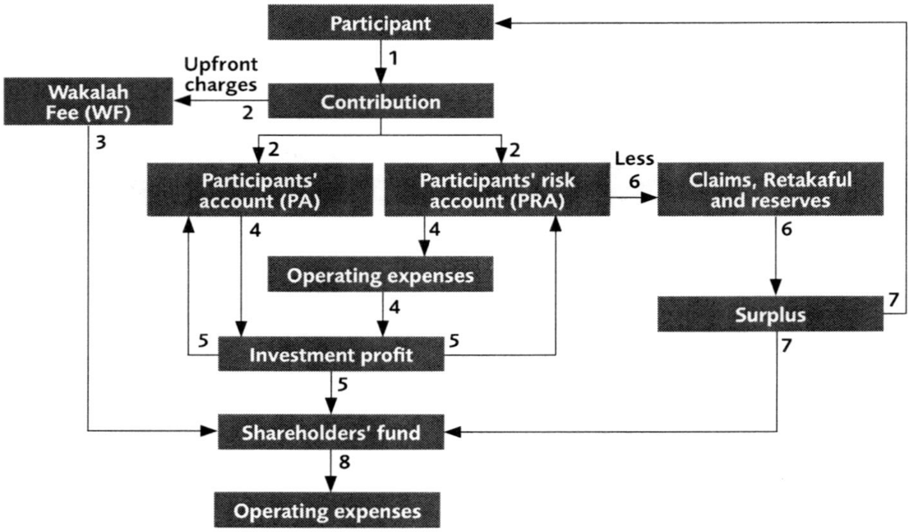

Description of operational flow:

1. Participant pays contribution under the scheme.
2. Depending on the model adopted by the takaful operator, the contribution will be divided into:
   – Wakalah Fee ('WF') (applicable for Wakalah model);
   – Participants' Account ('PA'); and
   – Participants' Risk Account ('PRA'), also known as Participants' Special Account ('PSA').
   The allocation between WF, PA and PRA is based on a pre-agreed ratio as specified in the contract.
3. WF that consists of commission and management expenses will be paid to the shareholders' fund ('SHF' i.e. the takaful operator).
4. The PA fund and excess in PRA after deducting operating expenses will be invested in Shariah-compliant investments.
5. Investment profits, if any, will be distributed between the takaful operator and the fund (participant) in the form of profit-sharing or performance fee based on the pre-agreed ratio between the takaful operator and participant. The amount in PA will be accumulated and paid to participant upon death, surrender or maturity.
6. The amount in PRA will be used to pay claims and retakaful, and to set aside as reserves.
7. Surplus in PRA at the end of the year (after deducting claims, retakaful and reserves) will be distributed to the takaful operator and participants under the Mudharabah model. The distribution of surplus will be based on the pre-agreed ratio as stipulated in the contract.
8. Shareholders will use the WF and investment profit to pay for operating expenses of the SHF and takaful funds under the Wakalah model (only SHF's operating expenses under the Mudharabah model).

Source: Bank Negara Malaysia

There are takaful companies in a number of countries outside the GCC such as Iran, Turkey and the Sudan, and even in some non-Islamic countries.

Popularity of Bancassurance

As the name suggests, bancassurance is the promotion of insurance and banking products and services through the same channel. Essentially, it is the distribution of insurance products through a banking network. The insurance products sold through these banking channels can range from life insurance (e.g. endowment, annuity and investment-linked insurance) to non-life or general insurance (e.g. motor insurance).

There are sales synergies in the use of common distribution channels. Some of these sales synergies are derived from the extensive customer base that banks have. Banks usually have a large customer base and can cross-sell insurance products to their banking customers. For example, some banks generally insist on life insurance for mortgage borrowers. While there may be no obligation to buy insurance from the lender, many do (despite it often being very overpriced) as they perceive it as an easy option. Another example would be selling cargo insurance to corporate customers along with trade financial facilities.

Bancassurance products are marketed through banks' extensive communication channels such as statement inserts, telemarketing and notices programmed into self-service terminals. By synergising the marketing activities of their banking and insurance products, some banks are able to offer insurance products to their customers at competitive prices due to their reduced cost per sales lead.

There are factors that strengthen the position of banks in selling insurance products. For a start, the value customers place on convenience/ease of use would lend credence to the hypothesis that banks have been able to capture market share in certain insurance products, given that they have established a competitive advantage on key factors of customer acquisition, such as the level of customer interaction.

According to the Capgemini World Insurance Report 2008, on average banks interact with their customers at least once a week on regular banking needs. They have been able to make the most of that connection to cross-sell other financial products, and grow their wallet share across the financial services spectrum.

The report also shows that banks have another weapon in their arsenal; they are perceived by customers to be credible providers of certain types of financial products. In an associated survey, 53% of customers said they would purchase insurance products through a bank, while only 26% said they would buy banking products from an insurer (see Figure 5.9).

Figure 5.8 Factors Influencing Future Decision to Purchase from a Bank in Mature Countries (%)

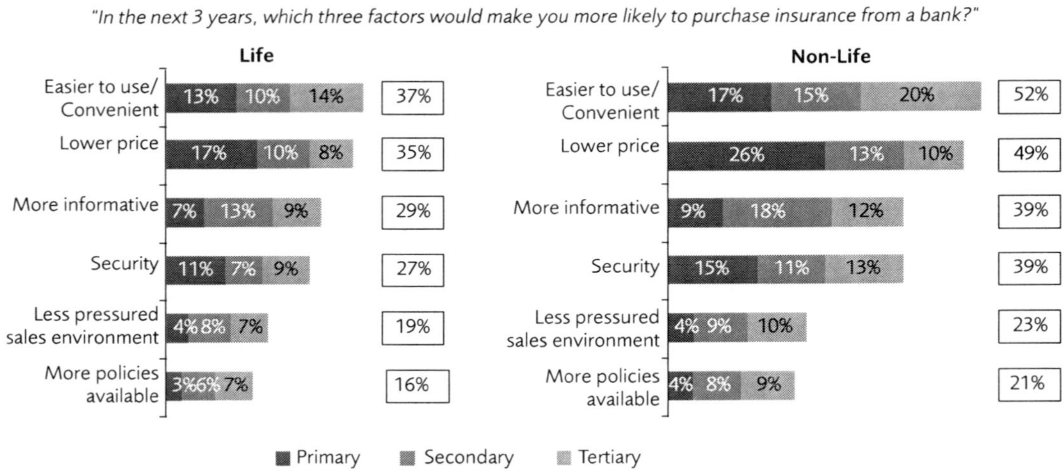

Source: Capgemini analysis, 2007.

Figure 5.9 Customers' Willingness to Buy Insurance from a Bank vs Purchasing from an Insurer in Mature Markets (%)

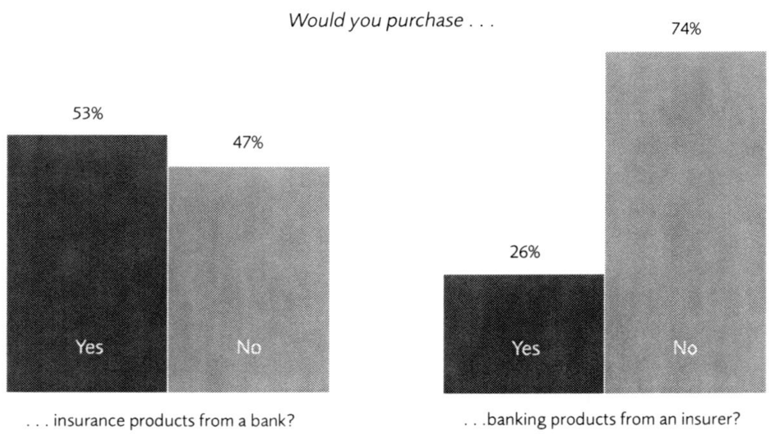

Source: Capgemini analysis, 2007.

Interestingly, while some banks have many competitive advantages in the insurance space, some insurers have managed to use them as a lever as opposed to a 'roadblock'.

Growth of the Insurance Securitisation Market

Insurance companies are increasingly transferring risks to the capital markets rather than relying exclusively on the conventional reinsurance market and investors have been turning to specialist insurance-linked products as an attractive alternative to traditional corporate and asset-backed securities. This has led to the growth of a market for structured insurance risk securities, which offer returns linked to the occurrence of catastrophes such as floods, hurricanes and earthquakes.

Given that catastrophe risk is inherently uncorrelated with financial markets, such instruments (securities) are potentially attractive to a wide range of investors. Therefore, an integration of the reinsurance and the capital markets appears to be mutually beneficial for both insurers and investors, providing insurers with reinsurance coverage at reasonable and stable prices, and offering attractive securities to investors.

Securitisation in the insurance industry is relatively new, with the first transaction recorded in the early 1990s. Ever since, the number of transactions has increased steadily.

Insurance-linked securities (ILS) are a vehicle used for ceding insurance-related risks to the capital markets. ILS can be categorised in two ways: by risk type – property/casualty (P&C) and life risks – and by catastrophe (cat) and non-cat risk. To date, P&C bonds have tended to transfer peak risk, while life bonds have typically provided financing backed by future premium flows. A cat bond transfers the risk of extreme events to the capital markets while a non-cat bond is more of a financing vehicle.

Raising capital through securitisation is also gradually gaining recognition within the life insurance sector, opening up opportunities to enhance returns, improve capital flexibility and provide new sources of funding for acquisition.

Structure of Insurance-linked Securities

In a typical structure, as used for cat bonds, the reinsured enters into a financial contract with a special purpose vehicle (SPV) (see Figure 5.10). This SPV performs two functions: (1) It provides reinsurance to a ceding insurance (or reinsurance) company, and (2) issues securities to investors. At the start of the risk period, the SPV gathers funds from the investors, which are put in a trust. At the same time, the SPV receives a premium from the cedant and in exchange underwrites reinsurance for the cedant. Funding for the interest payments that the investors receive is provided by the premium and the income on the trust. If it happens that there is no trigger event causing losses above the attachment point of the reinsurance, investors will have their principal refunded at maturity. Nevertheless, should a loss above the attachment point of the reinsurance contract happen, then the funds are used first in its place to make payments to a ceding company under the agreement, leading to partial or total loss of principal to investors.

Figure 5.10 Structure of a Catastrophe Bond

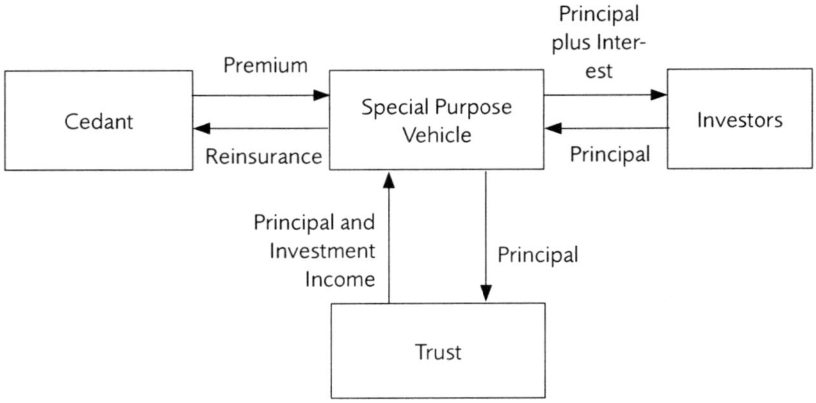

Source: Analysing Insurance-Linked Securities, Canabarro et al., 1998

The Life and Cat Bond Markets

Strong yields and good credit ratings have helped to make life securitisation increasingly popular with investors. In recent times, industry reports have shown that the issuance of life bonds exceeded that of cat bonds. Interest in life securitisation has grown as a result of the need to: (1) fund growth of new business, and (2) transfer catastrophic mortality risk to capital markets. The outstanding volume of insurance-linked securities as of 2006 had grown to nearly $23 billion, from about $6 billion in 2001 (see Figure 5.11). It is worth noting that the $23 billion is only for bonds. Thus, it significantly plays down the involvement of fixed-income investors in the market, given that it excludes swaps, industry loss warranties (ILWs[45]) and private transactions.[46]

As for cat bonds, the volume of outstanding and newly issued P&C cat bonds grew strongly in 2005 and 2006, especially after hurricane Katrina.[47] Between 2001 and 2006, the outstanding volume of cat bonds had more than trebled from $2.4 billion to $7.7 billion (see Figure 5.12). Demand for cat bonds from investors remains strong, in spite of the potential triggering of a one-rated bond after Katrina.[48]

45 These are a type of reinsurance or derivative contract through which one party will purchase protection based on the total loss arising from an event to the entire insurance industry rather than on their own losses.
46 Swiss Re, Securitisation – New Opportunities for Insurers and Investors, Sigma 7/2006.
47 Katrina was an extraordinarily powerful and deadly hurricane that caused catastrophic damage and inflicted large loss of life. It was the costliest and one of the five deadliest hurricanes to ever strike the United States. (Knabb et al., Tropical Cyclone Report 23-30 August 2005).
48 Swiss Re, Securitisation – New Opportunities for Insurers and Investors, Sigma 7/2006.

Figure 5.11 Total ILSs Issued and Outstanding, USD billion: The market is taking off

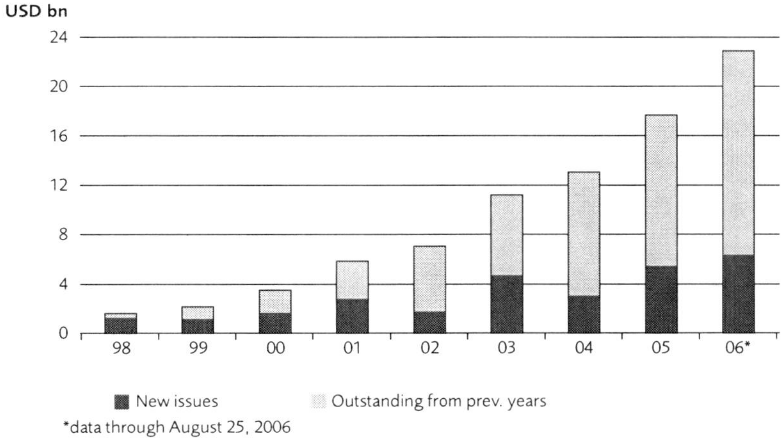

Source: Swiss Re Capital Markets

Figure 5.12 P&C Bonds Issued and Outstanding, USD billions

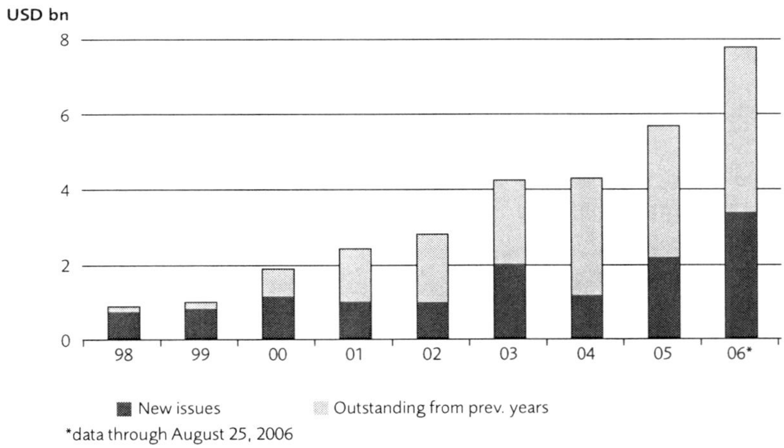

Source: Swiss Re Capital Markets

Who Buys Insurance-linked Securities and Why?

Investors are the primary purchasers of insurance-linked securities and they include insurance and reinsurance companies, money managers, cat funds and hedge funds.

The addition of cat bonds to a portfolio enhances the performance and lowers the risk of the portfolio, given that cat bonds yield reasonable returns, typically with less volatility than comparable quality corporate bonds, particularly if the seasonal volatility of hurricane and windstorm bonds is excluded (i.e. year-over-year returns).

Rise of Sovereign Wealth Funds (SWFs)

Undoubtedly, Sovereign Wealth Funds (SWFs) are emerging as major players in global capital markets. Most of these funds are based in the Middle East and Asia. SWFs are state-owned asset management firms funded by the accumulation of foreign exchange reserves; for instance, from oil exports in the Middle East and trade surpluses in Asia. All countries have foreign exchange reserves, but when a country, by running a current account surplus, accumulates more reserves than it feels it needs for immediate purposes, it can create a sovereign fund to manage the excess resources.

According to the International Monetary Fund (IMF), sovereign funds have been in existence since at least the 1950s, but their total size worldwide has increased dramatically over the past 10–15 years. In 1990, sovereign funds probably held, at most, $500 billion; the total as of September 2007 was an estimated $2–3 trillion and, based on the likely trajectory of current accounts, could reach $10 trillion by 2012.

The investment strategies adopted by SWFs have been observed to be either a passive approach or strategic approach. Typical examples of SWFs with strategic investment approaches include Dubai International Capital, Qatar Investment Authority, China Investment Corporation and Abu Dhabi Investment Authority. Strategic funds are looking for gains beyond a typical return on their investment. For instance, they may engage in negotiations with a company in which they have invested with a view to opening a local operation or setting up its headquarters in their home country or city. As a result, they tend to invest in firms that operate in lucrative industry sectors such as financial services, energy and telecommunications in the hope that these investments will help strengthen these sectors in their home economies.

Interestingly, these SWFs appear to have a fondness for financial services companies. In 2007, SWFs engaged in a 'shopping spree', acquiring mostly firms in the financial services sector. According to a Deloitte Research Paper entitled 'Insurance Firms: The Missing Link in the Sovereign Wealth Fund Acquisition Spree', between March 2006 and February 2008, 14 of the 15 SWF deals were in the financial services industry, from hedge funds, private equity funds and banks to stock exchanges. The size of the deals ranged from

Figure 5.13 Top Sovereign Wealth Funds

Sovereign Wealth Funds	Assets ($ billion)	Year of Inception
UAE: Abu Dhabi Investment Authority	875	1976
Norway: Government Pension Fund – Global	380	1996
Singapore: GIC	330	1980
Saudi Arabia: Various	300	NA
Kuwait: Reserve Fund for Future Generations	250	1953
China: China Investment Corporation (CIC)*	200	2007
Singapore: Temasek Holdings	159.2	1974
Libya: Oil Reserve Fund	50	2005
Qatar: Qatar Investment Authority	50	2005
Algeria: Fond de Régulation des Recettes	42.6	2000
US: Alaska Peramanent Fund Corporation	38	1976
Brunei: Brunei Investment Authority	30	1983
Other	171.4	–
Total	2,876.3	

*Includes Central Huijin Investment Co. The CIC is the umbrella organization.
Note: Much variation surrounds the estimation of SWF assets.

Source: Morgan Stanley (as reported in 'Asset Backed Insecurity' The Economist, January 17, 2008)

approximately $1 to $13 billion.[49] The total value of investment by SWFs in OECD-country (Organisation for Economic Co-operation and Development) banks and other financial services firms is over $60 billion.[50]

What seems uncanny is that SWFs' attraction to financial services companies is restricted to banks, private equity funds, hedge funds and exchanges and does not extend to the insurance firms. While capital cities of SWF operators such as Dubai, Abu Dhabi and Doha (Qatar) and cities such as Shanghai in China have huge ambitions of becoming top-notch financial centres to rival the likes of London and New York, it is unlikely that they can realise their ambitions without luring a number of insurance and reinsurance firms.

What the future holds for SWFs, as they target insurance firms as a route to incorporate the insurance sector in their grand plans for developing world-class financial centres, will be discussed in Chapter 12.

49 The details of SWF financial firm deals are available at http://online.wsj.com/public/resources/documents/infolaunch.html?project=foreignSWF08,w=980,h=530.

50 'Sovereign Wealth Funds', Joint Economic Committee, Research Report # 110-21, February 2008.

Insurers Targeting the High Net Worth Market Segment

In recent times, many of the bigger life insurance companies that have sizeable, better-established agency forces are increasingly committing to a strategy that involves targeting the high net worth customer segment of the financial services industry.

Industry observers refer to the strategy as private client strategy, wealth management strategy or high net worth strategy; all sharing a common impetus.

Life insurance companies are attracted to this market segment in a similar way to their investment management and private banking counterparts because of the high-margin, stable, low-risk fee income associated with managing and/or protecting the assets of high net worth individuals the world over.

The allure of a fast-growing high margin has enticed a wide range of competing firms, each with its own individual set of strengths and weaknesses. The challenge, however, for life insurers that are seeking to compete successfully with the investment bankers, the private bankers, the broker-dealers, the larger retail banks, and the independent financial planners has been to seek out the most effectual method to leverage their strength as life insurers against their offsetting weakness in distribution, manufacturing and brand.

The following is a summary of some of the challenges faced, categorised according to distribution, manufacturing and brand.

Distribution

- Life insurance agents usually don't have access to the high net worth.
- They normally are not adept at selling into and servicing the high net worth.
- Their competitors – private bankers, investment bankers, broker dealers, financial planners – are better equipped to serve this segment.

Manufacturing

- The carriers (i.e. insurers) do not manufacture (design and produce) the range of products and services demanded by the high net worth.
- They also do not have the relationships with those who have the capability; that is, many of them they see as competition – the private banks, investment banks, commercial banks etc.
- In the case of products they do produce, they are usually incapable of delivering through their normal customer service/call centres the sort of service that meets the expectation of the high net worth.

Brand

- Customers' perception of them – both the carriers and agents – is as no more than providers of insurance, annuity and retirement products, usually questioning their cost and quality of service as well as their relative investment performance.
- Similarly, distributors perceive them as mere manufacturers of insurance products, and annuity and retirement products.

Industry observers assert the objective fact that most life insurers' agents normally lack both the access and financial sophistication of many of their competitors, private bankers etc., when it come to dealing with the high net worth, such as self-made entrepreneurs and inheritors of wealth. Even the mass affluent, who may not necessarily use private bankers, will typically have retail mutual funds, unit trusts etc. and will most likely have an existing relationship with a tax professional and/or financial planner.

The competitors typically have the requisite experience and skills honed through persuasion of their clients to purchase not only their own proprietary products and services, but also financial products from other producers.

In recognition of the above challenges, the insurance industry has intensified its effort to find ways to either enlarge and/or alter its existing distribution network through:

- Partnering;
- Mergers and acquisitions;
- Converting insurance agents into financial advisers/planners.

To this end, insurance companies are increasingly seeking to forge partnerships and looking to closely align themselves with organisations who have both access to and experience selling to as well as servicing the high net worth market segment.

6

Business Processes in Insurance

This chapter discusses some of the business processes in insurance including underwriting and claims administration.

Introduction

Insurance is a process business and a rules business. Insurers underwrite, and make, claims payments consistently. The ability of an insurer to make smarter decisions than the other company is an essential characteristic that can guarantee success. In addition, insurers depend heavily on financial and human capital for the production of insurance services as financial capital supports all operations.

The insurance marketplace continues to challenge even the most established industry leaders in the face of competition from new entrants into the market, increasing customer demands, increasing complexity of regulatory compliance and the growing pressure to improve overall performance.

Streamlining business processes from underwriting to claims administration can give an insurance company a competitive edge. A number of the insurance business processes will be briefly discussed in this section.

Before the discussion on business processes, it will be prudent to discuss the role of capital and surplus in insurance.

Role of Capital and Surplus

Financial capital serves as a cushion for insurance companies against the likelihood that actual losses, expenses or investment results may deviate in a negative manner from assumptions that insurers factor into the pricing of their products. A somewhat unusual characteristic of insurance policies is their reliance on pricing inversion which implies that product pricing occurs ahead of the insurer gaining knowledge of the exact production costs. Thus, it would be logical for insurers to provide margin for adverse pricing deviations to ensure that they inspire confidence in the marketplace of their ability to meet their obligations. To make this happen, insurers can source additional capital through borrowing, thereby enlarging their capacity through the purchase of reinsurance. By and large, an insurer's leverage, i.e. its capital compared with its premium writings and liabilities, is inversely proportional to its perceived security. An insurer with relatively low leverage will be well received by knowledgeable purchasers and their representatives.

This exemplifies one of the most noteworthy consumer issues in the insurance industry, given that consumers pay at the present moment for the agreement of future payment, according to terms of the binding contract. This is not as straightforward as it seems, given that the purchaser is not certain of the ability of the insurer to pay and the strength of its capital position.

An insurer's net worth is something that consumers are not fully aware of. As with other types of business, an insurer's net worth is denoted as:

Net worth = Capital + Surplus

This is essentially the difference between its assets and liabilities.

One issue that springs to mind is that while a consumer may be privy to the insurer's capital position, there is no guarantee that the position is not estimated by asset overvaluation or liability undervaluation. This could be especially true when consumers have dealings with foreign insurers whose home country's accounting standards, used in preparing their financial accounts, differ from the accounting standards in their host country.

Underwriting

Underwriting is one of the most important parts of the insurance process. The underwriting process helps the insurance company determine the rate the insured pays, based on the level of risk the insured poses.

Car insurance helps illustrate the concept. Good drivers generally pay less for coverage than do poor drivers. Also, young drivers, who have more accidents, typically pay more than mature drivers. The amount of premium is based on the amount of risk.

Definition of Insurance Underwriting

Insurance underwriting is the process of choosing who and what the insurance company decides to insure. This is on the basis of a risk assessment. It is, in practice, regarded as the 'behind the scenes' work in an insurance company, where underwriters determine who is insured and how much in insurance premiums they will charge the insured person. Insurance underwriting also involves choosing who the insurance company will not insure.

It is the process used by insurance companies for issuing insurance policies.

Underwriters carry out an assessment of risks and decide whether to accept or decline applications for insurance cover. They are skilled practitioners who determine, based on the application, whether to issue insurance (known as selection) and if so, the price and terms and conditions (known as classifications). This is a core skill, given that it is the essence of insurance – and if performed well, will minimise losses for an insurance company and boost its profitability. As a result, underwriting capability has a major influence on the competitiveness of insurance companies.

Underwriters, who often specialise in one type of insurance, determine policy terms and conditions, and calculate premiums based on risk assessment, and statistical and background information – looking at the potential for a loss, based on their experience of a particular trade or industry.

Main Task of an Underwriter

Insurance is based on risk. When a policyholder gets an insurance policy, the insurer is taking on some of their risk. For example, if the policyholder drives a car, they have a risk that their car will be damaged in an accident. Having car insurance means that if the car does get damaged, the insurance company will pay for the repairs. By having a policy, the policyholder's risk is lower.

The insurance company compensates for the risk it takes on by charging premiums and setting deductibles. If a company charges too little, it could go bankrupt when large claims are filed. But if a company charges too much, the consequence is loss of business to its competition.

An underwriter's job is to ensure that the insurer charges just the precise amount for the coverage it provides. They figure how much risk an applicant for insurance represents, how much coverage the company can offer them, and how much that coverage should cost. Their job involves a lot of complexity, depending on the type of applicant and the scope of coverage desired. When tackling complex cases, an actuary's assistance is usually sought.

An underwriter typically pulls together information about the applicant (or the insured in the case of policy renewal) and the subject of insurance so as to measure the loss potential. The complexity of the underwriting process is increased for large or unusual risks as well as global insurance initiatives. Therefore, strong knowledge of local conditions and the local legislation is required. Also required is a local presence in the event that continuous monitoring and gaining local knowledge is essential, which is usually advantageous in personal lines of insurance. As for complex cases, it is usual practice for underwriters to approach local engineers, surveyors etc. and brokers for the required selection and classification information.

Why Insurance Underwriting is Important

It is every insurance company's intention to stay competitive and stay in business for as long as possible. Thus, underwriting is important to them.

But why is it important to the applicant? Underwriting is important because when an applicant is applying for an insurance policy, their application is going to be examined by an underwriter. And that underwriter's opinion is going to establish how much the applicant will pay for insurance. And based on the condition of his or her health – or even a mistake on the application – they could decide to deny the application entirely.

It would appear that an applicant can get round it but in practice, it isn't that easy as applying for insurance leaves a record. And if an applicant is denied coverage, it will show up on that record. Once an applicant has been denied coverage at one company, other companies are more likely to deny them, too.

The Application Process

The application process illustrated in this section is for life insurance. When an applicant applies for life insurance, the company will examine a number of factors based on its own particular underwriting standards and guidelines. These factors include:

- The applicant's current health and physical condition;
- His or her medical history;
- His or her vocation (a racing-car driver, for example, presents a higher risk than an office worker);
- Personal habits (including tobacco use and a history of alcohol or drug abuse);
- His or her avocations and hobbies (bungee jumping, for example, is a high-risk pastime that could increase an applicant's premium);
- Age (a 60-year-old applicant will pay a higher rate than a 35-year-old);
- Gender (except in jurisdictions with unisex rates, rates for women are lower than those for men since women enjoy longer life expectancies).

How an Insurer Processes Information

Once an insurance company receives the application, all personal and financial information on the form is held in strict confidence. A specially trained underwriter reviews and evaluates these factors and develops a risk profile of the applicant. This risk profile relates to the life expectancy of the individual and possible reductions due to medical history. The final premium is based on the risk profile and the risk of death.

Experts usually point out that premiums are not set arbitrarily. There is a clear objectivity to the process in that risk selection must be based on actuarial projections, medical advances and expected or anticipated claims experience.

Risk Classifications

Each insurance company sets its own underwriting standards of what it considers to be acceptable, insurable risks. Then each application for insurance is reviewed to establish if the individual meets those standards. The following are four popular categories:

- **Preferred** – If the applicant is a better-than-average risk (i.e. in good health, with no dangerous hobbies or history of health problems) they may be charged a preferred or lowest rate.
- **Standard** – If the applicant is considered an average or typical risk, they will be charged the standard rate.
- **Rated** – If the applicant poses an above-average risk (maybe they have high blood pressure, smoke cigarettes or engage in rock climbing every

weekend), they may be classified as an increased risk and charged a higher premium. A typical example is an applicant that is 50 and has had a heart attack; actuarial statistics may show their life expectancy to have been cut short by 10 years. Thus, they will pay the premium of a much older person, say a 60-year-old.

- **Declined** – If the applicant is rated as uninsurable (maybe due to a serious illness), they will probably be denied coverage entirely.

Claims Administration

Insurance policyholders exercise the right to make a claim when something unfortunate happens – for example a flood, fire, storm damage or a vehicle accident.

Insurance claims handlers are responsible for the investigation of incidents and the payment of claims. They make decisions on the extent and validity of the claim, helping to reduce the impact of loss by arranging for appropriate action to assist the claimant. At the same time, they determine a claim's genuineness, and are on the lookout for fraud.

Their work involves the co-coordination of the services that may be required by policyholders following an incident; for example getting in touch with builders to repair damage to a factory or an approved car mechanic to repair a car or lorry. The claims inspector's primary intention is to quantify and settle claims quickly, resolving issues and negotiating settlements with policyholders or legal representatives.

Claims administration includes processes such as:

- First notice of loss;
- Claims/loss adjustment;
- Subrogation/salvage;
- Litigation management;
- Catastrophe management.

Claims/Loss Adjustment

In an ideal world, after a loss, the insurer and policyholder collaborate to measure and settle a loss. An amount is agreed upon and the claim is paid. Unfortunately, in practice there are many factors that make this apparently simple process complicated. It is understandable that after paying insurance premiums for many years, policyholders expect to be made whole for their losses quickly and fully without a lot of effort or hassle. However, policyholders often become disenchanted once they find out that they have to prove their claim, prepare it, substantiate it and then eventually negotiate a settlement with the insurance company. All of these events are closely monitored by the insurance company, adjusters, underwriters, supervisors, accountants, engineers, experts and often attorneys. There are many reasons why an insurer might bring down the value of a loss or refute all or part of a claim. There are also a number of methods by which a claim may be resolved including negotiation, appraisal, arbitration, mediation and/or litigation.

Subrogation/Salvage

When an insurer pays a policyholder for a loss, the insurer has a right of subrogation against any person or persons accountable for the loss. The right of subrogation arises out of a car insurance policy, which is an indemnity contract. The right of subrogation essentially, allows the insurance company to pay its policyholder and then pursue the responsible party for the payments made. When the insurance company collects against the responsible party or its insurance company, the policyholder will receive its pro-rata share of the deductible applied to the original loss payment made to the policyholder. In the event that the subrogation claim is unsuccessful, then the accident may become a chargeable accident to the policyholder and possibly result in a premium increase.

Subrogation refers to the business process an insurer uses to ask for reimbursement from the responsible party for a claim it has already paid. When an insurance company covers a loss that's not the insured's fault, as stated above, they may pursue the 'at-fault' party, which often is the other insurance company, to recover payments made for the insured's damages and injuries. Insurance companies can only subrogate other parties if their policyholder is not at fault for an accident.

For instance, suppose James Klame's car is involved in an accident with Clare Salvo's car, but his insurance company is taking too long to get back to Ms Salvo. Salvo's car isn't drivable, and she doesn't want to keep asking friends to run her around town, so she decides to use her own insurance to repair her car. She pays her $1,000 collision deductible, fixes her car, and is back to normal in a couple of weeks.

However, Ms Salvo still paid $1,000 out of her own pocket and her insurance company paid thousands of dollars for an accident that wasn't her fault. In situations like this, her insurance company will subrogate James Klame's insurance company to recover the money paid for the accident – and that includes attempting to recover her $1,000 deductible for her.

Subrogation is vital because the policyholder is recovering claim payments previously paid by the insurance company, or the self-insured entity, which entail losses (or partial losses) not caused by the policyholder's negligence. If the policyholder does not pursue subrogation, insurance premiums will increase as a result of poor loss experience. The loss ratio[51] is calculated by

51 The loss ratio is calculated by dividing the incurred losses by the earned premium. Incurred losses are the claim payments plus outstanding reserves less recoveries. Earned premium implies that the premium is earning over the policy period. A 24-month policy earns at a rate of 1/24 each month.

dividing the losses by the premium. The lower the loss ratio, the more favourable the loss experience. If the losses were $200,000 and the premium was $400,000, then the loss ratio is 50%. If the policyholder recovered $150,000 of the loss payments as a result of subrogation, then the net losses are reduced to $50,000 and the loss ratio will be reduced to 12.5%.

Catastrophe Management

An insurer has to grapple with significant financial hazards that include the risk of becoming insolvent, an immediate reduction of revenue and statutory surplus, the likelihood of enforced asset liquidation to meet cash requirements, and the risk of their rating becoming downgraded, when presented with catastrophe. Property and casualty (P&C) insurance companies usually formulate catastrophe risk management strategies that are a combination of the determination of their appetite for risk, measurement of exposures, pricing factors, business processes to confine exposure, and the use of reinsurance or capital markets for the transfer of risk to third parties.

Figure 6.1 shows five steps that insurers take to manage catastrophe.

Figure 6.1 Five Key Steps to Address Catastrophe

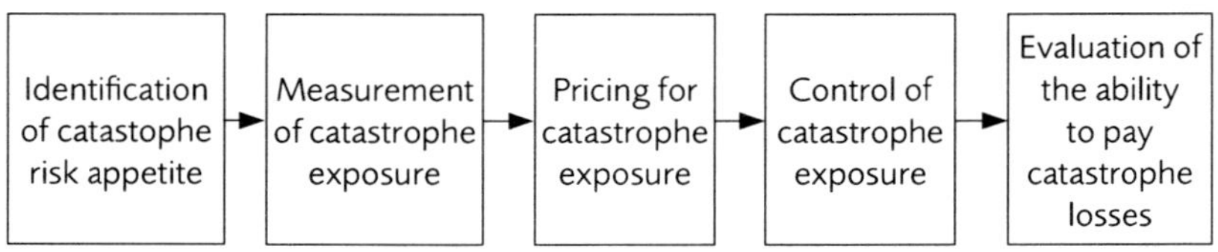

Identification of catastrophe risk appetite

When managing catastrophic exposures, insurers begin the process by gaining an understanding of the extent of the loss over a period of time that they are capable of absorbing and which will not have an unacceptable adverse impact. Each insurance company's appetite for risk is unique and a function of factors including the following:

- Accessibility and cost of reinsurance;
- Market pricing;
- Evaluations by ratings agencies;
- Tax considerations;
- Volatility of revenue;
- Cash flow requirements;
- Regulations relating to solvency;
- Financing needs;
- Rate regulation;
- Sundry lines of business written by the insurance company.

A company's appetite for risk is usually denoted as a maximum acceptable reduction to surplus (or income) from a single event or multiple events in a year. The management team may, instead, stipulate a maximum loss that can be permitted within a certain time frame, like '£200 million of loss that could possibly be exceeded only once in 100 years'. Underwriters use expressions such as this as a guideline for monitoring the likelihood that the catastrophe risk in the insured portfolio is within acceptable limits.

Measurement of catastrophe exposure

As soon as a company has determined its appetite for risk, it is essential that an inventory of its current exposures is completed. Historically; this may be achieved by the evaluation of the company's loss potential resulting from the aggregate policy limits written in a catastrophe-exposed area. In the wake of significant losses from catastrophes such as earthquakes and hurricanes, the insurance industry has witnessed an improvement in catastrophe modelling technology and, as a consequence, increased thoroughness in the measurement of catastrophe risk.

A term that readers will come across during this process is 'probable maximum loss' (PML), which can be defined as the amount of loss that is associated with a specified amount by which the loss exceeds a standard or permissible probability over a defined period of time. Insurers use PML in a context that is applicable to their catastrophe risk management strategies.

Pricing for catastrophe exposure

Insurance companies, unlike most businesses, are unaware of the majority of the costs for their products when they are sold. Most insurance costs don't occur until much later. Indeed, a number of claims may remain unreported until a long period, months or even years, after the policy has expired. Insurance premiums may be determined by the regulatory process or by the operation of the competitive marketplace and vary from jurisdiction to jurisdiction. The following costs are factored into premiums in either case:

- **Net cost of reinsurance** – This is the premium needed by the reinsurance company to accept the catastrophe exposure, less the expected loss transferred to the insurance company.
- **Cost of capital** – This represents the provision for profit required to attain the insurance company's rate of return on capital that is proportionate to the risk present in the exposure profile.
- **Underwriting expenses** – These are costs associated with gaining new business or the retention of the insurer's existing book of business that include commissions, other acquisition costs, and general expenses, salaries, rent and so on.
- **Premium taxes, licences, and fees** – These areas represent the

premium taxes enforced by the relevant jurisdiction as well as costs for licences and fees.

- **Expected loss and loss adjustment expenses** – These represent payments that an insured receives for first-party coverage or a third party receives on behalf of an insured in addition to claim settlement expenses.

Control of catastrophe exposure

As soon as a company has ascertained its appetite for risk, evaluated its current loss exposure and determined the optimum price for a product, the next logical step is to contain its risk. The management process entails steps including:

- Identification of the area in which the company can grow its portfolio without going beyond its capacity limitations;
- Reduction of exposure through reinsurance, capital market substitutes, deductibles and other endeavours for mitigation of loss;
- Reduction of property exposures where the company has exceeded its capacity for the region.

There are different approaches that insurers adopt for the management of the amount of a specific product or aggregate catastrophe exposure it will write in any given area. Nevertheless, there are common characteristics in all effective catastrophe risk management programmes. For instance, a company that chooses to write equal amounts of product in two dissimilar locations, covering particular perils such as earthquakes, will have a bigger capacity than a company that writes twice the exposure in one location.

Evaluation of the ability to pay catastrophe losses

There are cash demands on the insurer that may vary considerably depending on the nature and intensity of the event. Insurance payouts to the insured are faster for catastrophes that produce observable damage, such as tornadoes and hurricanes, than for earthquakes. In addition, the timing of the monetary requirements is a function of the magnitude of the event.

The time frame between the catastrophic event and when repairs are completed gives insurers time to finance the loss through underwriting cash flow, normal cash flow from investments, liquidation of assets, debt financing, or advance funding from reinsurers. In general, the liquidity, or lack of, of an insurance company following a catastrophe does not result in insolvency. It is the size of the event and the fact that the company has insufficient surplus for claims payments that are the crucial factors.

Insurance companies with catastrophe exposures typically establish contingency plans for handling cash demands. These kinds of plan commonly include the following steps:

- Determination of the potential size and timing of cash demands for catastrophe claims;
- Determination of the willingness and ability of the company's reinsurer to advance funds;
- Determination of the above cash resources which might also be impacted by the catastrophic event;
- Determination of the gap, if it exists, between potential catastrophe cash needs and cash sources that are readily available;
- Determination of the dependability and flexibility of current sources of cash including daily cash flow from insurance and investment operations;
- Development of a plan that will plug the gap when a catastrophe happens, including decreases in other spending, liquidation of assets or tapping equity or debt markets.

Pricing and Product Development

Pricing or ratemaking is the most important business process in the insurance industry. Ratemaking is essentially the process of calculating a premium in order that it is:

1. Sufficient to make payment of losses in accordance with expected frequency and severity, thereby protecting against the insurance company becoming insolvent;
2. Reasonable to the extent that the insurance company is not able to generate an excessive profit;
3. Equitable and fairly discriminatory.

In theory, each insurance applicant should pay a unique premium that is a reflection of different expectation of loss, but this would be unrealistic. Rather, classifications are created for grouping of applicants according to similar expectation of loss. Statistical studies of a large number of nearly identical exposures in each underwriting classification allow for the projection of losses after adjustments for future inflation and statistical irregularities. The adjusted statistics are used to calculate the pure cost of protection, or pure premium, to which the insurance company adds extra for agent commissions, premium taxes, administrative expenses, contingency and profit margin reserves, other acquisition costs, and profit margin. The result is the gross premium to be charged to the insured.

Insurance pricing is a major aspect of actuarial science.

Premium Rating

Insurance companies charge premiums based on:

- Their profitability requirements;
- The level of risk associated with the policyholder;
- The cost of the acquisition and administration of the business;
- The level of exposure of the policyholder and the insured goods or services to the various perils.

The process of setting an appropriate rate for the cost of certain future contingencies of unpredictable timing, frequency and magnitude is an imprecise science that requires approximation of future cash flows, including claims, investment income, various costs (including the cost of reinsurance), and tax as well as profit. Additionally, the pricing structure adopted can greatly impact on the volume and the kind of business attracted, and certain categories of business exhibit more price sensitivity than others. It is worth noting that the demands in commoditised insurance markets, such as personal lines car insurance, exhibit particular price elasticity. Foremost, market participants can exert influence on the decisions centred on pricing that are taken by competitors. Whilst this is true, it is important to note that in well-informed and liquid markets, competitive advantage is eroded in a short space of time. Therefore, corporate aspirations, apart from the achievement of a sufficient level of profitability or return on equity, be it for an individual policy or across a group of policyholders, as well as the long-term survival of the firm, might include the following:

- Achievement of a target premium growth rate;
- Attainment of a minimum market share;
- The writing of a certain premium volume;
- The reduction of lapse rates, and especially retaining the more profitable business;
- Realisation of an overall operating ratio across the entire portfolio;
- Attracting a wider spread of business by, for example, geographical area, industry mix, or policyholder type.

The premium calculation can therefore be considered to be a two-stage process:

1. The costing exercise, i.e. the computation of a theoretical price for the risk and all associated costs; and
2. The pricing stage, i.e. the commercial adjustment to the theoretical cost that takes into consideration the broader objectives of the business.

An important element of premium rating is the design of the insurance product itself, which involves the precise specification of the extent of the exposure to be underwritten. Input is required from a number of other professionals: lawyers, underwriters, actuaries, loss adjusters and claims managers.

An insurer's ability to manage its uncertainty over the cash flows that emerge from an insurance policy or a portfolio increases if the policy coverage can be controlled. The policy might simply limit the maximum amount of money that is paid out in a certain calendar period. Insurers could carefully design the administrative workload of servicing the claims and enhance the profit signature of the business. For instance, the frequency of small claims and the relevant inconsistent claims handling can be lessened by:

- Specifying an appropriate level of deductible, which is a retention of part of the claim cost by the policyholder for each claim;
- Enforcing an experience rating system in a way that the premium is adjusted in accordance with claims experience. This system is known in insurance as a bonus-malus system (BMS). Bonus is typically a discount in the premium which is applied on the renewal of the policy if no claim is made in the previous year. Malus is an increase in the premium if there is a claim in the previous year. Bonus-malus systems are very common in personal lines insurance such car insurance. This system is also referred to as no claim discount (NCD) or no claims bonus in Britain and Australia.

Brokerage

A discussion on business processes is incomplete without a brief discussion on brokerage. Insurance brokerages act as intermediaries between insurance companies and insurance buyers, advising prospective policyholders on the most suitable product for their needs, helping to manage and mitigate potential risks and arranging to put cover in place.

Faced with a vast choice of insurers and different types and prices of cover and policy, customers – both individuals and companies – need professional advice. Brokers use their wider knowledge and experience to assess a client's risk profile and find the appropriate cover.

In the primary insurance market, brokerages augment product and price competition by setting right, to some degree, the imbalance in the flow of information between buyer and seller.

Although they usually receive their commission from the insurance company, brokerages are required to be client-focused and manage client relationships effectively. In larger brokerage firms, brokers may specialise in specific areas, while those in smaller organisations will carry out a broad range of functions.

Risk and Insurance

7

This chapter discusses risk from the perspectives of both insurance and reinsurance.

Introduction

People have always looked to manage uncertainty and in so doing have sought security. Experts opine that a sense of security may be the next fundamental goal after fulfilling the need for food, clothing and shelter. A person with economic security is fairly sure that they can satisfy their basic needs at the moment and in the future. Economic risk can be described as the possibility of losing economic security.

A common measure of risk is the standard deviation of the possible outcomes. For instance, two different types of car, say an Aston Martin and a Ford, may have the same expected value of repairs, say £2,500, in the event of an accident. But, the standard deviation for the Aston Martin is 1000 while that of the Ford is 400. Should there be a normal distribution of the cost of repairs, then the probability that the repair work will cost more than £3,000 is 31% for the Aston Martin and just 11% for the Ford.

A number of examples can be seen in modern-day life. For instance, damage to a person's car results in them suffering a potential economic loss. In the case of a homeowner, they face a large potential for variation associated with the possibility of economic loss caused by a house fire or any other types of structural damage.

In the past, the management of economic risk was achieved through informal agreements within a particular community. For example, in the event that a farmer, George Van Reesk, has his barn destroyed by fire and the herd of cows that provide milk for the farmer's dairy business killed, the community would donate funds for rebuilding the barn and allow the farmer to purchase a replacement herd of cows to enable him to replenish the milking stock. Industry experts point out that it is this type of cooperative (pooling) concept that became formalised in the insurance industry. A formal insurance contract arrangement entails each insurance policy purchaser (i.e. policyholder) implicitly pooling their risk with all other policyholders. In modern times, it is, however, unnecessary for any individual policyholder to be aware or have any direct connection with any other policyholder.

Definition of Risk in Insurance

Before defining risk in insurance, some fundamental concepts of risk have to be discussed.

Risk is typically a condition in which there is a possibility of an adverse deviation from the desired outcome that is expected or hoped for. Thus: (1) risk is not subjective, (2) risk can exist whether or not it is perceived, (3) risk can be imagined where the possibility of loss does not exist.

The degree of risk varies with the possibility of deviation from what is expected in the case of aggregate data and from what is hoped for (i.e. no loss) in the case of an individual. The degree of risk may or may not be measurable.

Risk differs from peril and hazard in that peril is the cause of loss while hazard is a condition that creates or increases that chance of loss. Examples of perils are fires, hurricanes, theft and heart attacks, while examples of hazards include smoking when taking into consideration potential healthcare losses, and poor wiring in a house when taking into consideration losses due to fires. Moral hazards, as opposed to the physical hazards described in the last sentence, refer to a change in human attitude increasing the likelihood of a loss.

Risk in insurance is defined as the uncertainty of financial loss; a term used to designate an insured or a peril that is insured against.

Financial loss may be defined as a decline in or disappearance of value due to a contingency.

Insurance professionals often use the term risk interchangeably with peril.

The Workings of Insurance

It will be prudent to recapitulate the workings of insurance as a prelude to the discussion on risk.

Insurance is essentially an agreement where an insurer agrees to pay to a policyholder or their designated beneficiary a specified amount, the claim benefit, should the specific loss occur, in exchange for a predetermined payment, the premium. This specified amount may be a fixed amount or a reimbursement of all or part of the loss that has occurred. There are considerations taken in to account by the insurer with regard to losses expected for the insurance pool and the potential for variation so as to charge premiums that, in total, will be adequate to cover all of the projected claim payments for the insurance pool. The premium that is to be paid by participants of the pool is equal to the participant's share of the total premium for the pool. There may be adjustments to each premium to reflect any special characteristics of the particular policy.

In general, only a small fraction of policyholders suffer losses. Insurers pay their losses out of the premiums they collected from the pool of policyholders. Therefore, the entire pool recompenses the unlucky few. In essence, each policyholder exchanges an unknown loss for the payment of a known premium.

Under this formal arrangement, the insurance company is the party that agrees to make the claim payments while the pool participant is the policyholder, i.e. the party that agrees to pay the premium. The insurance contract is the policy and the risk of any unanticipated losses is transferred from the policyholder to the insurer, who reserves the right to spell out the rules and conditions for participating in the insurance pool.

The insurance company may impose restrictions on the particular kinds of loss covered. In some instances, the policy (contract) may define specific perils that are covered, or it may cover all perils with certain named exclusions.

Risk Classification

The following are common classifications of risk:

- **Financial and non-financial (operational)** – Financial risk arises from an individual's or organisation's ownership or use of financial instruments. There are a number of economic factors that can give rise to financial risks including changes in interest rates, extensions of credit, issuance of stock, foreign currency transactions and the use of derivatives. Therefore, the extension of credit to customers by businesses such as credit card companies gives rise to the risk, financial risk, that some will default. Investment activities of individuals and the borrowing they undertake when making purchases of capital items such as cars, houses etc. also give rise to financial risk.

  Non-financial risk, including operational risk, arises from the existence and activities of an individual or from the operations of an organisation. For organisations, operational risk may arise directly or indirectly through inadequate internal processes, accounting, human error, systems or business continuity failures, fraud or inadequate legal and other documentation.
- **Static and dynamic** – Static risk can be described as risk arising from damage or destruction of property and/or property that is illegally transferred as the result of misconduct of individuals. The risk is insurable.

  Dynamic risk results from exposure to loss from changes in the environment, such as changes in price levels, output, fashions, people's tastes, and regulatory requirements. Dynamic risks are not insurable.
- **Fundamental and particular** – Fundamental risks are essentially societal risks that can be described as impersonal in origin and consequences.

  Particular risks are associated with losses that arise out of individual events and impact on individuals as opposed to the entire society. Individuals are normally responsible for addressing particular risks.
- **Pure and speculative** – Speculative risks involve the possibility of loss or gain and are freely accepted because of the possibility of gain.

  Pure risk is a type of risk that involves the possibility of loss or no loss only. Traditionally, insurers deal primarily with pure risk only.

Pure Risk Classifications

Pure risk can be classified according to the generic nature of exposure as follows:

- **Personal risk** – This is uncertainty associated with loss of health, incapacity, death and an individual outliving their financial resources.

- **Property risk** – This is the uncertainty associated with loss of wealth resulting from damage or destruction of property.
- **Liability risk** – This is the uncertainty related to financial instability that can arise from bodily injury (including health) or loss of wealth that an individual or an organisation causes to others.
- **Personnel risk** – This type of risk is associated with the loss to a firm as a result of death, incapacity, loss of health, prospect of harm to or unexpected departure of key staff.

Insurance from a Risk Perspective

The burden of risk that an insurer bears is inherent in the inevitability that some losses will occur. This also includes the cost of accumulated reserves and the deterrent effect on capital accumulation.

Insurers typically deal with risk using methods such as avoidance, reduction (loss control), transfer and sharing.

That said, from a risk perspective, insurance has two fundamental characteristics:

1. Transfer of risk from the individual to the group;
2. Sharing of losses on a given equitable basis.

Insurers reduce risk through pooling and the following are fundamental facts about this practice:

- The risk an insurer faces is not simply a summation of risks transferred to it by individuals (policy holders).
- It is possible for an insurer to predict within narrow limits the amount of losses that will happen.
- If an insurer could forecast future losses with absolute precision, it would have no risk.
- The precision of insurers' predictions is based on the law of large numbers.

Experts are divided on the issue of whether insurance is about risk transfer or pooling. Below are some industry viewpoints on this debate:

- The viewpoint which asserts that the fundamental nature of insurance is risk transfer stresses the individual's substitution of a small certain cost for large uncertain loss.
- Emphasis on pooling or risk sharing accentuates the role of reducing risk in the aggregate.
- Insurance can exist without pooling, but not without transfer.

Insurance can also be compared to gambling. The following are some interesting comparisons:

- In insurance, there is the possibility of loss whether or not insurance is purchased.
- As for gambling, there is the chance of loss (hence no risk) prior to the bet.
- Gambling brings about risk, while insurance provides for the transfer of risk.

The Risk Management Process

It is a given that all individuals, businesses and government must deal with risk. The management of risk is the identification, analysis and economic control of those risks which can threaten the assets or earning capacity of an entity.

Existing risk management practices, whether carried out by an individual, a company or a government body, appear to follow somewhat standardised steps. These steps are referred to as the risk management process and they entail:

- Risk analysis, which is the identification and assessment of the possible outcomes related to events and activities;
- Risk control for the explanation of techniques to control adverse outcomes;
- Risk financing, which involves decision making on how the costs of adverse outcomes that happen are financed.

Risk management increases the probability of success, and reduces the probability of failure and the uncertainty of achieving the organisation's overall objectives.

Theoretical Underpinnings of Risk in Insurance

Probability Theory

Probability theory is the basis of the insurance industry, in the form of actuarial statistics. The central objects of probability theory are random variables, stochastic processes, and events: mathematical abstractions of non-deterministic events or measured quantities that may either be single occurrences or evolve over time in an apparently random fashion.

Example

An example of the application of probability theory in insurance is as follows.

Consider an important insurance market segment – young drivers. Many young people pass their driving test prior to going to university and consider the possibility of running their own car, only to be put off by the very high insurance premiums they will be required to pay. An 18-year-old that has just passed their driving test can pay several times as much as their parents for apparently identical insurance.

This is not a practice that discriminates against the young, but merely a consequence of conditional probability theory. Prior to the discussion of the premiums paid by young drivers for car insurance, it would be prudent to consider a straightforward example to demonstrate the concept of conditional probability. This is the probability of some event X, given the occurrence of some other event Y. It can be written as P (X/Y).

One important formula in conditional probability is:

$$P(X/Y) = \frac{P(X \cap Y)}{P(Y)}$$

P(Y) is the probability of Y occurring. $P(X \cap Y)$ is the probability of X and Y both occurring and is referred to as the joint probability of X and Y.

In order to make conditional probability operational, consider the 7 days of the week. Let X be a weekday and let Y be a day with a letter n in its spelling.

$P(X) = {}^{5}/_{7}$ (Monday–Friday out of 7 days)
$P(Y) = {}^{3}/_{7}$ (Monday, Wednesday and Sunday)
$P(X \cap Y) = {}^{2}/_{7}$ (Monday and Wednesday)

$$P(X/Y) = \frac{{}^{2}/_{7}}{{}^{3}/_{7}} = {}^{2}/_{3}$$

This is intuitive as you are given Y, which is a day with an n. There are three of these days. Two of these three days are weekdays.

Now back to the discussion on the premiums of young drivers. The main reason an insurance company charges, for example, five times the premium for a new young driver is that they believe that the new young driver is about five times as likely to make a claim.

There are two reasons for this. Firstly, the conditional probability of having an accident if the driver is 18 years old is significantly higher than the conditional probability of having an accident if the driver is over 40 years old.

Secondly a person over 40 may have a significant 'no claims discount', whereas an 18-year-old will not have had the chance to build up a 'no claims discount'. The logic behind this is that the probability of having an accident, given that the driver has not claimed for five years, is significantly less than the probability of having an accident if the driver is opening a completely new policy.

Variations in the prices of car insurance occur mainly as a result of the above two types of conditional probability.

Law of Large Numbers

The law of large numbers (LLN) is a theorem in probability that describes the long-term stability of the mean of a random variable. Given a random variable with a finite expected value, if its values are repeatedly sampled, as the number of these observations increases, their mean will tend to approach and stay close to the expected value.

The rolls of a dice provide a simple illustration for LLN. That is, outcomes of a multinomial distribution in which the numbers 1, 2, 3, 4, 5 and 6 are equally likely to be chosen. The population mean (or 'expected value') of the outcomes is:

$$(1 + 2 + 3 + 4 + 5 + 6) / 6 = 3.5$$

To apply this theory to the insurance business, it is first worth mentioning that in the insurance industry, the majority of insurers would find it difficult or unreasonable to go back to their policyholders for additional payments if losses happen to be larger than expected. They must depend on a cushion of working capital (supplied by the shareholders in expectation of an investment return in a proprietary company) to meet such losses.

The sharing and pooling of risk is still, however, crucial. In the real world, the pattern of losses (cars stolen or houses burning down) is unsteady. That said, the following is an illustration of the application of the LLN in car insurance.

Suppose that statistics in a particular country show that, on average, 1 car in 20 is stolen each year. If the thefts are independent of one another, an insurer who had only insured 20 cars would discover that there was a 1 in 4 chance that 2 or more would be stolen, which would double their expected outlay on claims.

This does not qualify as good business practice.

However, if 100,000 cars are insured, the probability that more than 10,200 (or less than 9,800) will be stolen is only about 1%.

In other words, the more cars the insurance company insures, the more accurately it can predict the number of cars likely to be stolen. It is this aspect of probability theory that enables insurance companies to handle variations in the pattern of actual losses.

Features of Insurable Risk

Individuals believe that buying insurance will give them an economic advantage. Insurers agree to the arrangement on the understanding that risk can be pooled and, if feasible, they will need some protection. That said, it will be prudent to discuss what makes a risk insurable and the kinds of risk an insurer is willing to insure.

Insurers acknowledge that the potential loss must be significant and sufficiently important that substituting a known insurance premium for an unknown economic outcome (given no insurance) is advantageous.

The loss and its economic value are usually well-defined and are not some elements that a policyholder can control. The policyholder is usually not allowed to cause or encourage a loss that will result in a benefit or claim payment.

Covered losses are usually realistically independent. It is acknowledged in the insurance industry that the fact that one policyholder suffers a loss should not have a profound effect on whether other policyholders do so. For instance, an insurer would not consider insuring all the office blocks in a particular business district against fire, given that there is a likelihood that fire in one office block could spread, leading to the insurer having to make many large claims payments.

If these criteria are fully satisfied, then the risk is insurable. It should be noted that the fact that a potential loss is not able to satisfy the criteria does not necessarily imply that insurance will not be issued, but special care or additional risk-sharing with other insurers may be required.

Limits on Policy Benefits

In all types of insurance, limits on benefits or claim payments may exist. To be more specific, there may be:

- A maximum limit on the total reimbursed;
- A minimum limit on losses that will be reimbursed;
- Only a certain percentage of each loss reimbursed;
- Different limits applied to particular types of loss.

In each of the above circumstances, the insurer does not pay back the entire loss. Rather, the policyholder must cover part of the loss themselves. This is often known as co-insurance.

The specific types of limits on policy benefits are discussed in the next two sections.

Deductible (Excess)

In an insurance policy, the deductible (North American term) or excess (UK term) is the part of any claim that is not covered by the insurer. It is typically quoted as a fixed quantity and is a part of most policies covering losses to the policyholder. The deductible must be paid by the insured, before the benefits of the policy take effect. As a general rule: the higher the deductible, the lower the premium, and vice versa.

In a typical automobile insurance policy, a deductible will be applicable to claims resulting from damage to or loss of the policyholder's own vehicle, regardless of the cause of this damage/loss. Third-party liability coverage generally has no deductible, since the third party will likely attempt to recover any loss, however small, for which the policyholder is liable.

Reasons for deductibles include the following:

- There is a reduction in claim payments by the amount of the deductible, which is translated into the premium.
- Small losses do not create a claim payment, therefore saving the expenses of processing the claim.
- The deductible puts the policyholder at risk and, therefore, provides an economic incentive for the policyholder to prevent losses that would lead to claim payments.

Problems associated with deductibles include:

- The policyholder may exaggerate the loss in order to recover the deductible.
- The policyholder may be disenchanted that losses are not paid in full. Certainly, deductibles increase the risk for which the policyholder remains responsible.
- Deductibles may make the marketing of the coverage more complex for the insurance company.

Example

A company BizCorp takes out property insurance with EssInsure that has a $2,000 deductible on their office building. Flooding now occurs in the district in which this office building is located. Floodwaters cause $12,000 worth of damage to this building, therefore EssInsure pays $10,000 since BizCorp has paid the $2,000 deductible.

Benefit Limits

A benefit limit sets an upper bound on the amount of money the insurer will pay out for any loss. The motivations behind placing a limit on the benefits include the following:

- The limit prevents total claim payments from exceeding the insurer's financial capacity.
- With different benefit limits, the policyholder is able to choose appropriate coverage at an appropriate price, given that the premium will be lower for lower benefit limits.
- From a risk perspective, an upper bound to the benefit reduces the risk borne by the insurer.

Generally, the lower the benefit limit, the lower the premium. In practice, a policy may have more than one limit, and overall there is more than one way to provide limits on benefits. Different limits may be set for different perils. Limits might also be set as a percentage of total loss.

The Role of the Actuary

The profession of the actuary is one of the oldest in the financial world. Actuaries apply financial and statistical techniques to solve real business problems. These business problems usually entail analysing future financial events, especially when the amount of a future payment, or the timing of when it is paid, is uncertain. A lot of actuaries' work might be perceived as risk management, assessing how likely an event may be and the costs associated with it.

As experts in measuring and managing risk, actuaries fill a significant need in society. Their contribution to society's psychological, physical and economic well-being is vast. If actuaries did not develop their own brand of risk management programmes, the growth of the global economy would be impacted. Consider the following:

- Would parents enjoy risky and adventurous recreational activities such as rock climbing or skiing if their children faced financial disaster in the event of an accident?
- Would people spend money today and still be confident about their future if there were no retirement programmes or social security?
- Would as many people be willing to own a home if fire insurance did not exist?
- Would a company build a factory that could be destroyed in an earthquake if it were not protected by insurance?

Actuaries are heavily involved in insurance because it is acknowledged that this is society's most powerful answer for managing risk.

What is an Actuary?

An actuary in the insurance sector is an individual who analyses important data such as mortality, sickness, injury and disability rates, and uses that information to aid those involved with insurance. An actuary is responsible for collecting the data to forecast future risks and seeing how these predictions will affect various aspects of insurance.

The following are some of the characteristics of actuaries:

- They are acknowledged experts in the analysis and modelling of situations involving financial risk and contingent events.
- They are concerned with both the asset and liability side of the balance sheet.

- They have the ability to provide realistic solutions to complex problems with a long-term forward look.
- They are practical, innovative and numerate.

Skills that actuaries typically possess include:

- Financial and mathematical modelling, including mortality and morbidity rates;
- Analysing and managing uncertainty;
- Evaluating financial consequences;
- Analysing of risk and risk management;
- Scientific pricing and reserving techniques;
- Asset/liability management;
- Overall financial management.

In insurance, actuaries determine the expected costs and risks in any given situation where there is financial uncertainty and data for creating a model of those risks. This includes developing net premiums (benefit premium), gross premiums, and the amount of assets the insurer should have on hand to assure that benefits and expenses can be paid as required.

The actuary would begin by attempting to estimate the frequency and severity distribution for a particular pool. The process entails, for a start, an analysis of past experience. The actuary will typically try to use data gathered from the insurance pool or from a group as comparable to the insurance pool as possible.

The actuary usually considers the reliability of past experience as a predictor of the future when analysing past experience. Based on the assumption that the experience gathered represents the insurance pool, the more data, the more the confidence that it will be a good predictor of the true underlying probability distributions. The following illustrates this concept:

Sally Van Reesk, an actuary, is trying to establish the underlying probability that Ferrari drivers will be involved in a car accident in one year. She collects data using a large random sample of Ferrari drivers from previous years and identifies the number of such drivers who were involved in a crash within one year. The probability is approximated by using the ratio of the number of drivers in the sample to the total number of Ferrari drivers in the sample. The Central Limit Theorem postulates that if the underlying distribution has an average of **p** and standard deviation of σ, this implies that the average of a large random sample of size **n** is approximately normally distributed with average **p** and standard deviation $\sigma/\sqrt{\mathbf{n}}$. The larger the size of the sample, the smaller the variation between the sample average and the underlying value of **p**.

The actuary, in the process of assessing past experience, must also look out for fundamental changes that will change the underlying probability distributions. A typical example is in medical insurance when healthcare costs are being estimated. In the event that new but expensive methods and drugs are discovered and implemented, then reflection of the use of the new methods will be evident in the shifting up of the distribution of healthcare costs.

The combination of the frequency and severity distribution developed from the analysis of past experience is used to develop the loss distribution. The claim payment distribution can be derived by adjusting the loss distribution to serve as the reflection of the provisions in the policies, such as deductibles and benefits limits.

If inflation has an effect on claim payments, there will be a requirement to estimate future inflation on the basis of past experience and information about the current state of a given country's economy. As for insurance coverages, where present-day premiums are invested to cover claim payments in the future, the actuary will also be required to estimate investment returns.

The tools to determine the net premium are at the actuary's disposal at this point.

The actuary is also able to use similar methods for estimation of an adequate amount of margin to build into the gross premium in order to cover both the insurer's expenses and a reasonable level of unanticipated claim repayments.

Risk Management in Reinsurance

As seen in Chapter 3, insurers cede part of their risks to reinsurers and this results in the reduction of their underwriting risk. In exchange, they bear the counterparty credit, i.e. the risk that the reinsurer would not be able to honour its financial obligations. It is therefore essential that reinsurers inspire the confidence of insurers in their financial security.

Reinsurers generally implement sophisticated risk management processes in order to strengthen their capability to meet financial obligations. The encompassing aim of their risk management practices is to ensure that the long-term survival of their company is guaranteed. Risk management fulfils the role of identifying, monitoring and modelling risks and interdependencies, and ascertaining that risks assumed by the company are not in excess of what it is capable of bearing.

Risk Modelling

Risk modelling entails applying different forms of quantitative and qualitative analyses. Figure 7.1 shows a number of risks affecting reinsurers. Analysis of these risks provides a basis for modelling, which takes into account possible interdependencies among the various sources of risk. A detailed discussion of risk modelling in reinsurance is outside the scope of this book.

Figure 7.1 List of Risks Affecting Reinsurers

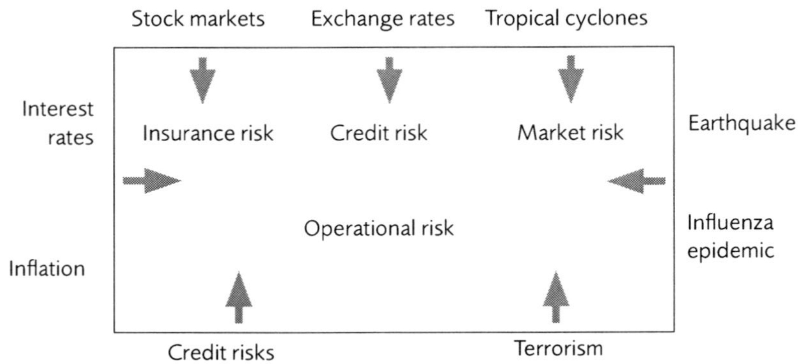

Source: Swiss Re Sigma

Underwriting and Risk

Underwriting[52] is the first step in determining the level of risk that a reinsurer is able to bear. The main task of the underwriting process is to ascertain that:

- Controls are in place for accumulation and peak risks;
- Risk are assessed in a proper manner and the terms and conditions are satisfactory;
- The limits of assigned capacity are adhered to.

Risk Assessment

Risk assessment begins with the assessment of the data supplied by the primary insurer and the determination of the need for, or lack of, the extra information regarding the characteristics of the insured objects or persons that is required. In non-life reinsurance, this includes information about the location, the value and the exposure of the objects to the risk. For example, in life reinsurance, risk assessment will take into consideration information that aids in determining the risk of death or illness like age, gender, genetic factors, and medical and lifestyle factors.

Only risks which meet the general conditions of insurability as listed below can be reinsured.

52 Underwriters assess the presence of additional risk factors to arrive at the underwriting decision. They are also able to classify the additional risk as increasing, decreasing or constant.

Principles of insurability[53]

Reinsurance can only function within the limits of insurability. There is no strict formula for determining insurability; instead there is a set of basic criteria which a risk must fulfil to be reinsurable.

The following can be used to classify these criteria:

- **Randomness** – The time at which an insured event happens must not be predictable, and the occurrence itself must be independent of the event to be insured.
- **Economic efficiency** – Primary insurers and reinsurers must be able to charge a premium commensurate with the accepted risk.
- **Assessability** – It must be possible to quantify the probability that the insured event will occur, as well as its severity, in order to calculate the potential exposure and the premium necessary to cover it. In addition, it must be possible to allocate the loss to a particular insurance period.

Capacity Allocation, Accumulation and Peak Risks

Reinsurers only accept risks if these are within the capacity limits that have been specified. Capacity is the maximum amount of coverage that a reinsurer can provide over a certain period. As for risks with low accumulation potential, such as a portfolio of different fire policies, underwriters are generally capable of committing to a defined amount of capacity for a certain line of product and client/country.

Some risks, particularly those in the field of natural perils, have a greater accumulation potential. Accumulation occurs from dependencies between individual risks. This can be the concentration of risks, for example real estate or automobiles, which may be affected by the same loss event such as a hurricane, or a concentration of shares in the same large risk, e.g. a biotechnology firm, through diverse reinsurance treaties, increasing the insurer's exposure to a single loss incidence.

Diversification and Risk Management

A solid risk management process will result in a reinsurer's portfolio whereby there is an alignment between the capital available and the underwriting and investment risks. This can guarantee the long-term survival of a reinsurance company. To ensure success in a competitive market, it is not only important for a reinsurer to be secure, but also to manage this security efficiently, which is achieved by diversifying risks. Reinsurers become highly diversified by operating internationally across a wide range of many lines of business and by assuming a large number of independent risks.

53 Source: Swiss Re. (2005), 'Understanding Reinsurance – How Reinsurers Create Value and Manage Risks'.

Figure 7.2 Dimension of Diversification for Reinsurers

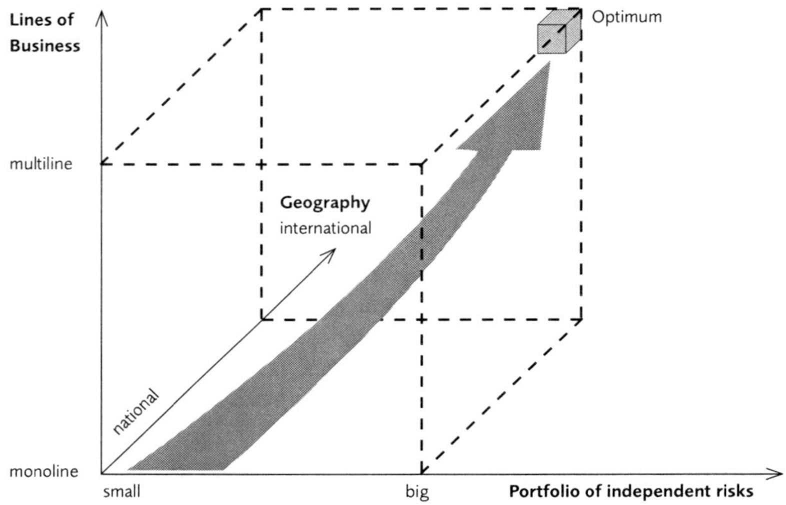

Source: Swiss Re Sigma

The law of large numbers (LLN) is the basic principle behind diversification. From a reinsurance point of view, the LLN postulates that the more risks that are added to a reinsurer's portfolio, the less the volatility of its results. From a capital requirement standpoint, lower volatility translates into lower capital needs and, in turn, lower capital costs, for the same capital protection. A better diversified reinsurance firm is therefore capable of offering reinsurance at a lower price and providing a higher level of protection for the level of capital.

8 Common Systems used in Insurance

This chapter discusses systems commonly used in insurance. The history of IT in insurance and legacy systems in insurance are also discussed.

Introduction

Of all of the revolutionary changes that have been witnessed in recent times in the insurance industry, one factor that has brought sweeping changes to the manner in which it will operate in the future is Information Technology.

With the advent of increased regulation that may result in increased mergers and acquisitions, IT is playing a pivotal role in insurers' ability to implement enterprise–application integration in a responsive fashion so as to introduce products to the market in a timely manner.

Alternative distribution channels are now required as supplements to the conventional agent/broker model to help introduce products to market. In addition, underwriting is assuming a new form, whereby it is increasingly geared towards profit making as opposed to dependence on the capital markets to hide underwriting losses.

As a result, underwriters require the right data to arrive at the appropriate pricing, terms and conditions, and in decision terms, can essentially refuse business if deemed unprofitable.

The influx in technology has resulted in the promotion of underwriting and rating, once classic back-office functions, to the front office. In recent times, more of the underwriting process is occurring in real time, i.e. while a customer is getting a quote, they are also being underwritten. This speed is especially beneficial in areas such as personal motor insurance, where consumers expect instant answers and will become increasingly impatient while waiting for a quote.

Data is also seen as an essential of the insurance industry, but accessing, managing and using data can be an overwhelming task, particularly when doing this requires the use of a variety of technology solutions, including data marts, data warehouses, extract-transform-load (ETL), customer relationship management (CRM) and so on. Nevertheless, technologies that are designed to collect, warehouse and mine data are now part of standard operating procedure as opposed to the erstwhile perception of them as cutting edge and should be used when the occasion calls for them.

The alignment of IT to business processes is becoming widespread in the insurance industry and with the use of modern systems, straight-through processing of policy submission and claim settlement is increasingly achievable, enabling insurance companies to trade electronically like their counterparts in the banking and capital markets.

History of the IT Function in Insurance

In this section, the history of the IT function in insurance is briefly discussed. Life insurance is used as the basis.

Well before the sale of computers for commercial applications, some life insurance actuaries had interacted with major vendors in the newly forming IT industry. They had a key role in educating their industry about possible uses of computers as well as communicating the needs of life insurers to computer vendors. The earliest use of IT was for data maintenance and accounting in financial operations activities. After this came the development of integrated systems for policyholder records and service. Actuaries in that era used such mainframe systems mainly for valuation and statistical reporting; however, they also began to have access to personal computing through time-sharing arrangements.

The invention of the personal computer (PC) made it possible for life insurers to give their agents direct EDP links to the company's systems. Eventually, this functionality was enhanced using mobile (laptop) computers. Using PCs essentially changed the way that insurance products were sold, and became an important source of competitive advantage for many companies.

Similarly, the PC also fundamentally changed the way actuarial work was carried out. The availability of spreadsheet software provided powerful and user-friendly tools for actuarial analysis. Setting up programming steps for actuarial work required relatively little effort using spreadsheets and related tools such as database management software. However, IT management was in two minds about the proliferation of desktop applications which required new support effort, and the IT function was often not in control of PC hardware and software purchase decisions made by individual operating units. The perception of the IT function was that PC systems were the representation of a host of rogue applications, which generated information outside the company's operational control of data. Actually, the informal use of desktop applications was often indicative of the shortcomings of IT in providing timely and effective business solutions.

The changing regulatory environment in financial services and the ensuing competition with mutual funds and banks were the basis of the response by the life insurance industry to develop more and more complex products.

The use of these products was not viable without the support of increasingly more complex systems. Actuaries in turn realised that they needed to respond by using more sophisticated modelling software, usually outside the firm's IT environment.

Companies adopted new technology, such as image processing and automated call processing, with a view to improving service efficiency. They found that in order to use these technologies, it was essential to re-engineer their business processes to achieve cost reduction and service improvement.

In recent years, the industry has witnessed a round of company consolidations and sales of blocks of business to achieve strategic objectives. These mergers and acquisitions, coupled with in-force business representing many generations of products, resulted in most companies using a variety of legacy systems to administer their heritage of policies from prior eras.

The introduction of e-business has presented new challenges to life insurance business models. Interactive systems give agents and customers access to company data, and many transactions are now possible online.

Legacy Systems in Insurance

In recent times, insurance companies have been seeking efficiency, agility and the ability to innovate; they quickly realised their legacy systems were a hindrance to the achievement of these goals.

There are obvious issues with reliance on legacy systems in the current and future business landscape. Most insurers' legacy systems have been in place for decades, with many in use since as early as the 1960s, and are based on ageing development standards with limited functionality and usability. In spite of their limitations, with green-screen interfaces and lacking the conveniences of modern applications – drop-down menus, instant help files, intuitive navigation, etc. – a large percentage of corporate business systems in the current marketplace are legacy applications. In fact, many are still depended upon to provide mission-critical business functionality.

The current competitive climate in the insurance landscape, however, requires insurers to be nimble, flexible and forward thinking, and to adopt reliable technology that is scalable and integration-friendly for growth and change to ensure their long-term survival. Given that legacy applications were developed in a different time, often to serve a single purpose, they hardly meet the criteria necessary to help an organisation in the long term.

That said, it is interesting to discover that some insurance firms – of varying size and location – continue to operate with legacy applications as their backbone. Yet, their successes are limited at best and at worst an utter liability.

The following are some the issues that insurers grapple with in their continued reliance on legacy systems:

- High maintenance and staffing costs continue to grow.
- Many legacy systems are loosely tied together and guarantee business silos.
- There is limited growth and innovation as a result of the limited functionality.
- Purely data-driven architecture excludes access to business content.

High Maintenance and Staffing Costs that Continue to Grow

For most insurance companies, whilst legacy systems are used to support core business transactions and capabilities that represent the source of revenue of the organisation, appropriate care of them is essential. However, that care involves huge expenses.

In addition to regular maintenance, there are a lot more emergencies associated with legacy applications than any other IT system. Emergencies result in an increased requirement for staff, which usually implies that an insurer is paying overtime to ensure the smooth running of its core systems. Given that insurance companies are combating these emergencies on such a regular basis, overtime costs can become a major concern for IT managers.

Apart from overtime costs that drive up the outlay of maintaining legacy systems, finding, attracting and simply paying the staff that care for them is a major issue. The maintenance of the original code can be a major cost, given that the original programmers have long since left the organisation and finding others with the relevant skill sets can be tricky.

In spite of the money that is specifically being used up, it is obvious that the maintenance of legacy applications is responsible for consuming a large percentage of IT budgets. In addition to merely being expensive, this diverts funds that could otherwise be used for innovative projects that ultimately attract and retain IT talent as well as policyholders.

Many Legacy Systems are Loosely Tied Together and Guarantee Business Silos

The ability to reuse data and avoid redoing or completely recreating work that's already been done allows organisations to achieve the largest returns on their IT investments. The absence of adequate interfaces linking systems means that reusability is greatly limited, if possible at all.

The wave of mergers, acquisitions, takeovers and reorganisations in the insurance industry, as a result of increasing globalisation that is being achieved by consolidation, can be witnessed in not only large insurance companies, but also the medium-sized and small insurance firms. While these changes bring about growth and revenue for these firms, IT systems are often part of the short-term damage that is unintended or incidental to the integration of two or more organisations and their respective systems.

As a consequence of the attempt to piece together systems that were never intended to integrate, long-term effects, including wasted time, loss of revenue and an inability to innovate, can continue indefinitely.

In an effort to achieve reusability, insurance companies still grapple with systems that have been weakly and loosely threaded together in an effort to achieve reusability, only to realise that legacy applications simply were not designed for it. Given that their unique and hard-coded interfaces were written with rigid functionality in mind, legacy systems make integration complicated. This further perpetuates existing silos of business information and prevents the sharing of information across departments and also various line-of-business (LOB) applications.

Even though the insurance industry is used to conducting business in a siloed environment, silos can present insurers with major problems.

Reusability of data is increasingly at the top of most IT managers' agenda, given that the interconnections in the insurance business are exemplified by a process such as the initial recording of customer information on a policy application that can be reused later in completing a claim submission and later in a renewal form.

The Limitation of Growth and Innovation as a Result of Limited Functionality

Insurance customers demand instant and easy access to as much information as possible and in response insurers, in a bid to be competitive and to attract and retain customers, require accurate information in real time and immediate availability from multiple sources. However, most insurers' legacy systems simply cannot meet such lofty demands, and this fact impacts negatively on both employees and customers. Legacy systems can be perceived as a hindrance to innovation as a result of the restrictions on efficiency and productivity for employees – both IT and business alike.

On the business side, the hard-to-learn interfaces and lack of functionality of legacy systems do not aid productivity. These result in business users frequently spending more time trying to figure out how a system works or actually completely avoiding using the system, choosing instead to complete tasks manually. Not only does this cost the insurer time and increase employee frustration (which leads to staffing and morale concerns on the business side as well), but when employees revert to manual processes, information security and access become key concerns.

As for IT, programmers spend so much time maintaining and rewriting legacy code with a view to keeping up with user demands that they have little, if any, time to create new or unique functionality for improving business processes. As a consequence, it is common for these IT staff to have low morale and high turnover. Because of the virtually limitless possibilities of technology that exist in the current marketplace, most programmers would prefer to create new and different applications and solutions, rather than simply fixing what is broken.

Purely Data-driven Architecture excludes access to Business Content

There are inherent difficulties in extracting business content from legacy systems since they are built with data-driven programming languages.

For example, it is almost impossible to identify process bottlenecks, or to easily balance or manipulate workloads, and legacy systems provide limited ability to see business trends without the need to pore over pages of reports. Insurers need exactly this kind of information to remain competitive.

While IT staff may be more than capable of designing a solution for monitoring business processes, the architecture of legacy systems may not have the capability to handle a newer, cutting-edge business perspective. The reason for this is that although the information contained in legacy systems may still be valid and relevant, the architecture of these programs isn't designed to assist business growth. Legacy systems are huge repositories of information, but they can be unreliable when it comes to drawing conclusions or making predictions based on the information contained in them.

Possible Solutions to these Issues?

It would appear that these issues can be addressed by simply approaching vendors and purchasing replacement systems. But this may not be the most sensible solution for the following reasons:

- Too much risk;
- Prohibitive cost;
- User reluctance;
- Limited business agility;
- Speed of delivery.

Too much risk

Replacement is the most risky solution to the problems associated with legacy systems in insurance. Insurers become vulnerable when they decide on replacing their legacy systems as some key questions appear to remain unanswered.

The most pertinent question is that of reusability. Outright replacements are often siloed in nature and these LOB applications are not intended to solve problems in multiple departments. Rather, replacement systems typically solve one or more business problems within one functional area of an insurance organisation, e.g., claims, underwriting, etc.

This LOB system becomes a repository for business knowledge within one group, but that knowledge seldom exists elsewhere in the organisation, given that replacements are not usually designed in a form that is ready to interface with multiple other LOB applications. This further perpetuates business silos, limits information and knowledge sharing and prevents reusability of data, all of which lead to less efficiency within the organisation.

In conclusion, replacing a legacy system only increases the amount of risk that an insurer needs to manage.

Prohibitive cost

In terms of cost, complete replacements are very expensive undertakings. In addition, by replacing a legacy system without replacing the underlying mainframe as well, insurance companies may still not be nimble enough to rapidly respond to changes in the marketplace.[54]

The deployment of a replacement system is expensive and resource-intensive, and many organisations basically underestimate the time and resources that are necessary. A case in point is implementing a replacement. Before committing to this, organisations must have an accurate understanding of both internal costs and processes – something many insurers are not used to measuring.

54 OnBase (2007), 'The Trouble with Legacy Systems', available from www.OnBase.com/insurance.

User reluctance

User reluctance to use a replacement is a bigger concern than most insurers think – especially IT leaders who are used to technology changes. User reluctance is an aspect of change that is difficult to quantify or completely foretell, but a factor that can still impair the success of replacement projects.

Historically, insurers have hesitated to change any systems out of fear of losing both short-term and long-term productivity from their often very experienced workforce – not to mention the unease about their potential incapacity to train employees in the new systems.

Business users in most insurance companies feel that replacement systems will essentially prevent them from growing and changing to improve processes, and gaining the confidence of employees and making them comfortable in their new environment are essential for management if their business users are to eventually accept change.

Limited business agility

Let us recap the main reasons why insurers need to address problems caused by existing legacy systems: efficiency in processes and agility to innovate and compete in the marketplace. The replacement of legacy systems with new LOB applications will eventually trounce these goals.

For a start, the ability to respond to needs quickly is required for the creation and maintenance of efficient processes, whether during the response to a customer question or for integration of two applications. In spite of providing more flexibility for efficiency than available legacy systems, replacement LOB applications often have rigid logic that requires expensive and time-intensive custom coding to alter. Even if at installation a replacement system's functions and inherent logic may exactly match the insurer's current processes, they often discover that any changes in the short or long term can be frustrating and expensive.

Additionally, an insurer's ability to make adjustments as business needs and technology change highlights the significance of flexible technology. Furthermore, the dexterity of a company dictates its overall capability to stay abreast of competition.

Speed of delivery

Insurers usually store huge amounts of data in legacy systems; hence the difficulty in rolling out replacements promptly. Given the longevity of the use of legacy applications in the insurance industry, which in some cases is 30 or 40 years from the time of writing, the extraction of that data and devising a way of integrating it into the new system could be an onerous task that necessitates extensive custom coding. Purely data-driven legacy systems are efficient at outputting numbers and reports, but devising the means to use that data in such a way that it makes good business sense often requires accurate data analysis to achieve the integration of multiple legacy systems.

In a number of cases, migration and integration efforts are less important than another problem that organisations commonly face during the implementation of a replacement. Custom coding not only limits business agility to integrate with systems and processes, it also consumes a vast amount of time and money. In such a competitive industry and difficult economy, insurers require a solution that can be implemented without aggravation or unnecessary cost. Complete replacements can guarantee neither.

While a complete replacement may sound like a model solution in theory, completing all of these steps requires more commitment in terms of effort than many insurance companies understand when the project begins.

Having said the above about legacy systems in the insurance industry, the following are some of the modern systems currently used in the industry.

Profile of a System

System: ALIS

Vendor: FIS-Software Limited

Overview

ALIS is a full end-to-end policy administration system supporting the full product life cycle from the design and configuration of a product, through the illustration of a potential policy, the creation of a new policy record, the administration of the policy record throughout its lifetime and finally the settlement of the policy. This full policy life-cycle management is provided within a single systems solution delivered via a number of integrated components.

One of the key strengths of ALIS, and indeed a key differentiator to other administrations systems, is that it has been designed to be truly product-agnostic (i.e. the system has not been designed to specifically support particular life and pensions products).

One of the strategic design principles behind ALIS was to decompose all life and pensions products into a core set of product features and business processes (for example covers, premiums, funds, limits, charges, commission, business activities etc.). ALIS was then developed to include a highly parameterised super set of core components that deliver the functionality to support each of the constituent parts of a life and pensions product.

With this component-based product structure, 'products' in ALIS are created by connecting together a set of independent components ('catalogues') that have no product-specific logic into a product frame to meet the needs of a particular marketed product. The same catalogue components are reused for the creation of multiple products. The parameters for each product can be defined differently. For instance, in the example of a death cover definition, the sum assured limits could be specified differently or the cover could be mandatory for one product or optional for another.

This approach enables completely flexible products to be created, utilising the existing core components within the system and tailoring the capabilities to meet a particular brand, sub-brand, distribution channel or medium.

Examples of some of the catalogues that can be altered to produce label-specific products include:

- Activities & Tasks (processes)
- Arrears
- Billing
- Bonuses
- Charges & Expenses
- Claims
- Covers
- Contributions
- Commission
- Events
- Funds
- Illustrations Investment
- Profiles
- Limits
- Loans
- New Business (incl. acceptance criteria)
- Payment Method
- Roles
- Reassurance
- Renewals
- Reinstatements

A number of user-friendly tools have been developed to make this process as simple as possible.

Products types supported by ALIS

This approach to product management enables ALIS to support a broad range of products in both individual and group business along with deep functionality. In addition to this breadth, the solution offers tremendous back-end flexibility on modern technology.

Country-specific configurations have been completed for the United Kingdom, South Africa, France, Greece, Spain, Russia, Belgium, Australia, Israel, Vietnam and India, with products delivered within the following product 'families':

- Whole Life
- Universal Life
- Variable Universal Life
- Individual Term Life
- Individual Annuities
- Group Term Life
- Group Annuities
- Individual Pension Products
- Group Pension Products
- Group Protection Products

Generic product features supported within ALIS

The following is an overview of the generic product features that are supported within ALIS. These features are available for selection and configuration to deliver a particular marketed product for management within ALIS.

Calculations

ALIS has a multi-purpose, user-defined engine (the **formula engine**) that allows the creation of all sorts of calculation routines for use in the policy life cycle.

The **formula engine** allows the user to define how a formula will be calculated and controls whether the formula uses the **rule-based engine** or the **Excel translator** utility or is hard-coded.

The **rule-based engine** is a metadata formula programming tool and has an online testing tool which allows the full calculation chain to be seen.

The **Excel translator** utility is a standalone utility for enabling Excel spreadsheets to be used by ALIS. It takes an Excel spreadsheet complete with macros and converts it to system object code (DLL).

The formula engine is independent of the product definition within ALIS but may be called by particular product components when a particular calculation is required. This can be used, for example, in the calculation of premium rates, the calculation of charges, the calculation of policy fund and surrender values etc.

Covers

ALIS supports both with profit and pure risk covers. Covers within ALIS may be defined as covering single, joint or multiple insured lives.

It is possible to define the sum assured in a number of ways including:

- Flat amount;
- Multiple of salary;
- Percentage of salary;
- Percentage of the sum assured of another cover;
- Flat amount based upon contribution levels;
- Calculated from a formula.

Within the ALIS product cover component, it is possible to define, through configuration of metadata parameters, whether the cover is mandatory or optional and the relationship between each cover. This enables specific covers to be defined as being linked to each other and for rider options to be defined depending upon a particular cover being selected.

It is possible to specify limits that apply to each cover in relation to minimum and maximum entry and maturity ages, minimum and maximum sums assured, minimum and maximum terms etc.

ALIS offers a flexible approach to calculating the cost of providing the particular cover and whether the premium rate is reviewable or guaranteed. This includes the ability to calculate the risk premium based on look-ups in mortality tables with the option to use a formula engine for pricing, actuarial or underwriting loadings.

The mortality tables used to calculate the premium rate may vary with the following parameters:

- Sex
- Age
- Term
- Smoker status
- Escalation
- Reviewable/Guaranteed
- Deferred period
- Claim Period
- Sum assured banding
- Benefit Payment Type
- Age at term of Cover
- Age at Final Premium
- Renewal Period
- Buy Back Option
- Interest rate
- Payment Frequency
- Disability definition
- SA % of Salary
- Length of Service
- Occupation Class
- Definition of Incapacity
- Term Duration
- Number of Lives

Once the premium rate has been calculated, ALIS supports the ability to meet the cost of cover by collection of premiums or by surrender of units under the policy.

The wide range of options available for configuration of a cover enables ALIS to support a wide range of pure risk and traditional product types.

Funds

The fund parameters within the ALIS configuration enable a fund to be specified based on:

- **Unit prices**: The configuration enables the determination of the pricing basis. This enables the determination of the frequency of pricing and, if applicable, items such as the maximum bid-offer spread. Unit prices for the funds can either be uploaded via a flat file into the system or manually inserted/overridden.
- **Interest**: The fund parameters within the ALIS configuration enable a fund to be specified to have a fixed interest rate, which will then be assumed to accumulate over time. In addition, ALIS also has a standalone expenses engine which can be called to calculate relevant values to allow for interest and mortality assumptions.
- **Asset management**: The ALIS fund's pricing parameters allow the specification of an AMC for a specific fund for a specific fund series. This approach enables the same fund to be charged differently for different product types, distribution channels etc. For externally managed funds, it is also possible to specify the additional AMC rates to incorporate the extra costs associated with third-party investments. In terms of deductions, the AMC can be specified to be deducted from the fund price or may be an explicit monthly deduction.
- **Dividends**: The ALIS system provides full support for dividend payments. In defining the product through the controlling parameters, each fund associated with the product can be established to be dividend earning. The definition enables a different dividend specification to be configured dependent upon the product, fund and contribution/premium type. For calculation of the dividend, the system can either be configured to have

a specific rate or to invoke the inbuilt formula engine in order to calculate the value.

Commissions

ALIS supports the definition of a wide range of commission options. The commission can be defined as being calculated based on either contributions or upon a cover.

All commission in ALIS is initially defined as being indemnified (i.e. payable in advance) or non-indemnified, and the period over which the commission is indemnified. Indemnification factors can be applied when calculating the commission amounts, and associated claw-back factors can also be defined in the event of unearned commission needing to be reclaimed.

Each commission option defined includes a minimum and maximum percentage and the period over which the commission is payable. It is also possible to define the commission as a fixed monetary amount.

ALIS supports initial commission, level commission, renewal commission (i.e. commission payable after the end of the initial commission period) and also fund-based commission. Each of these commission options includes the ability to forego an amount of allowable commission in exchange for enhanced benefits.

Charges

ALIS has a flexible 'expense engine' that defines which charges are taken, what their trigger is, and how they are taken (e.g. from premium, from investments, from actuarial expense account).

The amounts are in turn calculated by the ALIS 'formula engine' (see above), which allows flexible definitions of calculation algorithms.

The expense engine permits both 'back-to-back' or 'transparent' models where, for example, the policy charge directly reflects intermediary commission, or independent models where the charging is unconnected to commission, or a combination of both.

ALIS also has the ability to define a number of different types of charge in addition to the expenses option described above.

Allocation rates

ALIS supports the definition of a complex allocation rate structure whereby the amount of a contribution to be invested in funds can be automatically reduced (or increased) based upon a number of parameters. It is possible to configure allocation rate tables that vary by the following:

- Premium frequency
- Selected commission style
- Policy term
- Contribution type
- Contribution amount
- Bid-offer spread

- Annual policy fee
- Term from commencement

Roles

ALIS is a client-centric system where a client record is added to the application once and then associated to the policy record via a concept of roles.

The type of role, whether they are mandatory or optional, the number of individuals who can perform a role and the type of information required for each individual is determined by system parameters.

ALIS has been utilised by various clients to establish the following types of role:

- Lives assured
- Employer
- Member/employee
- Payer
- Beneficiary
- Agent
- Policy holder

The nature of the system ensures that ALIS can be configured to match requirements in respect to role types.

Limits

The ALIS controlling parameters provide numerous options for specifying limits and controls to validate the data entered into the system. Some examples of the limits within the system are specified below:

- ALIS can validate the date of birth to ensure that the lives assured are within the age range for the specific product.
- For transaction charges, the default, minimum and maximum can be specified in the parameters for each type of event, thus providing complete flexibility.
- For investments, the minimum and maximum investment amounts or fund percentage can be specified, as can the minimum residual value to be retained in the fund.

Premiums

ALIS allows the definition of different contribution types within a product. A contribution type may be defined as being used for charges (e.g. payment for cost of a cover) or as an investment contribution (e.g. to be invested in funds).

It is possible to specify whether a contribution type is mandatory or optional and whether it is a monetary amount or a percentage of salary. It is also possible to specify the minimum and maximum amounts for the contribution and for any subsequent increases to the contribution amount.

Claims

ALIS has been built to deal with claims generically. The claims definition uses parameters that allow each company the freedom to define the process to match their business model.

All claim types can be configured to have up to four stages:

- **Initial notification** – This can be used to start the claim when minimum information is received.
- **Full claim details** – This would apply once full details to process the claim have been received.
- **Claim payment** – This is the stage where all information has been received and the claim payment details have been confirmed.
- **Completed** – This is the stage where the claim and the payment have been authorised and the process completed.

These claim stages enable the claim process to be controlled depending on the amount of information received. For example, at each stage of the claim process it is possible to define items such as whether to suppress the production of output documentation, stop billing and collection and whether to change the policy status.

For each claim type, product parameters control how the value to be returned is calculated (i.e. return of premium, value of units or whether surrender penalties apply) and whether a commission claw-back applies under the policy. It is also possible to define the minimum amount for the claim and the minimum residual value following payment of the claim.

It is also possible for each claim type to specify the required documents to enable the claim to be processed. This will provide a prompt for the ALIS user to make sure that all of the appropriate documentation has been received. It will not be possible to proceed with the claim unless it has been confirmed that the required documents have been received.

The ALIS follow-up mechanism can also be used in conjunction with the claim to trigger output documents at each stage of the claim process, in order to chase documentation or to inform of progress. Screen prompts can also be generated for the ALIS user to ensure that they are aware of any manual process steps required.

The approach to claims enables the system to be configured to support:

- Surrenders
- Withdrawals
- Paid up
- Cooling off
- Death
- Maturity
- Transfer out

Loans

ALIS provides functionality to support policy loans. At product level it is possible to define whether loans are allowed for the product. The definition of the loan enables the specification of limits including the minimum and maximum loan amounts, maximum percentage of the asset value of the policy that can be loaned against and the minimum and maximum loan period. In addition, it is possible to specify whether there are restriction periods when the loan cannot be taken out.

The configuration of the loan also allows for the definition of the interest type to be applied (if applicable), including whether the interest is fixed or variable rate, how the interest should be applied and whether it is simple or compound interest.

Other Systems

System	Vendor/ Provider	Uses
LifeSystem	eBao Technology	An end-to-end life insurance core system that supports all mainstream products (whole life and endowment, annuity etc.), sales channels, and whole life-cycle functionalities in an all-in-one manner.
Takaful System	First Apex	Used for surplus distribution, fund flow, regulatory compliance.
Eclipse Underwriting	Sequel	Underwriting system used by insurance and reinsurance companies to support their underwriting processes.
Elixir	Mastek	Insurance Enterprise Platform used for, amongst other things, policy administration and claims management.
Indus Renewal & Retention	R Systems International	This web-based solution is used by insurers for managing customer servicing and retention across all insurance business (Life, Non-Life). The module supports the processes involved from premium due date reminder to policy lapse management and beyond.
InsuranceEX	Exari	Used by Brokers and Carriers, for web-based access to document templates required for placing business in the USA and London for all lines of business that need contract-certain documentation, including open market, binders, facilities and treaties.

Partner XE	Strategic Insurance Software, Inc.	Agency management system used by insurers for management of policies and commissions.
CEM for Insurance	ResponseTek	Customer experience management software that allows insurers to manage the entire customer life cycle from initial awareness and purchase to claim settlement and renewals.
Claims	Fineos	Used as a fully automated claims and case management system for automated electronic transaction handling and workflow.
Fractal	Claims Analytics	Models built by this system are used by insurers to obtain scores on claims based on their probability of a successful recovery as well as based on the potential magnitude of the recovery. The system also assists insurers in automating their claims processes, replacing manual registration, claim forms and their underlying processes.
TalisLife	Bravura Solutions	Used for the administration of life insurance products.
SDT Life	SDT Financial Software Solutions	Life assurance administration system used for supporting all processes within a life assurance company.
Dragon Policy Administration System	OneShield	Used for policy administration of all lines of property and casualty, including personal, commercial and specialty lines.
Premia Property & Casualty	3i Infotech	Used for supporting underwriting/policy administration, rating, billing, claims and reinsurance, as well as financial accounting, reporting and analyses.
Synergy	Eurobase	A single solution used by insurers for supporting the full business life cycle right from product definition and rating, quotation and underwriting, through transaction processing, to the processing of claims and the recovery of outward reinsurance.
SAP for Insurance	SAP	Used by insurers for integrating their core insurance processes with back-office operations and customer-facing functions.
Diamond	Insuresoft	Used by property and casualty insurance carriers for policy processing automation.

Oracle Insurance Policy Administration	Oracle Corporation	Insurers use this system to support sales, new business, and policy processing across multiple lines of business including annuities, life, property and casualty, and reinsurance.
Oasis Reinsurance Management	Delphi Technologies	Used by insurers to automate the calculation of ceded premiums and claims, manage cash and produce a wide array of reinsurance management reports, including proofs and notices.
ID^3	StoneRiver	Used for policy administration, billing, and premium and claims administration.

IT Projects

9

This chapter discusses IT projects that can be undertaken in insurance companies.

Introduction

The fortunes of the insurance sector are linked to its ability to manage risks. This ability is galvanised by the effective use of technology, which ensures that even in a shaky economic climate, insurance companies can continue to thrive.

Experts predict an increase in the proportion of insurance that will be purchased online in the future. They predict that the insurance sector will continue to create new ways of delivering products. Thus, the importance of IT projects that insurance companies can execute to help them to achieve these objectives cannot be overstated.

However, despite the growing importance of the IT function, the majority of the major insurance companies have not gained a full understanding of their competitive IT positions. For most institutions, the performance level of IT remains well hidden.

As a consequence, insurance companies are seeking out levers that could help sharpen their IT efficiency and effectiveness. IT projects can offer the desired leverage and a number of projects that can be executed in insurance firms are discussed in this section.

Green IT

Over the past few decades, information technology has grown to become an indispensable business tool for insurance companies around the globe. Digital solutions are unquestionably playing a key role in the race to prevent global warming – but the proliferation of data centres, desktop equipment and mobile technology is also having a major environmental impact.

To ensure that technology does not become a net contributor to the problem, the IT industry and end-user communities are focusing on minimising the resources consumed by the manufacturing, running and disposal of IT equipment, whilst working together to realise its huge potential to deliver more sustainable business practices in the future.

Background to Green IT Practices

CO_2 emissions, or rather their reduction, are getting higher on both the economic and the political agendas of world leaders. According to experts, climate instability and global warming, as well as CO_2 emissions, are becoming the key expressions characterising what is considered to be the most significant threat to humankind and the environment.

Rising energy costs and increasing environmental damage are responsible for significant increases in the cost of living, and will continue to raise the costs of business. If insurers want to operate as green entities, they should be prepared for the substantial and expensive changes that are involved.

According to industry sources, eminent scientists have shown clear evidence that there is an obvious relationship between the level of CO_2 in the atmosphere and planet surface temperature, i.e. the 'greenhouse effect' that is characterised by more heat from the sun being trapped at higher CO_2 concentrations. Sir Nicholas Stern's report, the Stern Review,[55] showed that the level of greenhouse gases in the atmosphere before the industrial revolution was 280 parts per million (ppm) CO_2 equivalent (CO_2e), while the 2006 levels were around 430ppm CO_2e. It recommended that the level should be restricted to 450–550ppm CO_2e and that anything higher than this could heighten the risk of the impact of CO_2 emissions. The report also warned that the cost of stabilising CO_2 levels at 550ppm will be about £200bn or 1% of GDP per year and that this figure will rise as world GDP increases, and could be three to four times its size by 2050.

Other experts have also suggested that it may be impossible to reduce the growth in CO_2 emissions appreciably to avert an environmental disaster. The parties deemed responsible for the catastrophe will be expected to shoulder the responsibility with respect to cost as well as blame.

How Does this Relate to IT?

In recent times, the IT function in all business sectors has come under the spotlight as an area where significant energy savings can be made, with some experts convinced that IT may become a polluter on the scale of sports utility vehicles (SUVs) and aircraft. IT in insurance is no exception.

All aspects of IT nowadays have to factor power consumption into both operational and strategic decisions. It is only a matter of time before clients will start demanding to know the green credentials of the IT function.

Business Justification for a Green IT Strategy

The IT function in general is tasked with increasing business productivity and efficiency as well as reducing costs. As stated earlier, the insurance business is becoming increasingly competitive and one way to remain competitive is to cut costs. Green computing offers an avenue to cut costs, especially if consumption of electricity is effectively reduced.

Adopting a power-based IT optimisation strategy is a medium for an insurer to boost its green credentials in the face of the rising costs of energy and infrastructure. This entails making power consumption an integral part of an IT policy that cuts across all of the processes that support an insurer's workflow.

The approach taken to ensure that the IT function is more environmentally friendly will depend on the other internal policies of individual insurers.

55 This is a report that was compiled for the UK government by Sir Nicholas Stern, a British economist and academic.

Nevertheless, there are basic practices that every insurer should adopt as building blocks to the implementation of their green strategies. These include decisions centred on whether to implement a distributed or centralised architecture and decisions regarding the purchase of hardware. For example, they may opt for LCD as opposed to CRT monitors for energy efficiency, and PCs and servers that run on the new generation of dual-core processors that consume less power than conventional processors and offer better performance. Other practices will be enforcing the use of power-saving modes on unused IT hardware, such as printers and PCs, and even switching off these pieces of equipment after working hours.

Server consolidation and virtualisation can also help in reducing costs, given that a large server can be used to replace several smaller machines. Power requirements are reduced as well as the overall heat that is produced.

Green Facts

- **Fact 1** – Switching a PC off overnight and at weekends can save up to £53 (in the UK for instance) in electricity costs.
- **Fact 2** – A single PC in office mode generates 1.094 tonnes of CO_2 per annum, equivalent to the CO_2 produced by a single passenger flying from London to Cairo.[56]
- **Fact 3** – During a PC's life, from manufacture to disposal, approximately 2 tonnes of CO_2 are generated. Up to 1 tonne of this amount is generated through usage over 3 years when the PC is switched on for 24 hours a day, 220 days a year.
- **Fact 4** – An office with 50 desktop PCs may generate up to 10kW of heat.
- **Fact 5** – Data centres require 0.5 to 1 watt of cooling power for each watt of server power used and a typical x86 server consumes between 30% and 40% of its maximum power when idle.[57]
- **Fact 6** – The EU disposes of 9 million tonnes of electrical and electronic waste each year, much of it into landfill.

Table 9.1 provides a basis for insurers to consider implementing IT projects that could not only save costs but also enhance their environmental friendliness.

In the next section, a project that entails implementing thin-client computing in order to realise green benefits will be discussed.

56 Green IT –The Next Burning Issue for Business, IBM Global Technology Services, January 2007.

57 Ibid.

Table 9.1 Typical power consumption and electricity costs at different levels of usage[a]

365 days a year, 24 hours a day (No switch off)						
	Desktop	Display	Desktop	Display	Total	Total
	kWh	kWh	£	£	kWh	£
PC + Display	569	175	52	16	745	68
220 days a year, 24 hours a day						
	Desktop	Display	Desktop	Display	Total	Total
	kWh	kWh	£	£	kWh	£
PC + Display	343	106	31	10	449	41
220 days a year, 8 hours a day						
	Desktop	Display	Desktop	Display	Total	Total
	kWh	kWh	£	£	kWh	£
PC + Display	114	35	11	4	150	15
Financial benefit, per PC + display, per year						**£53**
CO_2 emissions reduction, per PC + display, per year						**374 kgs/CO_2**

[a] This is based on a desktop PC consuming 65 watts and an LCD display consuming 20 watts.

Source: Computacenter

Implementation of Thin-Client Computing

The growing importance of green IT has given most businesses a reason to have a rethink about the implementation of thin clients. IT staff responsible for sourcing computer hardware for insurance companies are beginning to reacquaint themselves with the authenticity of thin-client provisioning in order to put together a proposal to the various stakeholders in the firm who are championing its deployment.

IT sourcing groups in businesses that are in the process of starting their next major desktop hardware refresh or upgrade need to be aware of the increasing importance of green IT. Corporate social responsibility (CSR) initiatives and the ever-increasing power consumption of IT systems prompt purchasers to increase the priority of sourcing greener, more energy-efficient forms of IT. In recent times, this range of issues has started to prompt a few lateral-thinking businesses to re-evaluate the value of implementing thin-client hardware to replace conventional desktop systems. Insurance firms will also benefit from such a thought process.

Why Should Insurers Re-examine Thin-client Computing?

Major thin-client vendors have been ardent advocates of the benefits of thin-client computing at the desktop, given its lower total cost of ownership (TCO) and more-efficient administrative management and security. Thin-client terminals, in a traditional server-based computing (SBC) model, are devoid of moving parts and operate purely by providing users a connection to applications and data hosted on a server (see Figure 9.1). The movement of the deployment, management, support and execution of applications from the desktop to central server farms allows for easier administration and reduces TCO in the longer term. In spite of the likely benefits of implementing thin clients, a number of end-user companies were averse to embracing the concept during

Figure 9.1 Diagram Showing that Conventional SBC Supports Complete Server Execution of Data and Applications

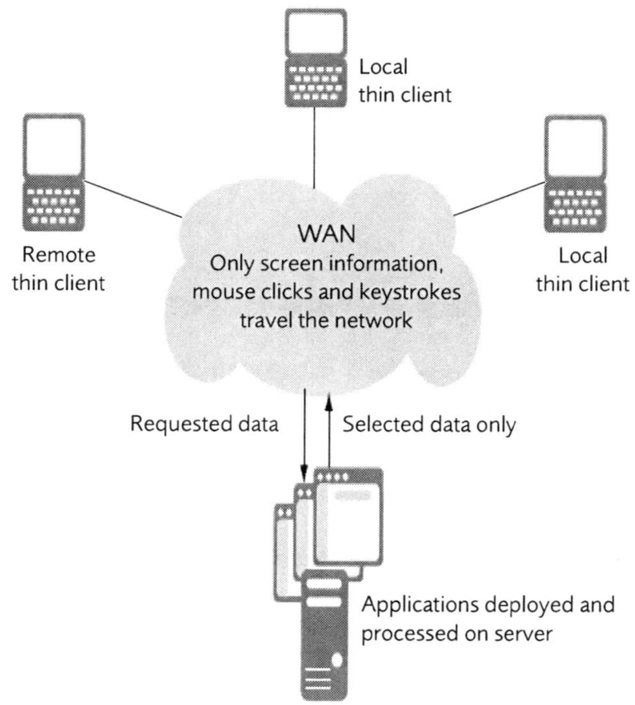

the 1990s, given the requirements of upfront cost investments in back-end infrastructure technologies such as servers, storage, and networking.

Companies encountered problems based on the perceptions around the integration, critical response time, and end-user acceptance of thin clients when compared with those related to traditional PCs running their own semi-autonomous applications (see Table 9.2).

Table 9.2 Major Thin-client Shortfalls[a]

Issue	Description
Incompatible applications	Not every application is equally suitable for utilisation on a terminal server. Computing-intensive applications that require complex mathematical calculations face unacceptable latency between the server and the client.
Connectivity constraints	The absence of a hard drive renders thin clients unusable without connectivity. Although this makes thin clients virtually useless to would-be thieves, professional road warriors caught without IP connectivity cannot access word processing, spreadsheets, databases, or other standard PC applications while on the move.
Lost computer sovereignty	Users accustomed to working in an unmanaged PC environment, where desktops are configured to personal preferences, often see thin-client deployment as a loss of personal control. Depriving user access to downloads, plug-ins, and a range of unnecessary non-corporate applications generates resistance against the controlling aspects of thin-client architecture.

[a] Contents of this table were slightly adapted.

Source: Forrester Research, Inc.

Why then are companies revisiting the implementation of thin clients in spite of its early limitations? The reason is that, increasingly, businesses are closely examining issues such as management, security, TCO and energy consumption, and in turn, IT management has begun to ensure that these items rank highly on their agenda. Given that most IT professionals signify that their operations planning will embrace environmental concerns such as energy efficiency and recycling, a shift in desktop hardware sourcing aligned to environmental effects merits further consideration. Thin-client terminals, when compared with their thick PC counterparts, lack hard drives and expansion slots, draw less power and need less complex components. In addition, they take up less space on a user's work space and in some cases are even integrated into the back of the display unit. The blending of these benefits has prompted some firms to change their attitude towards thin-client technology and insurance firms are likely to follow suit.

Figure 9.2 Implementation of Thin Client Results in Reduction of Power Draw and CO_2 Emissions

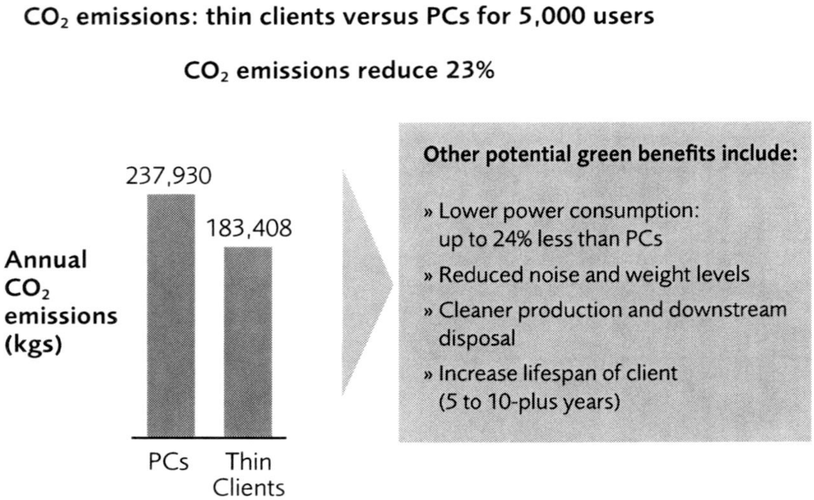

Source: Forrester Research, Inc.

Going Green Provides Further Impetus for Thin-client Acquisition

Relatively large-scale deployment of thin-client architecture, driven by centralised servers in a traditional SBC model, can provide functionality akin to that of desktops with local processing, with the added benefit of considerable power savings (see Figure 9.2). A desktop that is running everyday office applications, such as Internet Explorer, MS Excel, or MS Outlook, seldom needs the most advanced, leading-edge chipsets that consume large amounts of electricity. A well-scoped thin-client implementation connects cost reduction to the environmental agenda through:

- **Lower emissions and power usage** – Energy efficiency is one of the hallmarks of the thin-client terminals and this differentiates them from conventional thick clients. Their consumption is in the neighbourhood of 6 to 50 watts, which is considerably lower than the 150 to 350 watts consumed by typical PCs. A standard desktop and emissions calculator would identify, conservatively, a 24% power reduction in a conversion of 5,000 PCs to 5,000 thin-clients with the required server cooling infrastructure factored in. A 23% decrease in associated CO_2 emissions could also be expected.

- **Improvement in product lifecycles and material sustainability** – Industry estimates show that thin-client IT environments lengthen the life cycle of IT legacy investments by at least three years. While traditional PCs and laptops usually have a three- to four-year replacement cycle, thin clients have an average life span of seven years. Given that they have fewer points of failure and seldom require upgrades, they reduce the well-known pace of technology's unavoidable slide into obsolescence. Furthermore, since they do not have hard drives and limited or no microprocessor and memory requirements, thin clients make use of fewer harmful materials upstream, minimise packaging material during transportation, and generate less ecologically damaging waste downstream. Their green credentials are also further boosted by the lack of moving parts, reduced noise levels and decreased weight.

Preparation for a Thin-client Implementation

From the discussion above, there are essential steps to be taken by insurers in order to leverage the green benefits of putting thin-client computing back on the desktop hardware agenda.

It cannot be overstated that thin clients provide a practical way of provisioning desktop hardware in low-intensity, standardised desktop environments and are attractive to stakeholders in a business that is keen to pursue a green IT strategy. Sourcing and vendor management staff of insurance companies need to prepare in advance for the role IT sourcing will play in the assessment and deployment of thin clients by fitting steps that respond to and back up each stakeholder.[58] A comparison of the TCO of thin-client and current desktop hardware provisioning can be vital to the evaluation of the value of thin-client proposals, and widening of cost analyses of thin-client strategies to include product life-span considerations would be beneficial to insurers.

Recommended preparatory steps

The following is a cross-section of the steps recommended by leading experts:

1. **Creation of a thin-client suitability template** – Ideally this process would be begun internally by:
    - Assessing the pattern of desktop use around the company;
    - Building a template to capture this;
    - Documenting the dynamics between the corporate applications and the employees within the firm that use them in their day-to-day jobs to understand which applications and employees work most efficiently in a traditional PC environment.

58 Stakeholders in this case include the Chief Information Officer (CIO), IT Strategy groups and Functional or Line-of-business (LOB) managers.

2. **Mapping of PC usage according to the template** – Fill in the template with a view to calculating the number of employees that could be switched to thin clients and to determine the potential power and emissions savings. This kind of information offers a strong platform for decision making as and when the stakeholders demand it. Some insurance firms' sourcing teams might have inadequate PC usage data on record to perform this exercise without seeking external help.
3. **Interviewing of potential suppliers** – Interviews can be conducted in order to identify which of the company's preferred desktop hardware suppliers have feasible thin-client offerings and ascertain if any of them will deliver resources – such as return on investment (ROI) models or TCO calculators – to aid in the evaluation of the company's migration options. Some detailed background research on current-generation thin-client technologies to become familiar with the relevant issues would also be useful.
4. **Drilling down for integration of green criteria into total cost of ownership** – It should be noted that acquisition costs should not be the sole drivers of the sourcing of desktop hardware. If deemed feasible, the cost analysis should be widened to include product life-span considerations for the manufacture (material resources), operation (power consumption) and disposal (landfill tax) of the product in question. If the main consideration is emissions, then it would be beneficial to gain an understanding of the power use and CO_2 emission ramifications of desktop hardware provisioning through the use of a standard desktop power and emissions calculator.

Conclusion

In conclusion, insurers, being major users of legacy systems, would benefit from the above steps when considering migration from these systems to conventional server-based computing. It would also boost their green credentials in an age when corporate social responsibility is increasingly at the top of most businesses' agendas.

Virtualisation

Companies worldwide are embracing a digital work style to remain competitive in a dynamic and increasingly global business environment. This work style requires that teams connect seamlessly across organisations and time zones, while success depends on speed, mobility and connectivity.

These trends place ever-increasing pressure on IT departments to provide rich, connected capabilities across the infrastructure and they are looking to virtualisation to address these types of challenge, improving the efficiency of their IT operations and enhancing their responsiveness to changing conditions. Virtualisation is one of the key technologies that can help an insurance company progress towards a dynamic state, providing more flexibility in IT systems and streamlining change.

One of the simplest descriptions of virtualisation is that it is essentially a method used by businesses to pool their IT hardware with a view to cutting the growing amount of money expended on IT. In its most basic form, virtualisation software allows a large number of employees to share a section of IT hardware, running numerous 'virtual machines' – or screens – off the same components. In broader terms, virtualisation represents the abstraction of a technology into some form of centralised, controlled environment.

A more technical definition is as follows:

> *Virtualisation in an IT environment is essentially the isolation of one computing resource from others. By separating the different layers in the logic stack, businesses enable greater flexibility and simplified change management and no longer need to configure each element for them to all work together.*[59]

The hypothesis behind virtualisation is as follows.

An underwriter in BizInsure, Greg Vertu, while carrying out a task on a PC seldom uses all of its resources; running an MS Excel program, for instance, only consumes a fraction of a PC's memory and processing power. Logic would suggest that it is more cost-effective to split that power for use by another user, Stella Azzure, in the organisation than it is to supply them with the same machine, which they will in turn underutilise.

This concept can be extended to scores of servers, responding to the entire number of requests made by a particular business or department such as underwriting. As with the example above, the likelihood of, say, 40 servers all being used to their full capacity – in terms of processing power, memory and storage – is improbable. Therefore, as opposed to purchasing 40, a virtual server environment can get 20 servers to split the load, pooling all their resources and swapping tasks to ensure that the computing requirements of the organisation are realised.

IBM has been credited with the first introduction of virtualisation with the announcement of VM/370 virtualisation in 1972, but had been using the technology internally years earlier. It originally used it to partition a server to consolidate numerous smaller servers.

Anyway, virtualisation can help insurers in the quick recovery from system failure, maintaining 'business continuity' in the event of a disaster.[60] Virtual server environments allow for instant movement of data from one server to another in the event that one loses power or some other type of fault is encountered.

59 Adapted from Microsoft Corporation's 'Virtualization from the Datacenter to the Desktop', 2007 Core Infrastructure Optimization.

60 It would appear that this is a logical fit with the insurance business, given that it is primarily about managing risks in the face of disaster.

It is worth noting that virtualisation is not just about businesses like insurance companies making savings on the cost of IT hardware. In an age when insurance companies are more reliant on vast amounts of data, the price of renting or buying the space for housing servers as required can increase significantly. In addition, there are advantages in terms of ease of management in 'virtualising' the desktop. Experts assert that new developments in the virtualised desktop space will allow all users to be provisioned from a single image, with a desktop that is refreshed from the image each time the user logs on.

Other advantages include the saving of employee time. In conventional computer networks, in the event that a PC breaks down, the employee that is the user of the PC becomes unproductive and will be subject to hours of waiting before a desktop support engineer sorts out the problem. This is not the case with a virtualised network as this employee can easily be switched to a different set of hardware components.

Desktop support engineers no longer have to be concerned with fixing the desktop or saving local data; they can easily swap out the device and fix or replace it at their convenience. Together with the lower hardware costs that are associated with thin-client devices, this can result in a significant reduction in support costs.

Despite all the advantages highlighted above, there are inherent risks that insurers may face when implementing virtualisation. Having fewer servers doing more work means that there is a possibility that a firm's network could slow or even fail, particularly during peak times or when there is an atypical amount of strain. For this reason, it is important for an insurance company to make sure that the virtualisation solution chosen is suited to the nature of the business.

Selection of the Right Virtualisation Technology

Selecting the right virtualisation technology will be one of the hottest issues in IT for years to come as the proliferation of virtualisation solutions gathers pace. Thus, it would be prudent to discuss the factors it is relevant to consider when trying to differentiate between the different virtualisation solutions. Below are some key considerations that insurance companies may find useful to examine when deciding whether a virtualisation solution is ideal for a specific environment.

Mobility and Motioning

Motioning, or the ability to move applications between physical servers without disrupting them, is one of the most thought-provoking capabilities to emerge from the virtualisation world. Insurance companies that have data centres and plan to adopt virtualisation technology will realise that if it is not possible to move systems in real time (or even as a relatively fast offline procedure), the operation of their data centres will be fundamentally impacted.

The problem associated with this is the introduction of volatility; the curse of any mission-critical application. In addition, there could be complications of incident and problem management and the creation of potential compliance risks if the appropriate polices are not in place.

That said, the following are a number of factors that help guide the insurance company's decision of whether motioning is a mandatory feature or a liability in a given IT environment.

Maintenance and Change Freeze

Maintenance can become intertwined when applications are combined on a single physical machine. There is also the advantage of not having overlapping application maintenance windows, therefore preventing hardware maintenance. This is also true of change freezes, where certain combinations of systems may result in applications not affected by the freeze becoming frozen because of their common hosting.

The ability to motion virtual machines can alleviate this constraint by allowing server software to be moved off physical machines scheduled for maintenance and/or subject to a freeze.

It is therefore important for motioning to be an important consideration as insurance companies will definitely have maintenance policies and change freezes.

Consistency of Workload Patterns

The reason for including this factor is that when working with a fluid pool, an insurance company can place workloads on physical systems based on fairly sophisticated optimisation criteria. This means that a certain number of applications can potentially be hosted on fewer physical systems. However, this advantage depends on the level of volatility in workload patterns – for highly volatile workloads, a model for leveraging spare capacity is beneficial, but for consistent, repeatable workload patterns, the advantage is reduced. If the mainframe environment is examined, it can be observed that very high utilisation levels can be attained for low-volatility workload patterns without motioning of any kind.

Security

Security zones

If an insurance company has security policies and procedures that prevent security zones being bridged accidentally or, in extreme cases, intentionally, then security zones are an issue that could influence the choice of virtualisation solutions.

Organisations rarely mix security zones when virtualising their infrastructure since most virtualisation technologies are not considered to have strong enough security isolation models to permit such combinations. A typical example would be the placement of systems connected to a sensitive internal network on the same physical host as systems connected to a demilitarised zone[61] (DMZ), which is seldom recommended for a number of reasons.

According to Hillier (2007), '*One of the biggest reasons is that certain virtualisation technologies have "thinner walls" between VMs than others. Technologies that use inter-VM memory page-sharing mechanisms are generally deemed to be less secure than those that do not (or that share only read-only text pages). Some virtualisation solutions have security accreditations that make certain combinations possible, but it is rarely advantageous to make configurations that are overly complex from a security perspective.*

Another reason not to mix certain combinations of servers on the same physical box is the "super super user" phenomenon. In physical environments, a "castle wall" security paradigm is used to protect disk information – if you do not authenticate with the operating system image then you cannot get inside to see the disk. This gives local administrators control of their boxes and prevents them from having access to others.'

Insurance companies may discover that many virtualisation solutions have administrator-level access rights that can allow users to view disk images of all the virtual images, and in some cases modify and control them. This novel and potentially dangerous role should be assessed in light of their security policies and procedures.

Network and firewall rules

Initially, this appears highly related to the security concerns discussed above, and it is. Given that a number of high-level security policies are put into practice in the network and firewall components, the connection between security zones and networking is obvious.

However, security problems at the network level are worsened by virtualisation technologies that are equipped with internal network switches to manage traffic between virtual machines on the same physical host. These types of technology let virtual systems completely circumvent all established port-level firewall filters, deep packet sniffers, and quality-of-service (QoS) rules governing traffic in the environment. In some ways, this has regressed

61 This is a physical or logical subnetwork that contains and exposes an organisation's external services to a larger, untrusted network, usually the Internet. The purpose of a DMZ is to add an additional layer of security to an organisation's local area network (LAN); an external attacker only has access to equipment in the DMZ, as opposed to the whole of the network.

the network security world back into the dark ages and opened environments up to threats that cannot be detected by network level security tools.

Information privacy

Insurance firms are usually subject to regulations, or have other strict information privacy requirements and must be particularly diligent when it comes to the system and network-level security of their environment. The 'super super user' effect mentioned previously is particularly dangerous in IT environments where concurrent access to certain combinations of information (such as names and dates of birth) is prohibited.

According to Hillier (2007), '*This same diligence also extends to offline image management. Many virtualisation technologies allow access to information stored in offline virtual images by simply "mounting" them as disk images. This makes the entire offline image catalogue a potential liability, and when combined with the increasing size of portable storage media, opens the door to the virtual equivalent of "walking off" with a hard drive. It also means that any applications that leave residual data in temp files or other local storage must be treated very carefully when being virtualised.*'

Insurance companies can consider all of these constraints if they are identified early enough in the planning phase, and technologies that have strengths or weaknesses in major areas can be identified before they are actually rolled out.

Overhead and Scalability Concerns

It should be noted there are definite parts of the operational model of a virtualisation technology that influence its appropriateness for a particular purpose. These include the way I/O is handled, the 'quantisation model' of virtual CPUs, the maximum number of CPUs per virtual machine, and even simply the method that vendors use to license their software on the platform.

Below are some factors that impact those which, if any, are a concern for insurance companies:

I/O rates

Software components that insurance companies use which are I/O intensive, such as database servers, may be better suited to virtualisation technologies that don't use virtual device drivers. This is simply because virtual device drivers overload the CPU with every I/O transaction they perform, resulting in the system hitting a limit of scalability before it otherwise would.

Insurance companies could assess CPU utilisation based on the I/O activity on their physical servers to influence their decision to implement virtualisation technology. This assessment could help them eliminate any workload types that are unsuitable for a particular virtualisation technology and, more significantly, it could aid in the assessment of whether the effect is even worth considering in a given environment.

Non-computing-intensive applications

Applications running at high CPU utilisation rates are generally easier to deal with than applications that are doing very little. This is simply because they are easier to plan for and usually translate into fewer virtual machines on the target system, therefore avoiding the risk of running into other technology and/or resource limits.

Insurance companies should take an inventory of non-computing-intensive applications when choosing the right virtualisation technology.

Software licensing models

This is another major factor that influences an insurance company's choice of virtualisation technology. The licensing of the software on the target systems is a major consideration. If a specific application is not supported on a specific virtualisation technology, then it will not be feasible in most environments. In fact, the effect of this can make everything else discussed in some environments appear small in comparison, especially when applications are in use from vendors that have been slow to embrace the virtualisation paradigm.

However, even if support is not a concern, licensing costs can be. Applications and infrastructure software that are licensed per physical CPU can negatively impact on virtualisation plans. Insurance companies have to be conscious of this when selecting virtualisation technology suited to their IT and business needs.

Financial Considerations

Licensing costs

Given the manner in which the virtualisation space has grown, there are a variety of ways virtualisation solutions can be bought. At one end of the spectrum, proprietary hardware systems can be bought that integrate the virtualisation function as part of the overall solution, some of which even come with separate hardware to manage the virtual images. At the other end of the spectrum, many solutions are emerging in the market based on the widely available open-source Xen[62] technology. The licensing models for these vary widely, from free to support-only to licensed per host.

62 Xen is a virtual machine monitor that allows several guest operating systems to be executed on the same computer hardware concurrently. Xen was initially created by the University of Cambridge Computer Laboratory and is now developed and maintained by the Xen community as free software, licensed under the GNU General Public Licence (GPL2).

Implementation costs

The attraction of virtualisation lies in part in its 'transparency' to applications. If an application is placed in a virtual environment that is similar in its characteristics to the physical one it came from, then the risk of the transition is minimised. While attractive from an implementation standpoint, however, this quality could often prevent an insurance company from making other very useful improvements along the way.

Hardware and software savings

One of the primary reasons that virtualisation technologies exist are the hardware savings that they can offer organisations. These savings, along with the attendant power and cooling reductions, can provide a significant driver in many insurance companies.

According to Hillier (2007), *'The level of savings, however, can vary depending on the type of technology used. Virtualising onto high-density physical architectures (such as blades) greatly reduces server footprint, but may require water-based cooling to prevent hot spots. The use of fat nodes and large, vertically scaled servers provides very high scalability and efficiency but typically has higher upfront costs. Commoditised rack-mounted servers are simple and easy to deploy, but they share fewer hardware components with each other and thus may not be as efficient with respect to economies of scale. In general, these concerns are more related to the hardware selection than the virtualisation technology, but because there are dependencies between the two, in many cases it is necessary to consider them.'*

As for software savings, the majority of the forms of virtualisation do not create the amount that is expected. Experts believe this is as a result of most 'below kernel' virtualisation solutions having each guest with a complete copy of every piece of software it had in the physical world (with the possible exception of backup agents), offering little advantage over the physical world.

Case Study[63]

The following is a case study on the use of virtualisation by an insurance company, BizInsure, as a foundation for innovation.

Overview

Business challenge

Faced with the need to build a new, multimillion-dollar data centre to cope with server proliferation, and seeking to streamline application development and daily operations overall, BizInsure Insurance instead made a strategic decision to move to a flexible, virtualised IT environment.

63 Supplied by IBM. The name of the insurance company and the manager for Linux were changed.

Solution

BizInsure deployed two IBM System zTM mainframes running Linux®. The solution is a cornerstone of BizInsure's strategy of moving all new development to virtualisation and J2EE as a means of 'future-proofing' its IT environment.

Key benefits

- US$15 million cost savings anticipated over three years.
- 85–90 per cent server utilisation.
- 80 per cent reduction in environmental costs.
- Web hosting costs lowered by 50 per cent.

The server proliferation issue

Most large corporations face the problem of server proliferation. With the servers in use at a major company typically numbering in the thousands, costs related to purchase and support can be very high, especially in an era of rising energy costs and increasing IT usage related to new applications and services.

BizInsure Insurance, a Fortune 500 company and one of the United States' leading underwriters, is no different. Like other large insurance companies, BizInsure has a mixed IT environment that includes both traditional, mission-critical mainframe-based applications and enterprise applications running on distributed servers.

This mixed environment comes from the nature of BizInsure's business. From an IT standpoint, the insurance industry requires high-speed transaction processing to handle the tremendous amount of activity, such as policy verification and claims handling, associated with serving millions of policyholders around the clock. This kind of workload is best done by mainframes. Other kinds of workloads, such as enterprise applications or Web servers, do not warrant the use of a mainframe, and so are normally deployed on smaller, distributed servers. As the business grows, however, the number and variety of these smaller servers begin to increase, until they become unsustainable.

'*We were facing the same problems that any company our size has to deal with*,' says Vince Vaughan, manager of Linux for BizInsure. '*We were running out of floor space, cooling and electricity, and our servers were drastically underutilised.*'

There were productivity issues as well. Server provisioning – the activity of allocating capacity to a new task – took anywhere from weeks to months, which was stifling application development. '*It simply wasn't worth the risk to try out new ideas most of the time*,' Vaughan says. '*The costs, should a given project not pan out, were too high.*'

Changing course to save money

In 2006, it became evident that unless a new direction was taken, BizInsure would have to update the power and cooling at its Tier 4 data centre and possibly build a new data centre at a cost of millions of dollars to accommodate growth. To avoid this expenditure and to address the underlying proliferation issue, BizInsure made a major strategic decision: to deploy a virtualised infrastructure.

The new environment is based on IBM System z mainframes and key technologies including IBM z/VM® virtualisation software, IBM WebSphere® middleware and IBM DB2® database, which BizInsure analysis had shown could deliver a much faster, and much greater, ROI than other platforms due to its inherent cost of ownership savings. These savings, according to Vaughan, come in large part from reduced licensing fees. In a situation like BizInsure's, where there are thousands of servers in use, the cost of software licensing is considerable. But because of the way licence fees are calculated – by processor – a solution that can employ a few very powerful processors to replace many individual servers can result in significant licence fee savings.

'*The software and maintenance costs add up to millions. And, of course, there are all the ancillary cost savings as well – floor space, cabling, switches, network administrators – it all adds up*,' Vaughan notes.

Virtualisation provides a significant performance boost for BizInsure's overall IT environment, which translates into reduced response times and greater productivity. The consolidated servers run a version of Linux compiled to run on IBM System z. Combined with z/VM virtualisation, this eliminates the physical separation of Linux servers and enables resource sharing. With a distributed infrastructure, enterprise and line-of-business applications on standalone servers interact with the mainframe via a conventional network infrastructure. But with Linux on z/VM, the virtualised servers are able to use the fast I/O of the mainframe directly, while at the same time taking advantage of the traditional mainframe strengths of reliability and high availability.

In addition to moving to Linux for new applications, BizInsure has also strategically decided on the use of the industry-standard Java 2 Enterprise Edition (J2EE) environment for all future application development, which is seen as a good way to ensure future extensibility and development of applications.

By consolidating workloads onto its virtualised infrastructure, BizInsure has replaced hundreds of standalone servers running various applications under several different operating systems, and also avoided having to purchase hundreds of new servers to handle growth. '*Our virtualised environment is configured to handle the most important applications, but we still have a distributed infrastructure*,' says Vaughan. '*We've consolidated servers where it made sense to do so, but with a business like ours, you're never going to completely replace all of the distributed servers.*'

The two System z mainframes that run the virtualised environment are located at two separate data centres. One of the mainframes runs the production environment consisting of enterprise, line-of-business and Web applications, and the other is devoted to application development and testing. The second mainframe also doubles as a disaster recovery resource. Data is replicated between the two sites on a 30-second delay. In this way, the investment in hardware is leveraged to provide business continuity with no additional outlay.

The combination of cost savings and performance increases made virtualisation on System z the best choice for BizInsure's needs, according to Vaughan. '*We anticipate saving approximately US$15 million over three years,*' he says. '*We're seeing dramatic improvements across the board. An 80 per cent reduction in environmental costs including power, cooling and floor space; hardware and OS support efforts cut in half; Web hosting monthly costs also cut in half through capacity optimisation and overall server utilisation running at 85 to 90 per cent.*'

Rapid provisioning changes the mindset of developers

While the initial reason to deploy a virtualised environment was related to money, the new IT architecture's flexibility has provided a significant added benefit. It gives BizInsure's application developers much greater freedom thanks to the ease with which computing capacity can be allocated, or provisioned, to new workloads. This enables them to bring new services to market more quickly, which in turn drives competitive advantage.

With a distributed infrastructure, provisioning a new project can take days, weeks or even months. Equipment must be retasked, or new equipment purchased. As a result, the costs involved in testing new ideas can be prohibitive, which tends to stifle development.

'*With the virtualised infrastructure,*' Vaughan says, '*we can provision servers literally in minutes. That gives us the benefits related to rapid scalability that you might expect. For example, we premiered a high-profile ad during the Super Bowl last year, and we knew it would result in a usage spike on our Web portal. So we temporarily added capacity to the Web servers to handle it, very simply and easily.*'

It's the indirect benefit, however, that Vaughan highlights. '*Rapid provisioning lets us try things that we'd never have considered attempting before. If something doesn't work out, well, no problem . . . we just take the capacity back and use it for something else, right away. The ability to flexibly add capacity wherever we need it changes the whole mindset of the developers. It promotes out-of-the-box thinking, because the risk cost is so low. What virtualisation really gives us is a strong foundation for innovation.*'

Conclusion

IT can become a true source of competitive advantage only if an insurer's IT strategy is well aligned with its overall business strategy. Convergence of IT and business strategies will help IT investments achieve maximum value.

Integrated planning, supported by organisational and governance structures designed to maximise the business value of IT investments, is essential in the bid to achieve appropriate alignment of IT with business. Integral to this process is a clear understanding of the IT implications of specific business decisions – such as the extension of sales channels, merger activities, and the redesign of business models or processes.

10 Methodology, Skills and Tools

This chapter covers the methodologies, methods used and skills required to work in the insurance industry.

Introduction

The methodologies, skills and tools used in the insurance industry will be discussed in this section to ensure that readers focus on what is required. As insurers have historically adopted mainframe technologies to support the business, a section will be dedicated to skills required to work with mainframes.

The array of tools on the market presents opportunities to insurance companies to put structures in place for their IT projects and, as a consequence, the choice of tools is increasingly a strategic decision. To this end, the tools on the market will be discussed.

An overview of mainframe technologies will be discussed to give readers an insight into the benefits of acquiring mainframe skills.

Overview of Mainframe Technologies

Mainframe technologies have been well known for decades and in recent times have been combined with distributed architectures to provide massive storage and to improve system security, flexibility, scalability and reusability in the client/server design. Mainframes are used intensively in insurance companies because they excel at simple transaction-oriented data processing to automate repetitive business tasks, such as claims administration and quotations of annuities, and also at being a secure, reliable repository of customer, financial and claims information.

In comparing mainframes with client/server systems, it could be noted that while client/server systems are suited for rapid application deployment and distributed processing, mainframes are efficient at online transactional processing, mass storage, centralised software distribution and data warehousing.[64]

As insurance companies have a relatively large number of customers and product lines, they prefer mainframes for big batch jobs and storing massive amounts of vital data. They also use the tools in mainframes for monitoring the performance of their entire system, including networks and applications, not available today on UNIX servers.

Methodologies

In software engineering and project management, 'methodology' is often used to refer to a codified set of recommended practices, sometimes accompanied by training materials, formal education programmes, worksheets and

64 Data warehousing and data mining provide executive decision makers with data analysis information to make informed business decisions.

diagramming tools. In insurance, the best methodologies are employed to ensure that business-critical systems are built to the sufficient level of quality required by the activities carried out in the industry.

Information Technology Infrastructure Library (ITIL®)

ITIL (the IT Infrastructure Library) is essentially a series of documents that are used to aid the implementation of a life-cycle framework for IT service management. This customisable framework defines how service management is applied within an organisation. It is also aligned with the international standard, ISO 20000.

How is ITIL organised?

ITIL is organised into a series of five volumes (the books): Service Strategy, Service Design, Service Transition, Service Operation, and Continual Service Improvement. These in turn describe a closed-loop feedback system that provides feedback throughout all areas of the life cycle. The volumes continue to provide a framework of best-practice disciplines that enable IT services to be provided effectively. (IT Service Management Zone)

RUP

The Rational Unified Process (RUP) is an iterative software development process created by the Rational Software Corporation, now a division of IBM. RUP is not a single, concrete prescriptive process but rather an adaptable process framework. As such, RUP describes how to develop software effectively using proven techniques. While RUP encompasses a large number of different activities, it is also intended to be tailored, in the sense of selecting the development processes appropriate to a particular software project or development organisation. RUP is recognised as being particularly applicable to larger software development teams working on large projects.

Capability Maturity Model (CMM)

The Capability Maturity Model (CMM) is a way to develop and refine an organisation's processes. It was developed by the Software Engineering Institute at Carnegie Mellon University in Pittsburgh. The first CMM was for the purpose of developing and refining software development processes. The latest version (1.2) of Capability Maturity Model Integration (CMMI) contains 22 key process areas, indicating the aspects of product development that are to be covered by company processes. The method by which a company chooses to adopt CMMI is called a representation. Both the staged representation and the continuous representation contain all 22 process areas. The previous version of CMMI (Ver1.1) had 25 process areas.

Figure 10.1 RUP

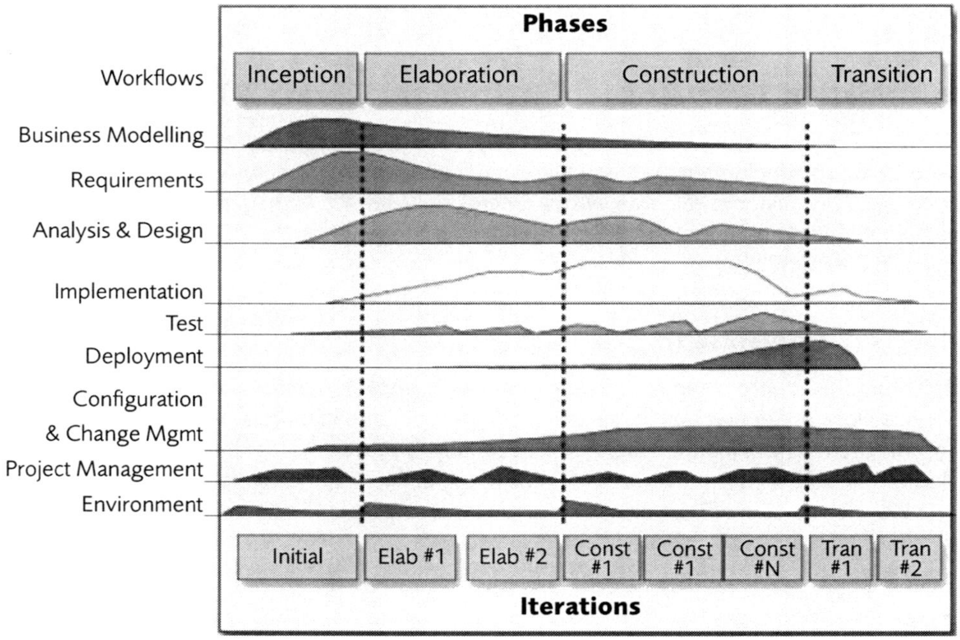

Source: Rational Software

A maturity model is a structured collection of elements that describe characteristics of effective processes. It is a layered framework providing a progression to the discipline needed to engage in continuous improvement, while the key processes mentioned above identify a cluster of related activities that, when performed collectively, achieve a set of goals considered important. The goals of a key process area summarise the states that must exist for that key process area to have been implemented in an effective and lasting way. The extent to which the goals have been accomplished is an indicator of how much capability the organisation has established at that maturity level. The goals signify the scope, boundaries and intent of each key process area.

There are five levels of CMM that an organisation can achieve and they are as follows:

- **Level 1 – Initial**: At this level, processes are usually ad hoc and the organisation usually does not provide a stable environment. Success in these organisations depends on the competence and heroics of the people in the organisation and not on the use of proven processes.

- **Level 2 – Repeatable**: At this level, software development successes are repeatable. The processes may not repeat for all the projects in the organisation.
- **Level 3 – Defined**: The organisation's set of standard processes, which are the basis for level 3, are established and improved over time. These standard processes are used to establish consistency across the organisation. Projects establish their defined processes by the organisation's set of standard processes, according to tailoring guidelines.
- **Level 4 – Quantitatively managed**: Using precise measurements, management can effectively control the software development effort. In particular, management can identify ways to adjust and adapt the process to particular projects without measurable losses of quality or deviations from specifications. Organisations at this level set quantitative quality goals for both software processes and software maintenance.
- **Level 5 – Optimising**: Maturity level 5 focuses on continually improving process performance through both incremental and innovative technological improvements. Quantitative process-improvement objectives for the organisation are established, continually revised to reflect changing business objectives, and used as criteria in managing process improvement.

PRINCE2

Prince stands for Projects in Controlled Environments. Prince2 is the latest version of Prince, released in 1996, and is a project management methodology for the organisation, management and control of projects.

Figure 10.2 shows Prince2 processes. The arrows symbolise flows of information.

Prince2 offers a process-based approach to key areas of project management. It is made up of eight high-level processes:

- Directing a project (DP);
- Planning (PL);
- Starting up a project (SU);
- Initiating a project (IP);
- Controlling a stage (CS);
- Managing product delivery (MP);
- Managing stage boundaries (SB);
- Closing a project (CP).

Figure 10.2 Prince2

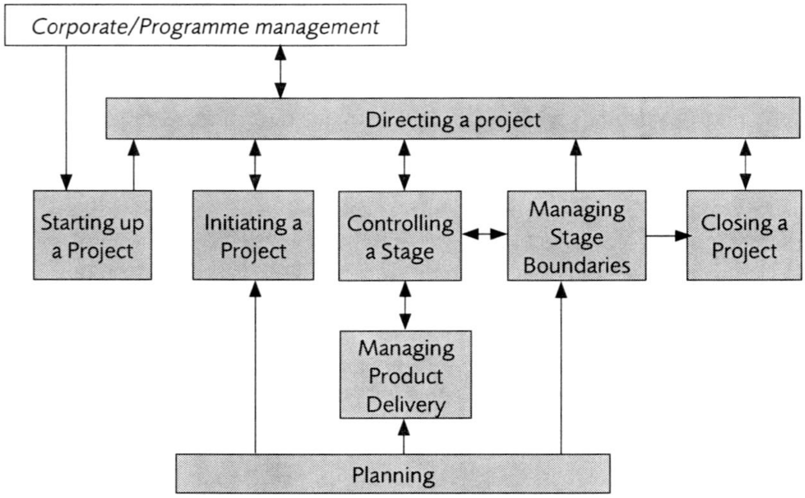

Source: Wikipedia

UML

The Unified Modelling Language (UML) is a non-proprietary object modelling and specification language used in software engineering. The UML model can be used to showcase the functionality of a system, the structure and substructure, and the internal behaviour. The following are artefacts that can be created using UML:

- Use cases;
- Class diagrams;
- Sequence diagrams;
- State activity diagrams.

The use case in Figure 10.3 shows different actors (employees and mainframe system of an insurance company) interacting with a special handling system.

V-Model

The V-model is a graphical representation of the system development life cycle. It summarises the main steps to be taken in conjunction with the corresponding deliverables during the life cycle.

The left side of the V shows the specification stream, where the system specifications are defined, while the right side of the V represents the testing stream, where the systems are being tested (against the specifications defined on the left side). The base of the V, where the sides meet, represents the development stream.

Figure 10.3 An example of a Use Case Diagram

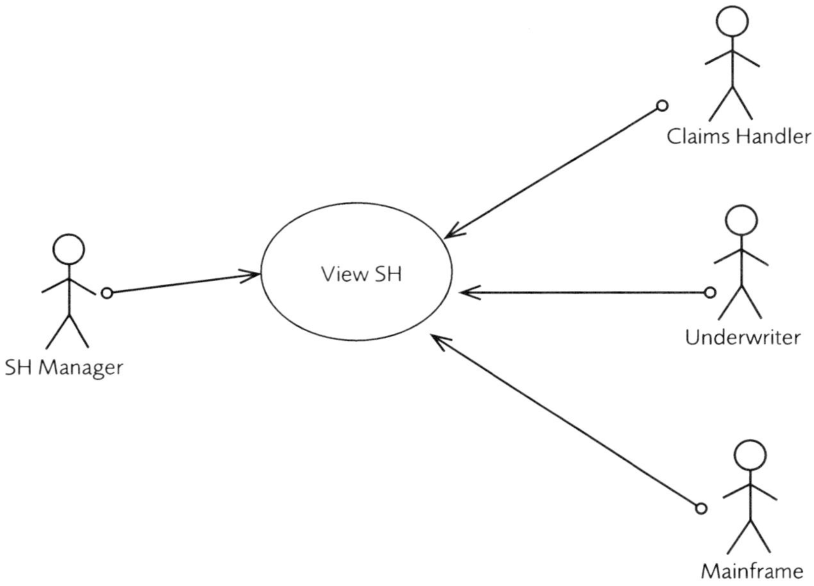

Figure 10.4 V-Model

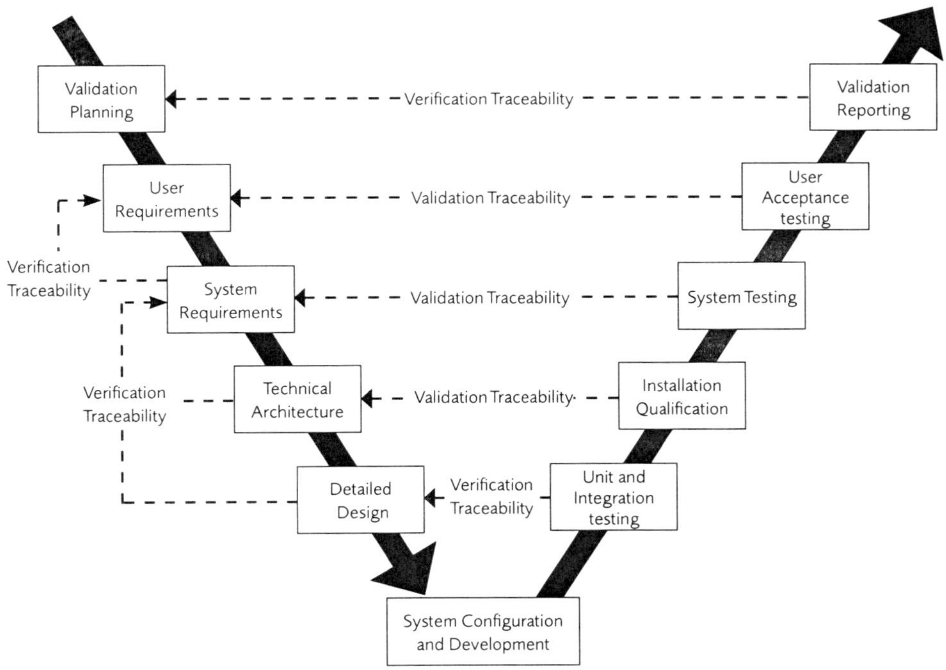

Source: Wikipedia

RAD

Rapid Application Development (RAD) is a software development process that involves iterative development and the construction of prototypes.

Core elements of RAD

RAD has six core elements:

- Prototyping;
- Iterative development;
- Timeboxing;
- Team members;
- Management approach;
- RAD tools.

Agile

Agile software development is a conceptual framework for undertaking software engineering projects. Agile methods attempt to minimise risk by developing software in short timeboxes, called iterations, which typically last one to four weeks. Each iteration is like a miniature software project on its own and includes all of the tasks necessary to release the mini-increment of new functionality: planning, requirements analysis, design, coding, testing and documentation. While iteration may not add enough functionality to warrant releasing the product, an agile software project intends to be capable of releasing new software at the end of every iteration. At the end of each iteration, the team re-evaluates project priorities.

Extreme Programming

Extreme Programming (XP) is a software engineering methodology for the development of software projects. It prescribes a set of day-to-day practices for developers and managers; the practices are meant to embody and encourage particular values and:

- Involve new or prototype technology, where the requirements change rapidly, or some development is required to discover unforeseen implementation problems;
- Are small and more easily managed through informal methods.

Pair Programming

Pair programming involves having two programmers working side by side, collaborating on the same design, algorithm, code or test. One programmer, the driver, has control of the keyboard/mouse and actively implements the program. The other programmer, the observer, continuously observes the work of the driver to identify tactical (syntactic, spelling, etc.) defects and also thinks strategically about the direction of the work. On demand, the two programmers can brainstorm any challenging problem. Because the two programmers periodically switch roles, they work together as equals to develop software.

Business and Systems Analysis Methods

Business and systems analysis methods adopted in the development of software in the insurance industry are vast and varied but the following are the most commonly used.

Business Rules Approach

The business rules approach is a development methodology where rules are in a form that is used by but not embedded in business process management systems.

The business rules approach formalises an enterprise's critical business rules in a language the manager and technologist can understand. Business rules create an unambiguous statement of what a business does, with information to decide a proposition. The formal specification becomes information for process and rules engines to run.

Entity-Relationship Diagrams

The entity-relationship model or entity-relationship diagram (ERD) is a data model or diagram for high-level descriptions of conceptual data models and it provides a graphical notation for representing such data models in the form of entity-relationship diagrams. Such models are typically used in the first stage of information system design; they are used, for example, to describe information needs and/or the type of information that is to be stored in the database during the requirements analysis.

Prototyping

The prototyping model is a software development process that begins with requirements collection, followed by prototyping and user evaluation. Often the end-users may not be able to provide a complete set of application objectives, detailed input, processing or output requirements in the initial stage. After the user evaluation, another prototype will be built based on feedback from users and again the cycle returns to customer evaluation. The cycle starts by listening to the user, followed by building or revising a mock-up and letting the user test the mock-up, then it goes back to the beginning again.

Testing Methods

The following are common testing methods adopted in systems development in insurance.

Equivalence Partitioning

Equivalence partitioning is a systematic process that identifies, on the basis of whatever information is available, a set of classes of input conditions to be tested. Each class is a representative of a large set of other possible tests.

Boundary Value Analysis

Boundary value analysis is a variant and refinement of equivalence partitioning with two major differences. First, rather than selecting any element in an equivalence class as being representative, elements are selected such that each edge of the equivalence class is the subject of a test.

Second, rather than focusing exclusively on input conditions, output conditions are also explored by defining output equivalent classes.

Error Guessing

Error guessing is an ad hoc approach, based on intuition and experience, to identifying tests that are considered likely to expose errors. The basic approach is to make a list of possible errors or error-prone situations and then develop tests based on the list.

Tools

Some of the most popular tools used in the insurance industry for software development, project management, test management and defect tracking are listed below.

IBM Rational Rose

Rational Rose is an object-oriented, Unified Modelling Language (UML) software design tool intended for the visual modelling and component construction of enterprise-level software applications.

IBM Rational ClearCase

ClearCase provides life-cycle management and control of software development assets. It is used in insurance companies for change management and control of source code and artefacts.

Mercury QTP

This Mercury interactive test automation tool is used mainly in insurance companies for the automation of regression tests and data-driven tests.

IBM Rational ClearQuest

ClearQuest helps to automate and enforce development processes, manage issues throughout the project life cycle and facilitate communication between all stakeholders across the enterprise software. It is used in insurance companies for defect management and change tracking.

Mercury Test Director (Quality Centre)

This Mercury interactive test management tool is used in insurance companies for storing requirements, test cases and scripts. Test Director is fast becoming the industry standard for test management.

Oracle Designer

Oracle Designer offers a toolset to model, generate and capture the requirements and design of web-based applications quickly, accurately and efficiently, and also to assess the impact of changing those designs and applications.

PowerDesigner

PowerDesigner is a business process modelling approach to align business and IT, is an enterprise data modelling and database design solution that helps implement effective Enterprise Architecture and brings a powerful conceptual data model to the application development life cycle.

PowerDesigner uniquely combines several standard data modelling techniques (UML, Business Process Modelling and market-leading data modelling) together with leading development environments such as .NET, Workspace, PowerBuilder, Java, Eclipse, etc. to bring business analysis and formal database design solutions to the traditional software development life cycle. Also, it works with all modern RDBMS.

Common IT Skills Required

IT professionals usually update their skills in line with technological advancements but to compete in the skills market in insurance, some specific skills are required in various capacities. These are some of the skills that employers in the industry demand:

- **JAVA** – Experience and knowledge of Java Collections Classes, threads, swing development, design patterns, messaging middleware concepts.
- **C++** – Experience and knowledge of C++ multi-threading, STL, design patterns, messaging middleware concepts.
- **BizTalk** – Good knowledge of Microsoft BizTalk.
- **ControlM** – Knowledge and experience of ControlM – a system that provides advanced production-scheduling capabilities across the enterprise from a single point of control – is desirable.
- **.NET** – Experience and understanding of Web services – small, reusable applications that help computers from many different operating-system platforms work together by exchanging messages – from technical and business perspectives.
- **J2EE (Java 2 Platform, Enterprise Edition)** – Appreciation and experience of this platform is essential.
- **Junit** – Knowledge of Junit – a regression-testing framework used by the developer who implements unit tests in Java – is desirable.
- **XP** – Proficiency in Microsoft XP is important and also Microsoft Vista.
- **Microsoft Excel** – It is essential to be proficient in Microsoft Excel. It is also desirable to have good skills in VBA.
- **Business Objects** – Knowledge of Business Objects and the ability to manipulate data for reports in Business Objects is an essential skill to have.
- **UNIX** – It is essential to have knowledge and experience of UNIX and Linux and associated scripting languages.
- **SQL** – Proficiency in writing SQL queries. Most insurance companies use Sybase and Oracle databases, therefore it is vital to have a good command of PL/SQL and also TransactSQL, and tools such as TOAD and Oracle Discoverer.
- **Messaging platforms** – Knowledge of IBM's MQ series, MINT, Tuxedo and Rendezvous ETX is desirable.
- **Cruise Control** – Knowledge of Cruise Control is desirable. Cruise Control is usually used for deploying software builds.
- **FIX protocol** – At least a basic knowledge of FIX (Financial Information Exchange) protocol is desirable.
- **XML** – A rudimentary knowledge of XML is required to work successfully in IT in insurance.
- **ISO 15022** – Knowledge of ISO 15022 – principles necessary to provide the different communities of users with the tools to design message types

to support their specific information flows – is important. It is necessary to understand the set of syntax and message design rules and the dictionary of data fields.

Mainframe Skills

As stated above, mainframe skills are invaluable for a career in insurance IT. In this section, popular mainframe skills and level of proficiency will be described.

Skill	Requirements	Level of Proficiency[a] (on a scale of 1–10)
COBOL	▪ Understanding of the structure of COBOL programs ▪ Ability to declare data in COBOL ▪ Ability to use XPEDITER to interactively test, debug, and analyse COBOL programs ▪ Ability to utilise and navigate Time Sharing Option (TSO) and its facilities	9
MVS ABEND	▪ Ability to use Abend-AID to debug COBOL programs ▪ Understanding of Hex arithmetic ▪ Understanding of Job Entry System (JES) job log information ▪ Ability to read COBOL compiler outputs (Maps, Clists, Xref)	7
CICS (Customer Information Control System)	▪ Understanding of the origin of online systems ▪ Ability to navigate the CICS environment ▪ Ability to create fields ▪ Ability to design and format the 'screen presentation' with BMS ▪ Ability to use COBOL to access files and communicate with other CICS application programs ▪ Ability to execute tasks with CICS commands ▪ Understanding of asynchronous processing ▪ Ability to create Virtual Storage Access Method (VSAM) files	9

[a] This our assessment of the levels of proficiency required.

COBOL II and OS 390	■ Ability to develop batch programs ■ Understanding of code of working storage entries using standard picture clauses, 88 levels and redefine clauses ■ Understanding of code of Procedure Division logic including Moves, IF, Perform ■ Understanding of code procedures and Data Division entries to handle sequential files ■ Understanding of code and manipulation of COBOL data stored in Occurs clauses ■ Ability to use a mainframe text editor such as Interactive System Productivity Facility (ISPF)	9
EasyTrieve Plus	■ Understanding of the use of EasyTrieve to create reports ■ Ability to code Easytrieve programs to read data and create reports using QSAM and VSAM data ■ Ability to update, add and delete VSAM data ■ Ability to create Queued Sequential Access Method (QSAM) and VSAM files ■ Ability to use DB2 data and Information Management System (IMS) data to create reports	6
Endevor	■ Ability to recognise the Endevor life cycle and logical structure ■ Understanding of the information displayed about system, sub-system, environment, types, and processors ■ Ability to recognise panel layout and navigate in Endevor ■ Understanding and the ability to use foreground and batch processing techniques ■ The ability to display/browse an element and to retrieve an element from Endevor	7
FILE-AID	■ Appreciation of the features and functions of the File-Aid product in a batch environment ■ Ability to use File-Aid with a focus on the features and capabilities as they pertain to DB2	7

IMS	▪ Understanding of IMS Database concepts & design ▪ Ability to write application programs that access and update DL/I databases ▪ Appreciation of the program specification block and the program communication block ▪ Ability to identify DL/I call function use ▪ Understanding of update call design considerations ▪ Appreciation of command codes and Boolean SSAs ▪ Appreciation of the major components of the IMS/DC environment including receiving and sending messages ▪ Understanding of conversational and non-conversational transaction processing and Message Format Services (MFS) ▪ Ability to test and debug with BTS utility	8
Job Control Language (JCL)	▪ Understanding of the concepts and principles of MVS JCL and how it relates to JES and the operating systems (O/S) ▪ Ability to execute basic JCL statements ▪ Ability to use JCL to submit batch jobs ▪ Ability to use debug and fix JCL errors ▪ Ability to interpret and understand JES output ▪ Ability to use standard MVS utilities	9
REXX Scripting	▪ Ability to code REXX programs in an OS/390 environment ▪ Understanding of the structure of REXX syntax ▪ Ability to develop constructs in REXX scripts ▪ Ability to browse an application with REXX ▪ Ability to manage data set and file I/O services EXECIO	7

Soft Skills

- **Numeracy** – Having numerical skills is important if readers want to work on insurance projects as there are usually complex calculations involved in developing and verifying the functionality of some applications.
- **Business acumen** – A solid business acumen and awareness is required to perform well in the insurance sector. Readers should make a habit of reading news in the financial pages of the broadsheets or periodicals such as the Wall Street Journal.
- **Good communication skills** – It is essential to be able to explain con-

cepts in insurance and risk management from both a technical and business point of view in order to gain the confidence of the business users.

- **Business analysis skills** – The ability to understand business requirements and be able to document them is a nice skill to have. Readers should learn the art of extracting vital information from workshops and meetings with business users.
- **Inductive thinking** – The ability to think inductively will stand readers in good stead.
- **Good writing skills** – Good writing skills are important in order to produce high-quality documentation.
- **Ability to withstand pressure** – The work environment in the insurance sector is highly pressurised and as such requires the ability to withstand pressure.
- **Ability to see the 'big picture'** – The ability to see the bigger picture is necessary in order to understand the wider implications of the work tasks for the profitability of organisations.
- **Basic understanding of economics** – A basic understanding of economics is required to work in the sector if readers want a fulfilling career in insurance.
- **Proficiency in different languages** – A proficiency in different languages would be beneficial as some of the projects could span different continents. The discerning IT professional should be able to communicate with business users and other IT professionals in another language.
- **Negotiation skills** – Good negotiation skills are important because of the aggressive deadlines to which projects are executed.
- **Time management skills** – IT professionals in insurance should have good time management skills to be able to prioritise work tasks to meet aggressive project deadlines.
- **Leadership skills** – Leadership, a critical management skill, is required to motivate other people towards a common project or organisational goal.
- **Project management skills** – These include scheduling skills, including the use of Gantt charts and critical path analysis, which are essential skills for the type of project work undertaken in insurance companies.

Commonly Used Terminology

11

This chapter contains a list of terminology commonly used in the insurance industry.

Introduction

The insurance industry is a unique sector of the financial services industry that is mature, has rich customer information, established distribution channels, favourable product positioning, and years of solid business practices and investment reputation.

Insurance business processes also tend be complex and increasingly so, as the rise in catastrophes, both natural and human-made, has brought about the need to make non-tradable insurance assets tradable in capital markets in order to boost reserves. In addition, insurers are increasingly taking a wealth management approach towards traditional pension systems as good health and lifestyles are allowing people to live longer lives.

All the above factors mean that the terminology used in the insurance industry is vast and varied and it is essential for IT professionals to be aware of some of the terms used in the industry to ensure effective communication with their business counterparts.

Below is a list of some of the terms used in the insurance and also the reinsurance industry.

List of Terms

A fortiori This means 'much more; with stronger reason'.

Ab initio This means 'from the beginning'.

Abandonment A notice given to an insurer indicating that a constructive total loss has been claimed.

Absolute net claim This represents premiums, plus additional premiums, less return premiums, less reinsurances, brokerage and commission.

Acceptance Notification by a party to a proposed contract that they accept the other party's offer of the terms proposed, or where an underwriter initials a slip. The proposer of a life assurance policy, on receiving an offer of cover from an assurer, signifies their acceptance by paying the premium.

Accident year The calendar or accounting year in which an accident or loss occurred.

Accommodation line An interest which the company accepts to assist a broker, which would ordinarily be declined/diverted if considered strictly in accordance with underwriting philosophies.

Accumulation The concentration of risk, such as where an insurer may find that they have many policies on properties in adjacent locations that could result in losses arising from one event, e.g. fire.

Acquisition costs The total costs incurred by an insurer in writing or issuing an insurance policy. Commission, plus all expenses (direct and allocated), excluding claims expenses.

Act of God This is an accident or event which happens independently of human intervention and due to natural causes, such as a storm, earthquake, etc. It will relieve from liability if it amounts to circumstances which no human foresight could provide against, and of which human prudence is not bound to recognise the possibility.

Actuarial valuation A valuation by an actuary of the present value of future liabilities using probability tables and other statistical techniques for evaluation of the long-term business liabilities.

Ad valorem According to the value.

Additional premium This is extra premium due from the insured because the insurance is more hazardous than normal, or there is a change in circumstances which gives rise to an endorsement or because additional benefits are added to the policy.

Adjustable policy An insurance policy where a premium is payable at inception and adjusted after expiry.

Admitted company This is a term used for either an insurer licensed to conduct business in a given state or a reinsurer licensed or approved to conduct business in a given state.

Advance deposit This is a rebate system to adjust premiums to the treaty loss experience (not to be confused with advance premium or deposit premium).

After-the-event insurance Insurance that is taken out only once the 'event' has occurred to insure the policyholder against the risk of losing their case.

Agency agreement This is a contract between the company and a broker, which itemises all the conditions which the company grants an agency upon appointment, i.e. commission terms, types of business etc.

Agent's account This is a statement of the period's business that shows each premium transaction, the policy number, the insured's name, the premium or return premium and claims in the appropriate column with commission, postage and other charges, and the balance due either to the company or to the agent, in accordance with the contract between the agent and the underwriter.

Aggregate excess of loss reinsurance This is a form of reinsurance providing excess of loss cover for losses arising from any one event (or vessel) in excess of the reinsured's retention up to an agreed limit, but only when the aggregate of claims otherwise recoverable under the excess of loss treaty exceeds a stated amount.

Aggregate stop loss reinsurance This is a wider application of the ordinary stop-loss treaty as it applies to the entire portfolio of one branch of the reinsured's activities.

Aggregation The process of accumulating claims as specified by an excess of loss reinsurance agreement for the purpose of establishing the amount recoverable.

All risk insurance Insurance of property against loss or damage however caused, subject only to stated exceptions.

Antedating Where a policy is expressed as operating from a date before final agreement was reached on its terms, it is said to be antedated.

Appointed representative Someone who carries out activities that are part of the business for which their principal has accepted responsibility in writing.

Arbitration clause A clause providing a means of resolving differences between the reinsurer and the reinsured without litigation. Usually, each party appoints an arbitrator. The two thus appointed select a third arbitrator, or umpire, and a majority decision of the three becomes binding on the parties to the arbitration proceedings.

Arranged total loss (compromised total loss) A compromise settlement where a total loss has not in fact occurred, but is deemed to have done.

As original A term used in reinsurance to indicate that the reinsurance is on the same conditions as the original insurance.

Automatic treaty An agreement between reinsured and reinsurer (usually for pro rata reinsurance, and usually for one year or longer), whereby the ceding company is obligated to cede certain risks as provided in the agreement and the reinsurer is obligated to accept.

Average cost per claim reserve Total claims outstanding divided into the total reserves (less payments) equal an average claim reserve. Reserves in this context means all amounts provided for all known claims less any deductions for subrogation.

Avoidance The right of the underwriter to treat an insurance contract as though they had never accepted the risk. This can occur in cases where there is a breach of good faith, a significant change in the actual risk involved or a delay in the commencement of a voyage.

Bad faith The failure of an insurer to settle within policy limits when there was an opportunity to do so (and a court award in excess of the policy limits).

Balance A concept in surplus share reinsurance, dealing with the relationship between the written premium under the treaty and the maximum limit of liability to which the reinsurer is exposed. The precise relationship will vary from treaty to treaty, but if the ratio desired for a specific treaty is achieved, the treaty is referred to as 'balanced'.

Balanced portfolio The total business of an insurer that has been so arranged by selection and reinsurance as to safeguard the financial equilibrium of the underwriter.

Brokerage commission* An amount paid to a broker for insurance or reinsurance placement and other services.

Brokerage market* A collective reference to those reinsurers which accept business mainly through reinsurance intermediaries.

Buffer layer* Used in casualty insurance to describe a stratum of coverage between the maximum policy limit which the primary underwriter will write and the minimum deductible over which the excess or umbrella insurer will cover.

Burning cost* The ratio of actual past reinsured losses to a ceding company's subject matter premium (written or earned) for the same period. Used to analyse past reinsurance experience or to project the future.

Burning ratio* In primary insurance, the ratio of losses suffered to the amount of insurance in effect. Thus, not a 'loss ratio,' which is the ratio of losses incurred to premiums earned.

Buy-back agreement* A negotiated contractual effort by an insurer writing primary insurance or excess insurance to limit further exposure to the insured for defence or indemnity by making a lump sum payment to the insured. Open questions exist as to how these agreements affect third-party beneficiaries of the original insurance policy.

Call This is a payment made by a member of a protection and indemnity club in consideration for a right to indemnity. Such initial payments may be followed by supplementary calls.

Capacity The percentage of surplus, or the dollar amount of exposure, that an insurer or reinsurer is willing or able to place at risk. Capacity may apply to a single risk, a programme, a line of business or an entire book of business. Capacity may be constrained by legal restrictions, corporate restrictions or indirect restrictions.

Capital redemption policy This is an insurance policy that provides a capital sum at the end of a term of years.

Captive company This is an insurance company set up by a (non-insurance) commercial/industrial company primarily to write the parent company's own insurances and obtain access direct to the reinsurance market.

Case reserves These are loss reserves established with respect to specific, individual reported claims.

Cash loss These are monies held by a cedant to pay claims in advance of the reinsurance recovery.

Cash reserve This is a provision made by an insurer where it is considered that liability could or will arise on a notified loss. This may be a known amount or an estimated amount depending upon the facts available at the time.

Casualty insurance or reinsurance This is a kind of insurance or reinsurance that is primarily concerned with the losses caused by injuries to third persons and their property (in other words, persons other than the policyholder) and the legal liability imposed on the insured resulting there from. Also referred to as liability insurance.

Catastrophe This is an event or series of events which, when added together, form a potential large claim.

Catastrophe cover This is a form of reinsurance that indemnifies the ceding company for the accumulation of losses in excess of a stipulated sum arising from a catastrophic event such as a conflagration, earthquake or windstorm. Catastrophe loss generally refers to the total loss of an insurance company arising out of a single catastrophic event.

Catastrophe excess of loss reinsurance This is a form of excess of loss reinsurance that, subject to a specified limit, indemnifies the ceding company for the amount of loss in excess of a specified retention with respect to an accumulation of losses resulting from a 'catastrophe'.

Cession This is a ceded line and is known as a cession.

Chose in action This is a personal right of property, which can be enforced only by action, e.g. a debt.

Claim This is any notified occurrence which it is considered can give rise to a payment or payments under any individual policy of insurance, e.g. if there is more than one claim made against an insured as a result of one incident, then it is still deemed to be one claim. If there are two separate insureds involved in one incident, then that is deemed to be two separate claims.

Claim expenses (loss expense or adjusted expense) These are expenses of adjusting claims, such as court costs, fees and expenses of independent adjusters, lawyers, witnesses, and other expenses which can be charged to specific claims.

Claims Death, injury, destruction, or damage covered by insurance gives rise to a claim, i.e. the mandatory indemnity payable to the insured under the terms of the policy.

Claims and claim expense ratio This is the ratio of claims and claim expenses to net premiums earned, determined in accordance with accounting standards such as GAAP.

Claims co-operation This is where the reassured agrees to consult and co-operate with reinsurers on claims handling and settlement.

Claims equalisation This is the amount set aside for the purpose of preventing abnormal fluctuations in claims due to the occurrence of exceptional events.

Class This is a category of insurance business defined by the nature of the cover provided or by the nature of the object at risk.

Closing reinsurance The reinsurance of an entire portfolio of outstanding liabilities and outstanding claims to close a syndicate's underwriting account by transfer of the outstanding liability to the next open underwriting account.

Collective policy This is a form of policy for several co-insurers sharing the same risk. The policy is issued by the leading insurer in the joint names of all co-insurers and on renewal a collective receipt will be issued for all co-insurers.

Combined ratio This is the combination of an insurer's (or a reinsurer's) loss ratio and expense ratio.

Commercial customer This is a person who purchases cover on behalf of their business, trade or profession.

Commission This is remuneration to an agent for services such as arranging an insurance policy.

Common account This is when an original insurer, who already has reinsurance, effects further reinsurance with another reinsurer. It may be either wholly for the original insurer's own protection or also for the protection of the first reinsurer. In the latter case, it is said to be reinsurance for the common account.

Commutation This is the finalisation of an outstanding loss by payment of an agreed figure in settlement.

Commutation clause This is a clause in a reinsurance agreement that provides for estimation, payment and complete discharge of all obligations, including future obligations between the parties for reinsurance losses incurred.

Composite company This is a company transacting most general lines and long-term business.

Cumulative liability The accumulation of liability of a reinsurer under several policies from several reinsureds, covering similar or different lines of insurance, all of which are involved in a common event or disaster.

Cut-off cancellation or termination This is a provision included in the termination clause (or endorsement) which provides that the reinsurer shall not be liable for losses occurring after the termination date.

Cut-through endorsement This is an addition to an insurance policy between an insurance company and a policyholder which requires that in the event of the company's insolvency, any part of a loss covered by reinsurance is to be paid directly to the policyholder or mortgagee by the reinsurer.

Declaratory judgment* A decision by a court in a proceeding, which can be brought by either the insurer or the insured, to determine the rights of the parties. In insurance, for example, a court decision may be sought to determine whether an insurance company has an obligation to defend, indemnify or pay on behalf of its insured policyholder under a policy with regard to a particular loss or losses.

Deemed (or so deemed)* A condition which is said to exist by agreement between the parties even though it may not exist in fact (e.g. 'all policy limits greater than $5,000,000 are to be reinsured on a pro rata facultative basis, or be so deemed.') To deem means to treat as if.

Deficit* As used in reinsurance, any excess of charges over credits at the end of any accounting period (which excess shall be a charge in the computation of the contingent commission for the succeeding period, or in computing various experience-rated reinsurance arrangements).

Direct Writer*
1. In reinsurance, a reinsurer which negotiates with a ceding company without benefit of an intermediary or broker.
2. In insurance, a primary insurer that sells insurance through licensed agents who produce business essentially for no other organisations.

Discovery period The period within which a loss covered by a policy has to be discovered and notified to the insurers. The period of discovery may extend beyond the term of the policy.

Diversifiable risk Risk that can be eliminated by investors by holding diversified portfolios.

Double indemnity Payment of twice the policy's normal benefit in case of loss resulting from specified causes or under specified circumstances.

Errors and omissions clause* A clause in a reinsurance treaty (requiring some affirmative act by the reinsured to activate the reinsurance protection) which stipulates that, in the event of inadvertent error or omission, the reinsured shall not be prejudiced in the fulfilment of the agreement, provided that such error or omission shall be corrected as soon as it is discovered.

Event loss trigger* An approach designed to deem that all loss from one occurrence had one date of loss, regardless of the type of coverage (i.e. occurrence or claims made), or the number of dates of loss there under, or the reinsurance contracts or periods involved.

Excess This is the first part of the cost of a claim which is not covered by a policy. It may be borne by the insured or by another party.

Excess of loss reinsurance* A generic term describing reinsurance which, subject to a specified limit, indemnifies the reinsured company against all or a portion of the amount of loss in excess of the reinsured's specified loss retention.

Excess per risk reinsurance* A form of excess of loss reinsurance which, subject to a specified limit, indemnifies the reinsured company against the amount of loss in excess of a specified retention with respect to each risk involved in each loss.

Exclusions* Those risks, perils, or classes of insurance with respect to which the reinsurer will not pay loss or provide reinsurance, notwithstanding the other terms and conditions of reinsurance.

Expropriation cover This is the protection of the risk of seizure of the assets of the insured by the government of the country in which the assets are located.

Extended coverage insurance This is protection for the insured against property damage caused by windstorm, hail, smoke, explosion, riot, riot attending a strike, civil commotion, vehicle and aircraft. This is provided in conjunction with the fire insurance policy and the various 'package' policies.

Facultative This is a contract setting out how facultative reinsurance shall be handled by an insurer and a reinsurer.

Facultative reinsurance This term can mean two things as follows:
1. The reinsurance of risks that the original insurer may elect whether or not to offer for reinsurance, the reinsurer being free to accept or reject the offer;
2. Reinsurance of a single risk negotiated and placed individually.

Fidelity guarantee This a type of cover offered to an employer against loss arising from dishonesty of employees.

Floaters These are insurance policies that cover property that can be moved from one location to another for both transportation perils and perils affecting property at a fixed location.

Follow the fortunes The clause stipulating that once a risk has been ceded by the reinsured, the reinsurer is bound by the same fate thereon as experienced by the ceding company.

Fortuitous loss The unforeseen and unexpected loss that occurs as a result of chance.

Frequency The number of claims occurring during a given coverage period.

Gross earned premiums Premiums received by or due to an insurer, without deduction of the cost of any reinsurance, but adjusted to take account of the differences between the unexpired risk reserves at the beginning and end respectively of the period concerned.

Gross line The share of insurance accepted by an underwriter before a deduction is made for any reinsurance by them.

Gross loss ratio This is the ratio of claims incurred after subrogation (but before reinsurance recovery) to gross premiums earned or deemed to be earned before reinsurance.

Gross negligence This means the act of intentionally failing to perform a duty, with reckless disregard of the consequences as affecting the life or property of another.

Gross net premium The gross premium for a marine insurance, before deduction of brokerage and discounts but less gross returns of premium.

Gross premium The total premium before deduction of brokerage or discounts.

Gross written premiums Premiums received by or due to an insurer without deduction of the cost of any reinsurance or any adjustment for the fact that some of the income has to be reserved for the unexpired element of the policy.

Hard market This is a market in which it is difficult to obtain insurance. This is demonstrated by high premium rates.

Hazard This is a physical or moral feature that introduces or increases the possibility of a loss arising from a peril or influences the extent of loss.

Held covered This is a marine term whereby the insured's interest remains covered in the event of a circumstance arising which would, without prior agreement, cancel coverage.

Implied condition This is a condition which does not appear in the policy, but which is understood to be incorporated therein and is equally binding as though it were expressed in the policy. Breach of an implied condition by the assured entitles the underwriter to avoid the contract from inception.

Implied warranty This is a warranty that is not expressed in the policy specifically, but which is understood by both parties to be incorporated in the contract.

Inception date The date when a risk commences.

Incidental non-marine This is a type of non-marine insurance written by a marine underwriter as an adjunct to their marine insurance account.

Incurred claims or losses This is the total, under the normal accruals concept, of paid and outstanding claims arising in a period.

Indemnity This can be either:
1. A principle under which the insurer seeks to place the insured in the same position after a loss as they occupied immediately before the loss (as far as possible). The principle does not apply to life assurance.
2. The cover given by an insurance policy or amount of claim paid to indemnify an insured.

Indirect business This is business accepted by way of reinsurance.

Insurable interest In order for a contract of insurance to be valid, the (prospective) policyholder must have an interest in the insured item to the extent that its loss, death, damage or destruction would cause the policyholder loss. This is called insurable interest and must exist as follows: marine insurance – at the time of the loss; life assurance – at the time the policy is taken out; other insurance – at the time the policy is taken out and also at the time of the loss.

Insurable value The value of the insurable interest which the insured has in the insured occurrence or event. It is the amount to be paid out by the insurer (assuming full insurance) in the event of total loss or destruction of the item insured.

Insurance agent This is a representative of an insurer, whether an employee or an independent contractor, who negotiates, effects and sometimes services contracts of insurance.

Insurance broker A person that advises people on their insurance needs and negotiates insurances on their behalf with insurers, exercising professional care and skill in so doing.

Insurance contract This is a contract under which one party, the insurer, in return for a consideration, the premium, undertakes to indemnify the other party, the insured, against loss upon the happening of a specified event that is contrary to the interest of the insured.

Intermediary This is an agent or broker through whom a transaction is arranged between parties.

Investment income This is interest and dividends arising from the investing of premium monies pending claims being made.

Knock-for-knock agreement This is an agreement between motor insurers that in the event of an accident involving their respective policyholders, neither party shall seek to recover the insured cost of repairing the damage caused to the vehicle it insured from the other insurer, whoever is to blame for the accident.

Known case reserves This is an amount set aside to cover claims notified to the company, but which are not fully settled (also known as 'outstanding claims').

Known outstanding losses This is where claim notifications have been received for potential loss.

Negligence Failure to use the care that a reasonable and prudent person would have used under the same or similar circumstances.

Net In marine insurance, the premium after all discounts have been taken off; alternatively the premium following the deduction of a return of premium.

Net earned premiums The premiums received or due to an insurer, less the cost of reinsurance, and after adjustment to allow for the cost of any unexpired risk.

Net loss ratio This is the ratio of claims incurred after subrogation and reinsurance recovery to net premiums earned after reinsurance.

No claim discount The reduction allowed in a renewal premium in recognition of no claims having been paid by the insurer during the recent past period of insurance.

Non-admitted insurance company This is an insurance company not licensed to do business in a particular state; such a company, however, may sell excess and surplus insurance in that state if admitted insurers lack the capacity or expertise.

Non-marine general This is business other than marine, aviation and transport business (motor business is also usually considered as falling outside the non-marine class).

Non-proportional reinsurance This is the reinsurance, such as excess of loss reinsurance, where the reinsurer's liability is not calculated as a proportion of the insurer's.

Occurrence basis This is the excess of loss reinsurance by which the reinsurer's liability is determined in relation to the aggregate net retained loss sustained by the reinsured as a result of a single occurrence.

Open cover This is the insurance (or reinsurance) where the insurer obliges themselves in advance to accept business of a specific kind.

Open market This is used to refer to a risk that is individually placed in the market as opposed to one that is covered under a binding authority, line slip or treaty.

Outstanding claims losses The total of losses or claims which have been advised but at a given time are still outstanding and as such are only estimated amounts.

Outstanding claims portfolio This is an amount payable by a cedant to a reinsurer in consideration of the reinsurer accepting liability arising under a contract of reinsurance in respect of reinsurance claims incurred and arising prior to a fixed date.

Overriding commission This is a discount allowed to an agent or ceding insurer in addition to normal commission. In reinsurance, it is commonly by way of contribution to the direct insurer's overheads. In direct insurance, it may be payable to an employee or agent in respect of insurances written within their territory, even without their mediation.

Paid losses or claims This is the total of claims or losses which have been settled during a given period.

Participating insurance* A designated class of insurance that shares in the dividends declared by the primary insurer to policyholders.

Participating reinsurance* The sharing of risks, as in quota share and surplus share reinsurance, in which the reinsured and the reinsurer participate pro rata in all losses beginning with the first dollar.

Payback period* A term used in rating, per occurrence, excess covers showing the number of years at a given premium level required to accumulate total premiums equal to the indemnity.

Per occurrence excess An excess of loss reinsurance where the reinsured company's loss retention and the reinsurer's limit of liability apply to the loss arising from a single occurrence, regardless of the number of risks or policies involved.

Per risk reinsurance* Reinsurance in which the reinsurance limit and the reinsured's loss retention apply 'per risk', rather than per accident, per event, or in the aggregate.

Personal lines Those types of insurance, such as car or home insurance, for individuals or families rather than for businesses or organisations.

Pool This is a pool created when several insurers agree to share all insurances of a defined nature in specified proportions.

Pooling This is the practice that entails sharing all business of an affiliated group of insurance companies among the members of the group.

Portfolio entry This is the mechanics of attachment of a reinsurance treaty which at inception may be arranged on varying bases – to new and renewal business or business in force, etc. – all referred to as portfolio entry.

Portfolio return This is the return of reinsurance premium and losses to the ceding company in respect of in-force business as of a specified date upon termination of a reinsurance treaty.

Portfolio return premium This is the premium payable for the reinsurance of a portfolio of insurance or reinsurance business.

Portfolio run-off This is the opposite of portfolio return – permitting premiums and losses in respect of in-force business to run to their normal expiration upon termination of a reinsurance treaty.

Portfolio transfers These proportional treaties are written on either a 'run-off' or 'portfolio' basis. Where treaties are written on a 'run-off' basis, the underwriting year is kept open until all premiums are paid and all claims are settled. Treaties written on a portfolio basis are effectively cut at the end of the underwriting year and the premium and loss portfolios transferred out to the ensuing year.

Pre-existing condition This is a physical condition that existed before the effective date of coverage.

Premium additions These are amounts payable to the company if the exposure under a policy is increased or the rate required by the insurer is increased.

Premium income Income of an insurer from premiums.

Premium portfolio transfer The reinsurers assume liability for claims occurring on all business in force under this treaty at the start of the year and are relieved of all liability for future claims on business in force at the close of the year.

Premiums – adjustments This is the amount due on the adjustable policy as in the case of employers' liability, or where a deposit premium has been paid.

Premiums – closed This is a premium having been received in full for the period of insurance.

Premiums – earned This is the proportion of the total premium under a policy which refers to a particular period normally calculated pro rata.

Premiums – gross This is the amount of premium after reinsurance, but before commission is deducted.

Premiums – net These are premiums shown after the deduction of commission (brokerage) and reinsurance.

Premiums – renewal This is the premium to renew an existing policy which is expiring.

Premiums – returns This is the amount due to the insured if a policy is reduced by rate exposure or cancelled.

Probable maximum loss This is the maximum amount of loss that can be expected under normal circumstances.

Quota share reinsurance This is a form of pro rata reinsurance. Treaty reinsurance provides that the reinsurer shall accept a certain percentage of all or certain classes of or parts of the business of the reinsured.

Rate The percentage or factor applied to the ceding company's subject premium to produce the reinsurance premium, or the percentage applied to the reinsurer's premium to produce the commission payable to the primary company (or, if applicable, the reinsurance intermediary).

Rebating This entails giving any valuable consideration (commission) to a prospect or insured as an inducement to buy.

Recapture Used often in life reinsurance as the action of a ceding company to take back reinsured risks previously ceded to a reinsurer.

Reciprocity This is a process whereby reinsurances are exchanged between two reinsurers.

Recovery This is money received by an insurer in respect of a loss, thus reducing the loss, by way of subrogation, salvage or reinsurance.

Reimbursement Payment of the expenses actually incurred as a loss covered by an insurance policy.

Reinstatement The restoration of the reinsurance limit of an excess property treaty to its full amount after payment by the reinsurer of loss as a result of an occurrence.

Renewal This is the continuation of an existing contract of insurance for a further period.

Replacement This is the substitution of insurance coverage from one policy contract to another.

Replacement cost This is the cost to repair or replace property without considering depreciation.

Representation These are statements made by an applicant in the application, which they represent as being substantially true to the best of their knowledge and belief, but which are not warranted as exact in every detail.

Rescission This is the termination of an insurance contract by the insurer on the grounds of material misstatement on the application for insurance. The action of rescission must take place within the contestable period or time limit on certain defences, but takes effect as of the date of issue of the policy, therefore voiding the contract from its inception.

Residual market This is a system through which insurance is made available to buyers that represent unusually high risks.

Retrocedent This is the reinsurer placing a retrocession.

Retrocession This is the term used to denote reinsurance of reinsurance.

Retrocessionaire This is a reinsurer who buys reinsurance on some of the risks they have agreed to bear.

Retrospective rating This is a plan or method which permits adjustment of the final reinsurance ceding commission or premium on the basis of the actual loss experience under the subject reinsurance treaty – subject to minimum and maximum limits.

Risk-based capital The amount of capital needed to absorb the various risks of operating an insurance business. For example, a higher-risk business requires more capital than one with lower risks. The calculation is intended to be unique to each company.

Risk basis This is the excess of loss reinsurance by which the reinsurer protects the reinsured against losses affecting individual exposure units.

Risk excess This is an excess of loss reinsurance where the contract is expressed 'excess of each and every loss, each and every risk'.

Self-insured obligation* An exposure of an insurance company within the classes of its reinsured business for which the company has issued its policy (or certificate) to itself, has made a premium declaration on its books, or has prepared an internal memorandum with details of the exposure, the purpose being to cover such self-insured obligation under its reinsurance contracts.

Setoff (noun)* The reduction of the amount owed by one party to a second party, under one agreement or transaction, by crediting the first party with amounts the second party owes the first party under other agreements or transactions, for the purpose of determining the amount, if any, the first party owes to the second.

Special covers* A general term used to describe reinsurance agreements written to protect the primary company against certain unusual situations, usually contingent in nature, rather than for the repayment of normal losses suffered under the primary company's policies.

Special termination* A clause in a reinsurance treaty providing that, if one or more conditions arise, the treaty or agreement can be cancelled immediately.

Spread loss reinsurance* A type of excess of loss property reinsurance which provides for a periodic adjustment of the reinsurance premium rate based on the reinsured's experience for preceding years (usually five), plus a loading for the purpose of compensating the reinsurer for a) its expenses, b) the possibility of unusual losses, c) those losses occurring at the end of the period of the treaty which the reinsurer might not have a chance to recoup if the treaty is not renewed, d) a catastrophe possibility, and e) the reinsurer's profit. In casualty reinsurance, adjustments to the above may be required for such other factors as economic and social inflation.

Structured settlement* The loss payment by the insurer in the form of a lump sum to the claimant (or its attorney), plus a discounted dollar amount (the premium) to an annuity company (affiliated or not with the insurer), which the annuity company agrees to pay the claimant (the annuitant) as an amount per year for either a period of years or for the lifetime of the annuitant.

Stub policy* An insurance policy written for less than one year.

Sunset* A provision in a contract limiting coverage to losses reported to the reinsurer within a certain number of years from a given point in time, such as the end of the contract year in which the loss occurs.

Syndicate An association of individuals or organisations to pursue certain insurance objectives.

Technical reserves* This is a collective term for the amounts set aside in respect of underwriting liabilities: unearned premium reserves, unexpired risk reserves, claims outstanding and the funds held for three-year and treaty business.

Termination clause* Continuous contracts remain in force until affirmative notice is given by one of the parties to terminate. This clause details the requirements of the notice.

Third party* This is a person claiming against an insured. In insurance terminology, the first party is the insurer and the second party is the insured.

Treaty* A reinsurance agreement between the reinsured company and the reinsurer, usually for one year or longer, which stipulates the technical particulars applicable to the reinsurance of some class or classes of business.

Treaty reinsurance* A standing agreement between reinsured and reinsurer:
1. for the cession and assumption of certain risks as defined in the pro rata treaty; or
2. for indemnity by the reinsurer only for the reinsured's losses above the reinsured's loss retention.

Turn* Referred to as 'the turn', this word describes the excess of reinsurance commission received by a ceding company over its actual costs incurred in producing the business ceded.

Ultimate loss ratio This is the ratio of net losses to net premiums assessed quarterly in respect of the open years for all lines of business, representing the ratio anticipated when all premiums are earned and all expired.

Ultimate net loss*

1. In reinsurance, the unit of loss to which the reinsurance applies, as determined by the reinsurance agreement. In other words, the gross loss less any recoveries from other reinsurance which reduce the loss to the treaty in question.
2. In liability insurance, the amount actually paid or payable for the settlement of a claim for which the reinsured is liable (including or excluding defence costs), after deductions are made for recoveries and certain specified reinsurance.

Unauthorised reinsurance* Reinsurance placed with a non-admitted reinsurer which is not licensed or approved in the jurisdiction in question.

Underinsurance This is insurance that is not adequate in terms of the sum insured to provide for full payment of a loss.

Underlying* The amount of loss which attaches before the next higher excess layer of insurance or reinsurance attaches.

Underlying premium The ceding company's premiums (written or earned) to which the reinsurance premium rate is applied to produce the reinsurance premium.

Underwriting capacity* The maximum amount of money an insurer or reinsurer is willing to risk in a single loss event on a single risk or in a given period. The limit of capacity for an insurer or reinsurer may also be imposed by law or regulatory authority.

Underwriting income* The excess of premiums earned by a reinsurer during any reporting period over the combined total of expenses and losses incurred by the reinsurer during the same period.

Underwriting leverage* The ratio of premium writings to surplus.

Underwriting-year basis* In rating, the use of all premiums written as arising from all policies written or renewed during the year and all losses relating to those same policies, whenever they may occur.

Unearned premium reserve* The sum of all the premiums representing the unexpired portions of the policies or contracts which the insurer or reinsurer has on its books as of a certain date. It is usually based on a formula of averages of issue dates and the length of term.

Utmost good faith* Firm adherence to promises made to another, including disclosure of all relevant facts, and complete trust in the fidelity of the other.

Vicarious liability The liability of one party which by law becomes the liability of another, such as the liability of an employer for the acts of an employee.

Vis major Irresistible force (act of God).

Voidable preference A payment made by an insolvent debtor which, by statute, is recoverable by the debtor's estate because it was either made within a particular fixed period of time prior to commencement of insolvency proceedings or it was in payment of a non-contemporaneous debt, and had the effect of giving the particular creditor who received it more than that creditor's pro rata share of the debtor's assets.

Voluntary excess This is an excess which the insured agrees to bear in consideration of a reduction in premium.

Working excess* A contract covering a type of excess reinsurance (per risk) in which loss frequency is anticipated, as opposed to loss severity. Thus, a working cover would usually have a low indemnity and would attach above a relatively low retention.

Written as such* Insurance written to cover a specific peril and specifically referred to as such, as opposed to insurance which may incidentally cover the peril, e.g. flood insurance written under a flood insurance policy vs a personal property floater, which would cover flood among a myriad of other perils.

Written premium This is the cumulative amount of premium income due to be received by an insurer.

Year free of premium Insurance offered by some insurers, especially household, under which a free year is granted from time to time, usually as a no claims bonus.

Year of origin This is the financial year in which a claim made against a company is known to have originated.

Zero or no-cost claims This is a term typically used in personal lines and denotes the claims which are settled or closed without indemnity payment to the insured or the claimant, except for possible service fees.

* Sourced from Guy Carpenter's 'Glossary Reinsurance Terms' available from www.guycarp.com/portal/extranet/utility/glossary_a.html.

12 The Future

This chapter discusses the future of insurance from both an IT and business perspective.

The Future: What does it hold for IT and Business in Insurance?

The future of the insurance industry from both an IT and business perspective is shaped primarily by factors that are out of the control of insurers. These factors, which could lead to an increase in catastrophes, include global warming, an increase in industrial complexity, a demographic shift towards dwelling on the edge of water (seaside resorts, riverside residential complexes, etc.), increasing conflicts and terrorism, and an increase in networking in the wider society. The following are three recent and notable catastrophes, human-made and natural, that exemplify the increased risks faced by insurers:

- Terrorists attacked the World Trade Center and the Pentagon in the USA on 11 September 2001. This event was a 'shot in the arm' for both insurers and reinsurers and provided an impetus for taking a radical view of risk management.
- A deadly tsunami hit the Indian Ocean on Boxing Day in 2004. This catastrophe, which was perhaps the most destructive tsunami in history, left more than 150,000 people dead or missing and millions more were homeless in 11 countries by the end of the day.[65] The scale of destruction was a stark reminder to insurers of the unpredictability of natural disasters.
- Hurricane Katrina hit the southern coast of the United States with devastating effect on 28 August 2005. It was reported that more than 1,800 people lost their lives, and more than $81 billion dollars of damage occurred.[66] This event also reminded both the insurance industry and the world of nature's capability to trounce human-made plans and defences.

These, along with corporate excess and scandals, have put identification and effective management of risk at the top of the agenda for insurance executives and boards of directors.

On the IT side, insurers are looking towards technology to help combat insurance fraud. Fraudulent and dishonest claims are a major problem for the insurance industry. Insurance fraud can be described as any act committed with the intent to fraudulently obtain payment from an insurer and has existed ever since the beginning of insurance as a commercial enterprise.[67]

65 National Geographic News, 'The Deadliest Tsunami in History?', 7 January 2005, available from http://news.nationalgeographic.com/news/2004/12/1227_041226_tsunami.html.

66 US Department of Health and Human Services, 'Hurricane Katrina', available from www.hhs.gov/disasters/emergency/naturaldisasters/hurricanes/katrina/index.html as accessed on 05/12/2008.

67 Coalition against Insurance Fraud, 'Insurance Fraud Hall of Shame: Mother Almost Blamed for Son's Arson', 31/12/2006, Coalition against Insurance Fraud, 13 December 2007.

According to 2007 research by the Association of British Insurers (ABI), one in ten adults admits to having cheated on an insurance claim. The research also revealed that dishonest customers were scamming insurers out of more than £4 million a day. The annual cost of insurance fraud to the British industry is estimated to be around £1.6 billion. This adds nearly £40 to the average premium paid by honest policyholders.[68]

Despite the well-documented problems intrinsic in dealing with fraud, fraudulent claims can be, and in fact are, detected. Industry experts suggest that detection normally occurs through the discovery of anomalies or inconsistencies in the information surrounding the claim (e.g. when the circumstances of the claim are inconsistent with the account given by the claimant), identification of patterns of claiming behaviour (e.g. repeated claims for similar losses), or recognition of inappropriate claimant characteristics (e.g. aggressive manner, uncertainty and hesitance in supplying information). Investigators, often based in special units in larger insurance companies, receive suspicious claims and investigate them further in an attempt to reject fraudulent claims.

The process of investigation normally involves looking for further information, either from the claimant or from third-party sources, and building up a clear account of anomalies and inconsistencies in the claim, coupled with potential motives of the claimant.

The responsibility for detecting fraudulent claims in insurance companies rests heavily with staff at the front line of the claims-handling process. Claims handlers are often inexperienced, with typical company lifetimes of less than one year, and they often lack sufficient or appropriate training in fraud detection.[69]

Specialist units and expert investigators rely upon others spotting suspect claims in the first place, and must therefore be able to discriminate quickly between claims that carry a high level of fraud likelihood and false positives, that is, genuine claims that appeared suspicious to an inexperienced staff member.

In order to increase the chances of inexperienced staff detecting fraudulent claims, insurance companies have traditionally provided claims handlers with lists of fraud indicators against which to check incoming claims. In recent times, technology has been the weapon of choice in fighting fraud.

That said, the following section contains a discussion on some of the factors that will shape the insurance industry in the future.

68 Mark Bridge. 'One in ten Britons commits insurance fraud', Times Online 9 May 2007, available from www.timesonline.co.uk/tol/money/insurance/article1767323.ece.

69 Doig, A., Jones, B. & Wait, B. (1999), The insurance industry response to fraud, Security Journal, 12, 19–30.

Future Insurance Demand and Supply Trends

The discussion of the future insurance demand and supply trends will be divided into sections: the private insurance sector and the public insurance sector.

Private Insurance Sector

The growth of the global insurance market will be dependent on the expected long-term economic growth of the emerging market economies of East Asia, Latin America and Central and Eastern Europe. Frontier markets in Africa could also contribute to this growth, as signs of economic growth in larger segments of the continent continue to be strong and this could lead to an increase in demand for insurance products.

Demand

While demand will vary from region to region, some factors will shape the trends in future. These factors include:

- Ageing populations, especially in more mature markets, which may lead to a decline in the demand for conventional death-based insurance;
- A decline in formal insurance arrangements;
- Increasing income and wealth, leading to an increased number of and higher-valued insurable properties;
- Proliferation of new, small entrepreneurial businesses, especially in rapidly growing emerging markets.

Supply

On the supply side, it is expected that it will be determined by overall demand. Factors that will shape future demand include:

- Growth of countries such as China, India, Brazil and Russia;
- The narrowing of the gap between banks and traditional insurers in terms of the innovative use of technology, quest for international expansion and marketing expertise;
- Consolidation in the industry, which is expected to lead to a decline in the number of major insurers and reinsurers worldwide;
- The proliferation of specialised niche firms that focus strongly on their core competencies and markets;
- The creation of larger more sophisticated reinsurers with strong capital positions as well as profitability and liquidity;
- The threat of global warming, which may impact on reinsurance pricing, policy limits, terms and conditions;

- The marketing role of information technology, especially that of the Internet.

Public Insurance Sector

Factors that will shape future demand for public sector insurance include:

- Possible changes in the social insurance programmes in many countries;
- Increasing life expectancy, which may lead to governments increasing normal retirement ages;
- The tendency for governments to link contributions more closely to benefits by allowing tax-deferred personal investment accounts to minimise long-term government liability for pension payments;
- The encouragement of individuals in certain countries by their governments to make greater provision for their own retirement using private market instruments;
- The inevitability that there will be future moves by governments in some countries towards increased cost sharing by patients as well as privatisation of many systems' operations and financing in light of their dwindling ability to sustain high-quality, fully financed public healthcare systems.

Continued Financial Services Integration

Financial services integration, i.e. a situation whereby a financial service that is customarily associated with one financial sector is produced and distributed by another, has become a noticeable trend in the financial services industry. A typical example is bancassurance, discussed in Chapter 5, which involves the selling of insurance (assurance) products by a bank.

In the past, insurance firms sold insurance, banks restricted themselves to providing traditional banking services, and brokerages and other investment firms stuck to dealing in bonds and associated advice and instruments. However, in recent times, the trend has been towards convergence, with players in one financial sector increasingly seeking a foray into other financial sectors.

Figure 12.1 shows the typical structure of a company that can deliver integrated financial services.

What does the future hold for financial services integration?

As financial integration gains traction in the financial services industry, insurance customers will be able to take advantage of the downward pressure on prices of insurance products, given that integration can result in economies of scale and scope as well as greater efficiencies, which in turn would allow financial conglomerates to offer products at reduced prices.

Figure 12.1 Integrated Financial Services via Holding Company

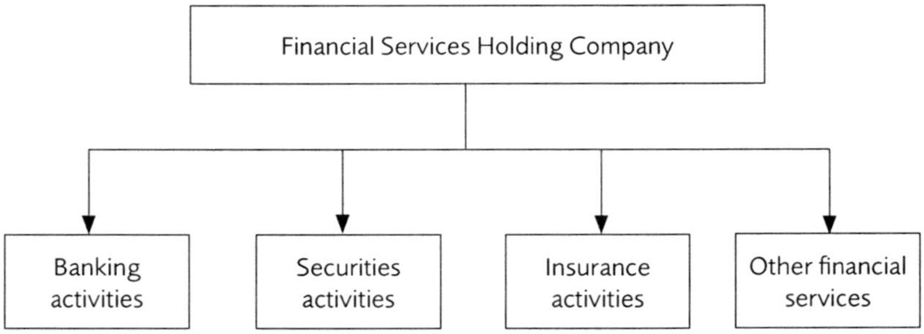

The degree of integration and its application to the provision of insurance products will be more advanced in some countries than others. The proliferation of financial integration can be limited or enhanced by the regulation and taxation that prevails in each country, and as insurance companies become increasingly global, they will seek to offer products and structure themselves in ways that will minimise their regulatory and tax burdens.

SWFs Investing in Insurance Firms[70]

Sovereign wealth funds were introduced in Chapter 5 and in this chapter a foundation was laid for discussion on how SWFs target insurance firms as a route to incorporate the insurance sector into their grand plans for developing world-class financial centres.

Industry observers have pointed out the absence of insurance companies amongst the financial services firms targeted by SWFs for acquisition, in spite of the well-documented role that insurance companies play in the development of financial markets and economies in general.

The Middle Eastern governments of countries such as Abu Dhabi, Qatar and Dubai, and Asian governments of countries such as China have in recent years stepped up their efforts in closing the gap between the current state of their financial sectors and the sophistication of leading financial sectors by accessing valuable resources and enhancing their skill base. Before drawing a conclusion on the chances that SWFs will invest in insurance firms, it would be prudent to gain an understanding of their special fondness for financial services firms. At the time of writing, acquirers have largely been the likes of Qatar, Dubai, Abu Dhabi and China, which experts believe have one thing in common: the ambition to develop world-class financial centres such as New York or London.

70 This section draws on a Deloitte Research paper entitled 'Insurance Firms - The Missing Link in the Sovereign Wealth Fund Acquisition Spree'.

However, it appears that the attraction to financial services firms is limited to banks, hedge funds or private equity funds, and exchanges. Industry reports show that out of the SWF acquisition deals that have been done, not a single one involved a pure insurance firm. Nevertheless, in order to realise the ambition of becoming world-class financial centres that could rival London or New York, SWFs must essentially attract a whole host of insurance or reinsurance companies.

It is expected that countries such as the Middle Eastern countries mentioned above and China, given the gap between the desired and the actual state of insurance services in their respective regions, will most likely seek to invest in western insurance firms in the future. These investments in European and American insurance companies through SWFs will allow these Middle Eastern and Asian economies to gain access to the skills and resources required to better serve individuals and enterprises as well as grow their position in their regional markets.

Increasing Role of Technology in Insurance

Insurers are seeking ways of using technology to help manage costs and remain competitive in the long term. According to a Boston Consulting Group report, they are no longer able to depend on extraordinary investment returns, focusing on identifying attractive markets and market segments, trying to achieve local leadership positions, and improving overall competitiveness. They are therefore concentrating on their core skills, reducing complexity, and systematically evaluating options to improve value creation within their companies. Achieving operational excellence has become an increasingly common strategic goal, one that requires superior management of IT resources. (Boston Consulting Group)

As they face external challenges such as the increasing burden of regulation and competition from other non-traditional insurance providers such as banks and the continued pressure on costs, they will be looking to technology to remain competitive in the coming years.

In addition, one of the most prevalent risks insurers face is a failure to keep their reporting systems current. In recent years, insurance companies in particular have felt this pressure rising through increased regulatory scrutiny. System modernisation is essential if an insurance company is to comply with new and future regulation and to avoid regulatory fines.

Insurance companies will take a more critical look at where their company stands within the industry where information technology is concerned and operate their IT systems as they would a business, measuring the value delivered by IT against the cost incurred. It will also become increasingly important to include chief information officers directly in the process in order to have the answers to questions raised by regulators about their IT 'health'.

Levers for Improving IT Performance and Cost Position

Industry reports suggest that most insurers have not harmonised IT and business strategies. The four levers briefly discussed below have been prescribed by industry experts for future improvement of IT performance and cost position with a view to tackling this disconnection:

- **Improvement of business and IT strategy alignment** – Achieving proper alignment is dependent on thorough integrated planning, supported by organisational and governance structures geared towards reducing total IT costs and maximising the business value of IT investments. To enhance business and IT strategy alignment, experts prescribe a three-step approach with feedback loops as follows:
  - Step 1 – the definition of IT requirements of the insurer's business strategy and formulation of a set of strategic IT initiatives accordingly;
  - Step 2 – drawing up a medium-term IT plan and an overall IT development programme that provides the method for transforming their current IT architecture into a target one from such strategic initiatives;
  - Step 3 – the design of a short-term IT road map with clear project definitions and planning aimed at achieving short-term objectives and laying of the groundwork for future steps from the medium-term plan.

  As a complement to these three steps will be other initiatives aimed at the integration of business and IT processes.
- **Reduction of complexity** – Whilst it is acknowledged that a degree of complexity in the IT landscape is difficult to avoid, greater maintenance and application development efforts will be required to address the typical drivers of excessive IT complexity in insurance companies, such as product complexity, new business demands, and mergers and acquisitions.
- **Optimisation of management of the IT project portfolio** – Emphasis is needed on the management of IT project portfolios with a view to enhancing IT performance. Managing of IT project portfolios can enable an insurance company to monitor incremental progress, budgets and the extent to which the planned business value of each IT project is essentially realised.

  Insurance companies will be using medium- and long-term IT project portfolios to drive a systematic skill-management programme for IT and relevant business capabilities.
- **Evaluation and pursuance of sourcing options** – Insurance companies that choose to pool procurement across business units can take advantage of economies of scale. This approach can be adopted for pooling IT equipment and services though this requires a degree of commonality across business units and is more of a challenge to achieve.

  Offshoring IT tasks that can be performed remotely to low-cost countries and outsourcing to third-party vendors can be of great benefit, especially in terms of costs, to insurance companies. Those that choose this option will, in future, need to follow a comprehensive evaluation of risk in the following four important areas: (1) brand value; (2) strategy; (3) vendors and markets; (4) operations.

The associated cost savings will differ from process to process and from insurance company to insurance company.

Service-oriented Architecture (SOA)

The rapidly increasing level of activity around the information technology (IT) methodology called 'service-oriented architecture' (SOA) is attracting the attention of systems groups in almost all industries. SOA can be described as the streamlining of business processes over time in order that these processes can be assigned ownership within an organisation. This means that all IT functions can be attached to a business process and, if advantageous, can be outsourced for efficiency.[71]

Progressive insurance companies are among those looking to exploit the potential of SOA with a view to increasing operational flexibility and the reuse of business-driven IT elements provided by this orientation to the 'services' model of information systems. SOA allows the IT function to become adequately flexible to serve business through the creation of minimal units of functionality known as services. The companion development for business is the identification and separation of its processes into logical networks of activities called 'components'. Thus, insurers offer more innovative products and services when armed with the capability of combining services and components in novel ways.

This opportunity is exceptional among recent IT innovations in that business units stand to benefit as much as IT departments or even more so. These business units have to have a serious commitment to the new approach, given the positive return on investment at several levels that has already been demonstrated at several insurance carriers.

The impending innovations in service-oriented IT and componentised business models will in future turn the spotlight of responsibility for performance a little more directly on the business side of insurance, as opposed to the IT function. Business managers will, in future, begin the process of strategic planning and scenario generation, with an emphasis on their ability to work as a team across the value chain to create new business opportunities. SOA will increasingly be relied upon as a true enabler of new business models and product innovations, which means that carriers will be planning for something beyond optimising existing processes.

71 David Piesse (Sept. 2006), 'The Role of IT in 21st Century Insurance', MIR IT in Insurance, available from www.meinsurancereview.com.

Telematics

Technology such as telematics will increasingly shape the future of the insurance industry. There is a likelihood that it will affect:

- Insurance business processes, i.e. how insurance companies conduct their business;
- Customer accessibility, which will potentially increase competition with other sectors and within the industry;
- The motoring environment, especially the number and nature of accidents.

The growth in telematics technology will in future result in a vast increase in the relevant and reliable information that can be accessed by insurance companies, which will result in dramatic changes in almost every part of the insurance process. A typical example could be insurers using this new data to assess risk in new and more accurate ways, to set premiums differently, to respond in real time to accidents involving their customers, and to revolutionise the claims process.

In the future, there will be an increasing number of insurance products available on the market that use telematics technology to calculate premiums based on actual determinants of risk – such as when and where the vehicle has been driven – rather than risk proxies. Given that telematics-based insurance relies on having a unit in the vehicle recording and transmitting to the insurer, or a third party collecting the records of vehicle usage on behalf of the insurer, expanding the uses to which the data involved is applied will increase the feasibiity that road charges could be generated as a by-product of the travel records used for insurance purposes.

Emerging Insurance Centres – Spotlight on Bahrain

The Middle East insurance market, as a whole, is attracting much international interest with many prominent market players choosing to locate in Bahrain. On the whole, rates of insurance penetration in the Middle East are not high. Nevertheless, Bahrain, having established its credentials as a financial services hub for the region, has been looking to boost its insurance sector by taking a proactive approach, both in terms of product development and implementing an effective regulatory framework.

Sound regulatory development and appreciable success have been notable features of the Bahrain insurance market in recent times. In spite of the relatively small market, the country has been able to successfully attract a number of international insurers looking to exploit the opportunities that exist in the local insurance market. The Bahrain Insurance Association (BIA) is equipped to effectively serve the interests of the domestic players.

Political and Economic Overview of Bahrain

As of August 2007, Bahrain's population was under 750,000 and experts assert that its eventual domestic growth potential is minuscule when compared to the like of its neighbours in the Middle East such as UAE and Saudi Arabia. However, as a gateway to the broader insurance market in the region, it is better positioned.

In recent times Bahrain has been characterised by the giant strides taken to update its economy and political system and has been particularly successful in positioning itself to become a major financial centre, mainly in the field of Islamic banking. Due in part to the fact that it has limited oil production, Bahrain has developed a more diversified economy than the other Gulf states. It undertakes the refinery of a large amount of Saudi oil and has the largest aluminium smelter in the Middle East. Bahrain also has a sizeable shipbuilding and repair yard and one of the area's busiest airports. On the other hand, wholly or partially government enterprises still dominate the economy. The most extensive recent political reform was the February 2001 referendum on the National Action Charter – the centrepiece of the Amir's political liberalisation programme.

Insurance Market Overview

Bahrain's insurance industry consists of conventional and Islamic (takaful) companies, which serve both the onshore and offshore insurance markets, primarily Saudi Arabia. The insurance sector in Bahrain is growing in importance as a part of the country's financial industry amid growing prosperity that is boosting demand.

According to industry experts, an economic boom in Bahrain and the region, large government infrastructure projects and strong private sector investment in real estate are fuelling the insurance boom.

According to industry reports, car insurance has in recent times been the most important segment of sales, but life insurance policies are gaining popularity as Bahrainis become more familiar with the concept.

Key data on the Bahrain insurance industry as of 2007:[72]

- Gross premiums: BD 135.6 million (US$359.7 million);
- No of firms: 33;
- Locally incorporated: 22;
- Branches of foreign firms carrying on direct insurance business: 11;
- Number of licensed insurance intermediaries and managers: 51 including 43 brokers (33 locally incorporated brokers and 10 brokers restricted to business outside the Kingdom of Bahrain), 7 consultants (including 2 consultants restricted to business outside the Kingdom), and 1 insurance manager;

72 Source: Central Bank of Bahrain, Insurance Market Review 2007.

Figure 12.2 The range of investments of Bahraini insurance firms

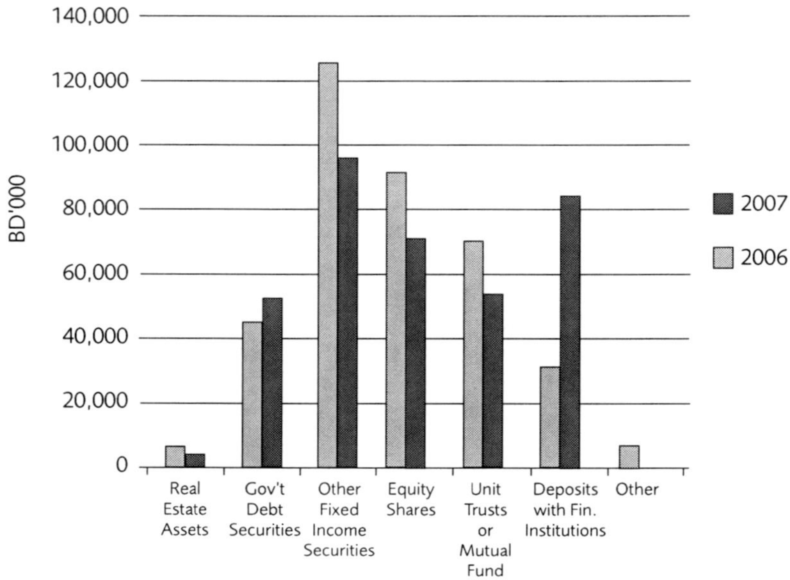

- Number of registered insurance experts: 10 loss adjusters, 18 actuaries, and 2 insurance ancillary services;
- Total assets of insurance firms: BD 965.5 million (US$2563 million).

It is also expected that the gross premiums of insurance companies in Bahrain will reach around US$1 billion by 2010 as a result of the increase in the number of insurance companies in the region and the opening up of new markets.[73]

Regulatory Environment

Bahrain has established a single regulatory body for the supervision of insurance markets as well as capital markets and banking. In a similar fashion to the UK's Financial Services Authority (FSA), the Central Bank of Bahrain (CBB) takes an integrated and standardised approach to supervision and licensing. Bahrain possesses an intricate regulatory framework created through active consultation with the industry, which is in contrast to some of the other countries in the Middle East.

73 Source: Central Bank of Bahrain, (February 2007) 'Insurance Potential Outstanding', Insurance and Takaful, pp2.

Future of Insurance in Bahrain

Despite challenges facing the Bahrain insurance market, such as raising public awareness to exploit the low penetration and promoting best practice in risk management, corporate governance and regulation aligned with international standards and expectations, Bahrain's future in the insurance arena appears to be sound.

Experts opine that Bahrain is at the forefront of insurance supervision and monetary expertise in the Middle East when it comes to the challenge of aligning its regulation with international standards. Industry reports also show that the country's central bank has developed rules purposely for takaful and retakful (Islamic reinsurance), helping to enhance Bahrain's status as a leading centre for Islamic insurance.

The discussion above provides more than enough evidence of the promise shown by Bahrain as an emerging insurance centre. It is expected that the country's insurance sector will continue to grow in the future as significant investment continues in infrastructure, real estate and industry.

Conclusion

While it is obvious from the discussions in the chapters of this book that the insurance industry is a mature one which will continue to thrive for years to come, it is the nature of events that will require insurance payouts that is more difficult to predict. The unpredictable nature of both natural and human-made disasters will strengthen the demand for insurance which will in turn provide numerous opportunities for business-aligned IT professionals to get involved in the various business processes required for the running of an insurance company.

Appendix

Bibliography

AIG 2007 Annual Report and New York Times. 'An Insurance Giant Brought Down'. Available from www.nytimes.com/imagepages/2008/09/27/business/20080928_MELT_GRAPHIC.html

American Academy of Actuaries (June 2001). 'Insurance Industry Catastrophe Management Practices'. Public Policy Monograph.

Anderson, J. and Brown, R. (2005). 'Risk and Insurance'. Education and Examination Committee of the Society Actuaries Study Notes.

Association of British Insurers. (September 2008). 'UK Insurance – Key Facts'.

Atkin, D. (2008). *Insurance*. Global Professional Publishing Ltd.

Attachmate. (2006). 'Turning Financial Mainframe Applications into SOA Building Blocks'. White paper.

Banks, E. (2004). *Alternative Risk Transfer: Integrated Risk Management through Insurance, Reinsurance and the Capital Markets*. John Wiley & Sons.

Barry, D. et al. (2003). *Insurance as Governance*. University of Toronto Press.

Bates, I. and Atkins, D. (2004). *Management of Insurance Operations.* Financial World Publishing.

Baur, P. 'Understanding Reinsurance: How Reinsurers Create Value and Manage Risks'. Swiss Re Economic Research and Consulting.

BBC Business News. (21 February, 2000). 'CGU and Norwich Union Merge'. Available from http://news.bbc.co.uk/1/hi/business/649600.stm.

Bennett, C. (2004). *Dictionary of Insurance*. Financial Times/Prentice Hall.

Blue Leaf Claims Inc. (2008). 'Claims Recovery'. Blue Leaf Claims.

Bisker, J. (2006). 'Creating Insurance Innovation through a Services Orientation'. IBM Global Business Services Insurance Point of View.

Booth, P. et al. (2005). *Modern Actuarial Theory and Practice*. Chapman and Hall/CRC.

Briys, E. and de Varenne, F. (2001). *Insurance: From Underwriting to Derivatives – Asset Liability Management in Insurance Companies*. John Wiley & Sons.

Burns, C. (5 December 2008). 'Are You Mastering your Data?'. Available from www.insurancenetworking.com/news/data_management_Celent_insurance.

Canabarro, E. et al. (October 1998). 'Analyzing Insurance-linked Securities'. Goldman Sachs Fixed Income Quantitative Research.

Capgemini and EFMA. World Insurance Report 2008.

Central Bank of Bahrain (February 2007). 'Insurance Potential Outstanding'. The Insurance and Takaful Review. pp2-3.

Crow, D. (29 October 2008). 'Virtualisation Can Save Money, and Will Help You Keep Going in a Crisis'. City A.M. City Focus Technology.

Culp, C. L. (2006). *Structured Finance and Insurance: The ART of Managing Capital and Risk*. John Wiley & Sons.

Cummings, D. J. et al. (2007). *Handbook of International Insurance:*

Between Global Dynamics and Local Contingencies. Springer-Verlag New York Inc.

Davenport, E. W.(May 1993) 'The Role of the Actuary in an Insurance Brokerage Firm'. Casualty Actuarial Society Discussion Paper

Davis, E. (10 March 2008). 'Green Benefits Put Thin-client Computing Back on the Desktop Hardware Agenda'. Forrester Research Inc.

Deloitte. (2008). 'Insurance Firms: The Missing Link in the Sovereign Wealth Fund Acquisition Spree'. Deloitte Research Paper.

Deloitte. (Summer 2008). 'Insurer, guard your own house – Why IT modernization is today's critical issue'. Forward Focus.

Dorfmann, M. S. (2007). *Introduction to Risk Management and Insurance*. Pearson Education.

Duffy, T. (2007). 'Insurance product life cycle management – Shedding light on product life cycle management for the insurance industry'. IBM Global Business Services Insurance Point of View.

Flaherty, S. (29 December 2008). 'More Mergers Likely Within Insurance Industry'. Financial Times Adviser.

Fujitsu. (2007) 'Modernize Your Legacy System AND Cut Costs?'. White paper.

Gartner, Inc. (21 September 2008). 'Legacy and IT Modernization in Insurance'. Kimberly Harris-Ferrante. Las Vegas.

Gartner, Inc. (24 June 2008). 'Legacy Modernization Among Insurers'. Kimberly Harris-Ferrante. (Podcast).

Hannover Re Factsheet. Available from www.hannover-re.com/about/index.html.

Hardy, M. (2003). *Investment Guarantees: Modelling and Risk Management for Equity-linked Life Insurance*. John Wiley & Sons.

Heydorn, S. et al. (April 2005). 'Creating IT Advantage in the Insurance Industry'. The Boston Consulting Group Report. pp8-9.

Heydorn, S. et al. (April 2006) 'Ensuring IT Excellence in Insurance'. The Boston Consulting Group Report. pp 4-6.

Hillier, A. (November 2007). 'How to Choose the Right Virtualisation Technology for Your Environment'. Cirba Data Center Intelligence White Paper.

Incisive Media. (November 2008). 'Bahrain Boom in 2007'. Reinsurance Magazine.

International Association of Insurance Supervisors. (12 December 2007). Global Reinsurance Market Report 2007.

International Financial Services London. (November 2007). 'Insurance 2007'. Available from www.ifsl.org.uk/output/ReportItem.aspx?NewsID=41

Johnson, S. 'The Rise of the Sovereign Wealth Funds'. Finance and Development. September 2007, volume 44(3). Available from www.imf.org/external/pubs/ft/fandd/2007/09/pdf/straight.pdf

Kenealy, B. (1 September 2008). 'The Technology Altering the Art of Underwriting?'.Insurance Networking News.

Knadd, R. et al. (December 2005). 'Hurricane Katrina'. Tropical Cyclone Report.

Microsoft Corporation. (2007). 'Virtualization from the Datacenter to the Desktop'. Core Infrastructure Optimisation Paper.

Miller, E. (19 May 2003). 'Technology and Insurance Fraud...A shared Responsibility'. Available from www.insurancejournal.com/magazines/southcentral/2003/05/19/features/29674.htm.

Munich Re Company Profile and 2007 Annual Report. Available from www.munichre.com/en/corporate/default.aspx.

Paehr, R. (November 2007). 'Legacy Modernization: Creating an Agile Enterprise. LOMA.

Paine, C. (2004). *Reinsurance*. Financial World Publishing.

Patrik, G. S. (1990). *Reinsurance Practices*. Insurance Institute of America.

Piesse, D. (September 2006). 'The Role of IT in 21st Century Insurance'. Available from www.meinsurancereview.com.

Potts, H. (29 October 2008). 'Insurer Remain Attractive Despite Strength Concerns'. City A.M.

PricewaterhouseCoopers. (May 2002). 'The wealth management challenge for insurers'. Insurance Digest Americas Edition.

PricewaterhouseCoopers. (September 2007). 'Sharing insights on key industry issues'. Insurance Digest European Edition.

PricewaterhouseCoopers. (January 2008). 'Sharing insights on key industry issues'. Insurance Digest Asia Pacific Edition.

PricewaterhouseCoopers. (April 2008). 'Sharing insights on key industry issues'. Insurance Digest European Edition.

PricewaterhouseCoopers. (May 2008). 'Bridging risk and capital – Countdown to Solvency II'. Edition 3.

Redja, G. E. (2007). *Principles of Risk Management and Insurance*. Pearson Education.

Rolski, T. and Schmidt, V. (2008). *Stochastic Processes for Insurance and Finance*. Wiley Blackwell.

Slaby, E.D. 'Technology in the Insurance Business Environment'. Available from www.soa.org/library/newsletters/the-actuary-magazine/2006/august/pub-technology-in-the-insurance-business-environment.aspx.

Smallwood, D. (June 2003). 'The Changing Competitive Landscape'. Available from Standard and Poor's. Global Reinsurance Highlights 2008 Edition.

Swiss Re. 'Securitisation – New Opportunities for Insurers and Investors'. Sigma 2006(7).

Vaughan, E. and Vaughan, T. (2008). *Fundamentals of Risk and Insurance*. John Wiley & Sons.

Zawya. (August 2007). Bahrain: Staying Ahead of the Game. Available from http://www6.zawya.com/story.cfm/sidZAWYA20070806070831/Bahrain:%20Staying%20ahead%20of%20the%20game as accessed on 07/01/2009.

Zurich Financial Services. (May 2008). 'Global Factsheet' and 'Zurich at a Glance'. Available from www.zurich.com/main/about/introduction.htm.

About the Bizle Brand

The Bizle brand represents the model approach to brand extension. This brand stands for excellence, quality, vision and innovation.

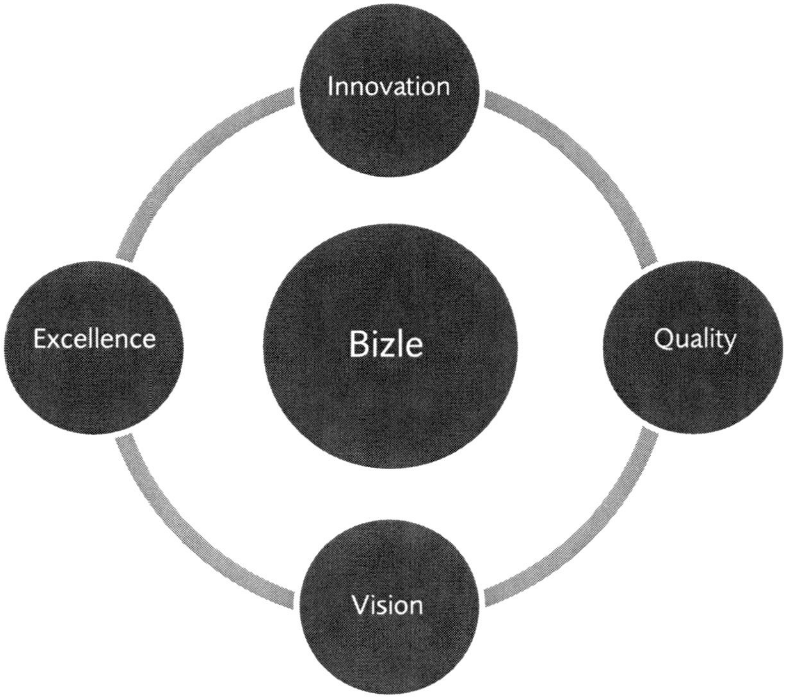

Bizle can be extended to any product that is related to fostering education, especially in the alignment of IT with business, such as the following:

- Training materials
- Training sessions
- E-learning tools such as CBTs
- Business software
- Conferences
- Boot camps
- Certification programmes
- Online portals such as the www.bizle.biz

At Essvale Corporation Ltd, we have a great vision for leveraging the Bizle brand equity and are looking for partners who share this vision to ensure that the brand fulfils its global potential.

Introducing Bizle.biz

Bizle.biz is the first online portal dedicated to the alignment of IT and business. When fully operational, Bizle will be the reference point for IT students and professionals that want to keep abreast of issues concerning IT and the alignment with the business community. It will also provide answers to "on-the-job" queries that professionals might have during the course of their everyday tasks.

Bizle.biz will have the following features:

- IT jobs adverts partitioned into the industry sectors to allow both candidates and advertisers to tailor their job requirements
- Recommended Books
- Industry News
- 'Ask' support service
- Glossary of Terms
- Forum
- Content in different languages

Introducing Global Real Estate Investment Series (GREIS)

The Global Real Estate Investment Series by Essvale Corporation Limited is designed to provide invaluable knowledge of the hottest property markets around the world. As real estate is now a bonafide asset class in its own right, private investors as well as investment managers are looking to exploit the undervaluation of emerging property markets in order to create well-diversified portfolios. This does not imply that they have turned their backs on the traditional markets such as the UK and USA; but savvy investors understand the benefits of diversification, especially in the realms of risk management.

These books will reinforce the widely held opinion that building a property portfolio is by far the safest form of investment over the medium to long term, because the fundamental market factors of supply and demand are always going to drive property values over the long term if investors choose to buy in the right market and at the right time.

GREIS books will provide an insight into the burgeoning property markets spread across the globe. They will provide readers with the benefits of investing in emerging markets, the pros and cons, the pricing structure, legal and taxations issues and much more.

The books will allow an investor to make an informed choice about their investment options around the world. The various investment strategies to be discussed will aid the investor in selecting the right approach for entry and exit from their chosen markets.

This series will cover the fledgling markets in the Middle East and South America as well as India and China. Established markets will also be covered as they deliver low-risk investments that are, as they say, safe as houses.

The maiden edition is due for release in 2010.

Other Titles in the Bizle Professional Series

Business Knowledge for IT in
Global Investment Banking

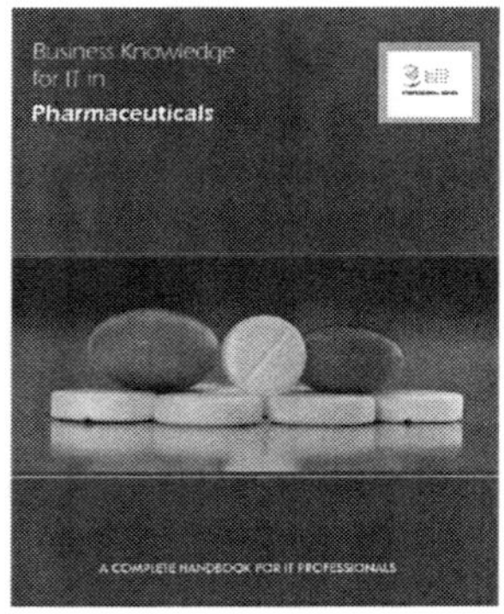

Business Knowledge for IT in
Pharmaceuticals

Business Knowledge for IT in
Private Equity

Business Knowledge for IT in
Foreign Exchange

Business Knowledge for IT in
Islamic Finance

Business Knowledge for IT in
Mobile Telecommunication

Useful Job Boards

Banking Technology Jobs	www.bankingtechnologyjobs.com
Career Center	http://jobs.careerzone.banktechnews.com
Career Center	www.finextra.com/finjobLIST.asp
Computer Weekly	www.computerweekly.com/Jobs
Cv Library	www.cv-library.co.uk
efinancialcareers	www.efinancialcareers.com
IT Job Feed	www.ciquery.com
Job Databases	www.jobdatabases.co.uk
Job Crawler	www.jobcrawler.co.uk
Jobserve	www.jobserve.com
Jobsite	www.jobsite.co.uk
Monster	www.monster.co.uk
Online Job Match	www.onlinejobmatch.co.uk
Planet Recruit	www.planetrecruit.com
The IT Job Board	www.theitjobboard.co.uk
Total Jobs	www.totaljobs.com

Index

Printed in the United Kingdom by
Lightning Source UK Ltd., Milton Keynes
141410UK00001BB/51/P

9 780955 412431